Hockey Tonk

The Amazing Story
of the Nashville Predators

CRAIG LEIPOLD
& RICHARD W. OLIVER

THOMAS NELSON PUBLISHERS®
Nashville

Published in Nashville, Tennessee, by Thomas Nelson, Inc.

All photographs are by John Russell and are copyright © Nashville Predators. Used by permission.

Library of Congress Cataloging-in-Publication Data

Leipold, Craig.
    Hockey-tonk : the amazing story of the Nashville Predators / Craig Leipold and Richard W. Oliver.
      p. cm.
    ISBN 0-7852-6841-3
    1. Nashville Predators (Hockey team)—History. 2. Nashville Predators (Hockey team)—Finance. 3. Hockey—Economic aspects—United States. I. Title: Amazing story of the Nashville Predators. II. Oliver, Richard W., 1946- III. Title.
    GV848.N35 L45 2000
    796.962'64'0976855—dc21

                                 00-034877

Printed in the United States of America

1 2 3 4 5 6 BVG 05 04 03 02 01 00

This book is dedicated to the city of Nashville,
which made the dream come true,
and to my family, Chris, Kyle, Connor, Curtis, Bradford,
and most important,
Helen,
who is sharing this dream with me.

Craig Leipold

For my nephew Mark,
who had more goals to score
and more words to write.

Rick Oliver

Contents

Preface

This is the story of a city and its hockey team.

The city, Nashville, Tennessee. The team, the NHL Nashville Predators.

For most of the histories of the city and of hockey, the combination seemed improbable.

Nashville is a midsize southern city with long and storied traditions in college football and basketball. It is a capital city, located in the geographic center of a state that many say is ruled by college football.

Hockey is a sport that was born and raised in the North, on frozen ponds in Canada and big city arenas in the American Northeast and Midwest. For all intents and purposes, Nashville and hockey don't, or didn't, belong together.

But in the late 1990s, a diverse set of events and a common set of minds combined to make hockey and Nashville one. This book tells the story of how that came to be, from the points of view of the majority owner of the team and one of its fans. It is a true story, but one full of twists and turns of events that make the story read like a novel.

To make it easy for the reader, this story was written in the third-person narrative form from the point of view of an informed observer, although much of the text contains firsthand accounts of the principals involved.

Readers are often interested in exactly how two people write a book together. Many authors suggest that it doesn't happen easily. The results often support that contention. In this case, it was easy, and we trust the reader will benefit from the two distinct perspectives.

Craig Leipold, the majority owner, tells the Predators' story in his own words, but is quick to point out that his is only part of the story. Coauthor Rick Oliver, a fan, puts Craig's story in the context of the many events that combined to make the Nashville Predators a reality.

The story itself is not so much about the team and its storybook first season as about the people behind the scenes—in the back rooms and the front office, in Nashville and New York—whose efforts allowed a group of twenty men to show a city how much fun and heart-pounding excitement they could pack into sixty minutes on a few square yards of ice.

In many ways the book is a formal record of the first year of the Predators, their 1998–99 inaugural season. More important, though, because the results of the team's accomplishments on the ice are a matter for the official record books, this book traces the exciting history of the people and events that led to the granting of the NHL expansion franchise to Nashville.

The story is told as faithfully as memories allow and as fully as modern publishing permits.

CRAIG LEIPOLD
RICK OLIVER
Nashville, Tennessee

Acknowledgments

I t takes an enormous amount of time and energy to write a book. No one could do it alone. We've been particularly blessed with a significant number of people who have helped make this book a reality. Although it is impossible to thank them all, several individuals and groups deserve special recognition.

First and foremost, there wouldn't be a book because there wouldn't be a Predators team without former Mayor Phil Bredesen, his staff, and the group of people who put the franchise application together: Terry London, Dick Evans and the Gaylord Entertainment staff, Tom Sherrard, Russ Simons, and Jenny Hannon.

Then, there is the growing Predators family: the players, coaches, hockey operations staff, and the business office staff who gave freely of their time to tell their parts of this story. In particular, we wish to thank Jack Diller and Gerry Helper, who helped keep the story straight, Greg Harvey, and photographer John Russell, whose excellent work graces this book.

On the editorial side, we wish to thank Tim Leffel, Peter Miller, Martha Redo, Kim, Russell, Beryl, Sutton Brothers, Carrie Oliver, our editor, Brian Hampton, and the people at Thomas Nelson Publishers who believed in the book.

Finally we wish to thank our families, and in particular, the two people who gave so much personal time to make this book a reality, our wives, Helen and Susan.

Introduction

HOCKEY 101

NASHVILLE COMES TO HOCKEY

Of all major team sports, hockey is the fastest. It is played by men traveling at speeds up to thirty miles an hour, using long, curved sticks to finesse a small, hard rubber puck on a small, hard icy surface confined by wood and glass. A hockey player requires great individual balance, agility, skill, and strength, all the while closely coordinating his actions with five other teammates. Together they execute their artistry in a strategic, free-flowing architecture of complex offensive and defensive maneuvers, carrying or deftly passing a puck that travels at speeds over one hundred miles per hour. It would be a virtual ballet on ice, were it not for an opposing group of fiercely determined players trying to do exactly the same thing, only in the opposite direction. Both sides are on an emotional high, intent on creating havoc by checking the play with sticks, skates, and crunching bodies.

Such conditions test the body and sharpen the mind.

Such speed, intensity, and skill have created a rich body of history and tradition, born of the emotion of the minute, where the heat and sweat of the coaches and players meet the frozen reality of the ice. The story of the NHL Nashville Predators is one of the latest to join the many stories of teams and players gone by.

Hockey is a game invented some hundred years ago on a small, remote Canadian pond. It was, for most of the next hundred years, lovingly nurtured by amateurs and professionals alike, but almost secretly, on a piece of geography stretching from Boston on the east to Chicago on the west, from Montreal on the north to New York City on the south. This small piece of geography was the breeding ground for a sport that is now enjoyed throughout the world and is growing so fast globally that it rivals the world-wide interest in soccer. Today, the language of hockey, English mixed with the French of Quebec, has been enlivened and enriched by fans speaking Swedish, Russian, Czech, Finnish, and many other tongues.

In the U.S., particularly in nontraditional markets of the South and West, hockey is slowly but surely encroaching on the other team sports as a favorite American pastime. Today, there are more professional hockey teams in Texas than in any other state or province. Everywhere its popularity is on the rise.

This is the story of one team in its magical expansion year, and the ideas and actions that brought it together.

HOCKEY COMES TO NASHVILLE

"It's a football town," they said. "Hockey will *never* make it!"

With no real hockey tradition, Nashville, Tennessee, was thought by many observers to be a poor choice for a National Hockey League (NHL) franchise.

But to a handful of people, people with vision, money, and a love for the city and the sport, it was worth the risk to bring a tra-ditionally northern sport into a southern town known primarily as the home of country music. How the country music establishment joined a wide cross section of the Nashville community to embrace the NHL's Nashville Predators is more than just a great sports story or even a "textbook" business story. It's the story of a city opening itself to something beyond its own traditions—something entirely new. It's the story of a city believing in itself enough to join the ranks of the country's biggest cities, cities perhaps with more people, money, and fame, but none with more pride, enthusiasm, and vocal cords powerful enough to be proclaimed "the loudest fans" in the NHL.

Less than a year before the Predators arrived in town, many couldn't imagine Nashville with a hockey team. By the time the season was over, however, the talk on the street, around the dinner table, and in the boardroom was about the Predators and the excitement they brought to Nashville. Most agreed that they couldn't imagine Nashville without a hockey team. In just one season, the Predators' fans established themselves not only as the loudest, but also among the league's most fiercely supportive. As an expansion team, the Predators weren't expected to win many games. But win they did, at home and away. By season's end, they had the third best record for an expansion franchise in the history of the league. They also set records off the ice, with more than 90 percent attendance and seventeen sellouts—accomplished primarily with young, previously unproven players, not aging veterans.

By the end of the season, it was easy to attribute the success of the Predators in Nashville to the fast, exciting, never-say-die style of hockey that General Manager David Poile and Coach Barry Trotz created on the ice. And in large part, that was true. But the story of the magical first season of the Predators really began more than a dozen years before most of the players had ever heard of Nashville. It began as a dream. A dream that Nashville would become a premier city with world-class venues for the arts, education, and sports. A dream shared by a small group of people who crafted their vision with patience and care. A dream that came forth not in any unified whole, but in a slow, constant progression of beliefs about how far and how fast Nashville might grow. It was a dream that was to infect and inspire politicians, businesspeople, community leaders, and eventually the public itself. More than just talk, the dream took shape in the form of buildings and institutions, and in Nashville's collective belief in itself.

The realization of the dream began with the building of the Tennessee Performing Arts Center, the Nashville Convention Center, the Bicentennial Mall, then the revitalization of Second Avenue and the renovation of the Ryman Auditorium, and finally the completion of the Gaylord Entertainment Center and the Adelphia Coliseum. It includes the emergence of Vanderbilt, Fisk, and Tennessee State Universities and several other local schools as nationally ranked and recognized educational institutions, and the growing prominence of Nashville as a business, arts, and economic center. And the dream continues to grow with the addition of a world-class library and museum.

Every dream, every vision, requires a catalyst, something special to bring everything together, to make it real. The Predators were that catalyst for the Nashville dream. They made it real. They made people believe that Nashville was in the major leagues, a first-class city among cities.

The Predators' preseason began before the funding and building of the arena, or the first face-off on the ice. It began with Mayor Phil Bredesen's visit to the NHL's office in New York to tell Nashville's story. It continued with building the arena, winning the NHL franchise, naming the team, and then surpassing the twelve thousand season ticket sales hurdle. It's a story filled with intrigue, excitement, emotion, and high finance. It's a story every bit as exciting as the game on the ice.

In the Predators' inaugural season, a group of hockey players from all over the world with little knowledge of one another came together for the first time in a city with little knowledge of their game. It became obvious fairly quickly that David Poile had chosen well, and that under the tutelage of Barry Trotz, the disparate group of players would hold their own in the world's roughest, toughest league. The Predators hockey players were joined by an equally interesting behind-the-scenes team. This team was led by owner Craig Leipold—an owner new to professional sports—and

President Jack Diller. They assembled a group of seasoned sports business professionals who rewrote the expansion franchise rule book in executing one of the finest marketing and business plans in sports history.

A sign over Predators marketing guru Tom Ward's desk reads, WAR IS HELL. EXPANSION IS WORSE! But not only did they survive and thrive; they succeeded beyond anyone's wildest expectations. These two Predators teams—one on the ice and one off—and a city ripe and anxious for major-league status matured together as a professional sports franchise and as a city. In academic terms, it was Hockey 101.

This book tells the story of that experience, about the magical storybook first season and the team behind the team that made it possible.

How Music City USA Became
Hockey Tonk Town

I can hear people around me yelling and screaming.
Sometimes that's as good as the show on the ice.

—BARBARA MANDRELL

After the first game I was hooked. They're such good guys
and they've got good attitudes.

—NATALIE MAINES,
DIXIE CHICKS LEAD SINGER

Most of our guys are country music fans, so we love getting
on the road and coming to Nashville. We're always hoping
to see some of the stars in the stands or on the street. And
the Nashville crowd is awesome. The players would much
rather play here than someplace where the fans are quiet.
We love the whole Nashville scene!

—#22, CLAUDE LEMIEUX,
NEW JERSEY DEVILS

Gaylord Entertainment Center*: 7:20 P.M.
Nashville Predators 0, St. Louis Blues 1
Less Than 10 Minutes into the First Period

"He shoots. *He Scores!*

So, with just 8:56 gone in the first period," Nashville Predators play-by-play announcer, Pete Weber, perched high above the ice at the Gaylord Entertainment Center, tells his radio audience, "St. Louis has now taken a *2-goal* lead."

"We still don't have much experience with this team," injects color commentator Terry Crisp, "but so far in this inaugural season, the Predators haven't been able to come back from an early deficit and win one. In fact, they've yet to come back and win when they've been just *1* goal behind. Let's hope they can hang on and not let this one get out of hand."

In the arena, sprinkled among the thousands of fans wearing silver-and-white Predators replica jerseys, sit about five hundred fans of the St. Louis Blues. Most are equally decked out, but with the Blues' home colors of royal blue and gold.

Over on the east side of the arena, country music recording star Deana Carter turns and whispers to the equally famous recording artists the Dixie Chicks. A few sections away, Vince Gill chats with nearby fans.

---

*The Gaylord Entertainment Center was called simply the Nashville Arena at this time. It became the Gaylord Entertainment Center on August 4, 1999.

After the second St. Louis goal, the Nashville fans are suddenly quiet, but their spirits remain high. They are ready for nights like this. These fans may be new to hockey, but they know the Blues are big, strong, and fast. They also know how hard it will be for a young expansion team to come back against a hockey team as experienced as St. Louis, particularly after going down by 2 goals so early in the first period. The next few minutes of the period see some back-and-forth action, but the Blues remain in control.

To support their new team, the fifteen thousand Nashville fans chant on cue some of the new mantras they've been taught. They've been carefully schooled in these new chants by the Predators event staff. Nothing has been left to chance. Everything has been orchestrated to inform, entertain, educate, and motivate.

On the ice, neither team seems to be getting the upper hand in the waning minutes of the first period. Neither is generating much offense, though; each team seems to be content to let the time run down. For the Predators, it will mean getting to the dressing room and regrouping.

Then St. Louis takes a penalty. As the Blues player skates to the penalty box, he turns and glares at the referee with a mocking body shrug that tries to say, "What did I do?" The Nashville fans stand in unison and stretch out both arms toward the penalized player. They point two fingers on each hand downward, mimicking the front teeth of a saber-toothed tiger.

"F*aaa*ng Fingers! F*aaa*ng Fingers!" they yell repeatedly, almost in a drawl. The loudspeaker supports their efforts. "F*aaa*ng Fingers!" it says. "F*aaa*ng Fingers!"

A shrill, rhythmic, pulsating whistlelike screech underscores the two-word assault on the Blues' indiscretion: "ReeeeReeeeReeee . . ." (the screeching sound from the shower scene in the movie *Psycho*).

With the power play over, the fans are still noisy, but have begun to quiet down somewhat, despite exhortations from the various promotional pieces on the Jumbotron. Just as the period seems to be over, first-year NHL winger Patric Kjellberg grabs a

4

pass from Tom Fitzgerald, streaks around the Blues' big defensemen, and puts it past the St. Louis goalie, Jamie McLennan.

The Jumbotron jumps to life again as Tim McGraw, on video, sings the Predators' song played after every goal, *"I like it. I love it. I want some more of it!"* The Predators are little more than three months old, but already the song is a classic. The fans seem to crave it as much as the actual goals.

Gaylord Entertainment Center: 9:05 P.M.
Nashville Predators 1, St. Louis Blues 2
5 Minutes into the Third Period

"Up to this point, the Predators have played the Blues extremely well, considering the various line matchups," intones Crisp, "but goalie Mike Dunham deserves a lot of the credit for keeping them in this game. He was flawless under that second-period barrage and just as good here in the opening minutes of the third."

Down on the ice, seemingly out of nowhere, Nashville winger Ville Peltonen, recently returning to the team from a shoulder injury, steals the puck and ties the score. The fans go into a frenzy.

Tim McGraw sings again. Soon after, another video breaks through on the Jumbotron.

This time it's Mel Gibson in the movie *Braveheart,* face painted and screaming a bloodcurdling battle cry to his troops. After raucous cheers for Mel, the fans settle into a loud, steady stream of encouraging chants. They feel good about this night, the game, the team, and this tie. "Hold on," they seem to be saying. "Just hold on another ten minutes for the tie."

Gaylord Entertainment Center: 9:46 P.M.
Nashville Predators 2, St. Louis Blues 2
1 minute to Go in the Third Period

Nearly a half hour of heart-stopping, back-and-forth, action-packed minutes later, the public address announcer tells the crowd, "One

5

minute to go in the third period," and the fans pick up the noise another couple of decibels. "We're going to do it! We're going to tie the Blues!"

It's not a win, but this is a division game and the Predators have played well against the Blues. The tie would be their first against a division opponent and bring their record to 6-9-2. Not bad at all for an expansion team that no one expected to do very well.

Down on the ice, the hastily assembled Predators line of Sebastien Bordeleau, Denny Lambert, and recently acquired center Cliff Ronning (on October 31, from the Phoenix Coyotes) are working hard to preserve the tie.

Terry Crisp, making notes for his three-star selection and getting into his postgame summary mode, says to his audience, "Well, folks, we've seen a classic tonight. The Predators are just fifty seconds away from a dramatic, come-from-behind tie against the Blues."

The game starts again, and although no one has left the arena, everyone's beginning to think about postgame activities. *Wonder how long the line will be to get out of the parking lot?*

On the radio, Pete Weber is describing the last few seconds of play: "They get ready for the face-off just outside the Nashville blue line, and Ronning wins the draw. Bordeleau picks up the puck and skates over the red line. Closely checked, he fires it into St. Louis territory. Blues defenseman Todd Gill corrals the puck behind his own net where he's checked there by Denny Lambert. Lambert feeds the puck to Ronning in front of the net. Ronning shoots. *He scores! He scores! He scores! Cliff Ronning puts the Predators ahead with just thirty-nine seconds to go in the third! Oh, man, does that David Poile trade for Ronning ever look good right now!*"

The noise in the arena becomes deafening. Everyone is cheering, screaming, at the top of his lungs. Where's the noise meter? It can't get any louder than this.

The loudspeakers are blaring with a rhythmic, thumping noise, a sound that is not so much music as a hypnotic electronic jungle beat.

Fans who hardly know each other turn and embrace or give each other high fives. Over in one corner, a two-story can of Edge® shaving gel spews smoke and white foam across the fans in Section 113.

The Jumbotron plays the song again. It's the Tim McGraw video for the third time tonight: "*I like it. I love it. I want some more of it!*" It seems louder than before, as if Tim has put more into it this time. The fans dance and jump in the aisles.

Then the Jumbotron erupts again. It's Godzilla, thumping away in symphonic beat, "THUMP! THUMP! THUMP! . . . THUMP! THUMP! THUMP!" The sound penetrates directly into the bone. Everyone's body seems to be vibrating along with the noise. "THUMP! THUMP! THUMP!"

Now public address announcer Bill Cody is saying something. He is announcing the goal scorer. Hardly anybody can hear him. They already know who scored the goal. To them, the announcement is meaningless in a moment of sheer exhilaration. And everywhere you can see it in the faces. "We're winning! Hold on, boys. Just thirty-nine seconds left. We can do this. We can beat the St. Louis Blues!"

The players are already lining up again for the face-off at center ice. Almost no one in the stands seems to notice or care. "We're ahead. We're beating the St. Louis Blues." That's all that matters. The people in Nashville, the people in this arena, in a whirl of emotion, acting like no crowd in Nashville history, have been waiting years for professional sports. This is our moment. Let's savor it. Yes, we've got the Oilers (the recently relocated NFL franchise now known as the Tennessee Titans), but they spent one season in Memphis and have just started playing at Vanderbilt Stadium, not their new home down the street and across the river. We'll cheer for them, too, when the time comes, but somehow this seems more special. "Our own team, in our own arena, and we're beating the Blues."

Once the NHL team nearest to Nashville, and thus a closely watched team for some of the die-hard hockey fans here, the Blues are now the dreaded enemy. And their players are big compared to our guys, the young, fleet, and much smaller Predators. It's easy to feel good about beating the Blues. We can't physically beat them, but tonight at least, we seem to be able to shake off their early lead, outskate 'em, and put the puck in the net. It's a great feeling.

On the ice, the third period is just seconds away from being over, but in the stands, the fans are singing, chanting, yelling, or holding their breath, still high from the emotion of the moment.

Gaylord Entertainment Center: 9:51 P.M.
Nashville Predators 3, St. Louis Blues 2
Game Over

Finally it's over. Blessed relief. We can relax now. We can breathe again. We've won. We beat the Blues.

On the radio, Weber and Crisp are almost talking over each other, anxious to portray the feeling inside the arena. These guys are professional announcers, good at their jobs, impartial. But everyone listening to the radio can tell from their voices, they're just as excited as the fans.

For the fifteen thousand screaming fans in the Gaylord Entertainment Center, it is truly a special moment. No one, it seems, has left his seat.

The inaugural game, October 10, will always be a special occasion, packed with memories of the dignitaries and official ceremonies, of the collective release of emotion that came after two years of waiting, hoping that our time had finally come. When they dropped that first puck, it was the start of a new era in Nashville. You could literally feel the energy in the air that night. And there were other moments as well. The first goal scored by the Predators, by Andrew Brunette on October 13, 1998. The first win, against the Carolina Hurricanes on October 13, 1998 (3-2).

But somehow, tonight, November 19, is something unique. We didn't know it could be this good. Tonight is electric. In the same division, everyone knew that St. Louis, Detroit, and Chicago would be special. The Blues, the Red Wings, and the Blackhawks, they'd be the teams to beat. Sure, we'd take a win from anybody, but these teams would be the real tests, of our team, of our city. But now, here we are. We beat the Blues!

Up in the owner's box just above the blue line, Craig Leipold savors the moment. He is on his feet, cheering along with the rest of the fans; he stands and shoots out his right arm during the Predators' victory song. He glances up at the scoreboard again. *Can that be right? Nashville 3, St. Louis 2?* Fans turn in his direction, give him high fives in the air. Everyone is excited, for himself, for Nashville, for Craig, and for the team.

Craig comments on the scene: "We won the game and it was our first division victory, so it was a big win for our club and very special for me. I had been in kind of a blur of excitement since opening night. So much had gone on. So much time and energy went into winning the franchise—selling our required twelve thousand season tickets, hiring the hundred or so staff, going through the draft, meeting with sponsors, publicity, and all the rest—that I'd hardly had time to let it all sink in, to enjoy the Predators for the sheer love of the game, to get emotionally carried away with the fans.

"It was a Thursday night, and the arena was packed. It was a wonderful feeling, the fans screaming and yelling, and there we were beating the St. Louis Blues. We'd won against some other big teams already, Colorado and Carolina, but to beat the Blues for the first time, at home, was something very special. It was a great night. That's the night I felt like we were for real. We'd made it. We deserved to be in this league."

The excitement in the arena was contagious, and many of the fans in the St. Louis Blues hockey jerseys caught it. "My guess is, hundreds of Blues fans from St. Louis were there that night," Craig remembers. "They have a big fan club that goes to games in close cities like Nashville. And there are a lot of people here who followed the Blues for many years before the Predators arrived. There were so many Blues fans in the arena that seemed to get

9

caught up in the moment. Of course, they wanted their team to win, but you could tell they knew this was a special time for us. Some of them looked over at me and gave a big cheer, waving and clapping."

Nashville, Tennessee: 10:25 P.M.
Wolfy's Restaurant

Craig says the celebration continued outside the arena after the game: "Afterward a lot of us went next door to Wolfy's [a restaurant near the arena], and a lot of the Blues' fans were there. They were thrilled for us, they were so happy. They said, 'You guys have the loudest arena we've ever been in. You understand what it's all about. Kiel Center doesn't have half of what you've got. We've had so much fun coming down here.' They just went on and on about what a great team we have, great city, and things like that. By the end of the night, some of them were still wearing a Blues jersey, but had a Predators cap on.

"I think the fans really appreciated how hard the players worked to win that game. I've been to a lot of sporting events in my life, including championship basketball games at the University of Arkansas, but nothing like this game. Nothing like this victory. Nothing like this night."

There had already been a series of big nights for the fans and Predators owner Craig Leipold. And before the season was over, there were to be many more: the Wayne Gretzky visit to Nashville, their first road win (over Calgary), their first shutout (Tomas Vokoun's 2-0 win over Phoenix), the surprise win over the Detroit Red Wings, and the homestretch that included six straight sellouts. And even when they lost, the Predators mostly kept it close. Forty of the season's games would be won or lost by 1 goal. In 8 games, they gave up another goal after pulling their goalie for an extra attacker (and another 4 games where they scored into an empty net). Always gritty, always determined, they never gave up. Five different times they came back to win in the third after being behind in the first two periods. They surprised just about everybody, tying powerhouse teams like the Toronto Maple Leafs and beating the mighty New Jersey Devils in overtime.

A defining moment for the Predators came early in the season, December 23 to be exact. Warned early on that Nashville was notorious for closing up at the slightest hint of snow, the Predators were prepared for a very small turnout against the visiting Red Wings when the weather turned icy. "We had heard stories about people clearing out the shelves at Kroger. In fact, it is so famous in Nashville that we used a preseason billboard with the headline 'Attention Kroger Shoppers. Ice coming!'" says Predators vice president of communications and development, Gerry Helper.

"Despite being sold out, we offered fans a truly unusual deal: we'd give them a ticket for another game if they didn't feel they could drive to this one. We were all making predictions about how many people might show up, given the ice and snow. The highest guess was five thousand people. The weather was bad enough that Craig's plane couldn't get into the airport. But we were astounded. Nearly fifteen thousand people got here for the game. It said to us that we had achieved broad, across-the-board fan support. They weren't coming for the novelty. They were here for the hockey!"

Off the ice, there was the Predators Foundation, holding fundraising events such as the Unmasked Ball, which raised $170,000 for local charities. Professional civic awards and accolades went to Craig, President Jack Diller, and the entire Predators management team. Knowledgeable observers were to proclaim that it was one of the finest, most successful launches of an expansion franchise in professional sports history. Underneath it all, though, was Nashville's growing fascination for its new sport and team.

An important part of that fascination grew out of the city's most globally recognizable business: country music. Nashville, like LA, is a *company town*. And the company is *music*.

From billboards to posters, from songs to videos, some of country music's biggest and brightest stars gave hockey their all. Whether it was blacking out their front teeth for season ticket billboards, participating in a telethon, or cheering for the Predators from their seats behind the bench or perched in a corporate box high above the stands, they became a vital part of the magic of that first season.

However, like many other aspects of this surprising expansion year, the involvement of country music stars didn't happen by accident. It took a fortuitous meeting in Maine years ago and some crazy twists of events here in Nashville to create the spark that ignited Nashville into Hockey Tonk Town, USA.

"GOT TICKETS?"

Sports Illustrated dubbed Nashville "Hockey Tonk Town" in its November 1998 article about the Predators and described what was happening in Nashville as a true love affair between the city and the team. "The marriage between country music and hockey represents a melding of Southern broken hearts and Northern broken bones," noted writer Michael Farber. What brought *Sports Illustrated* to town was not only the success of the team on the ice in the early going, but also the team's spectacular relationship with the country music industry.

The relationship was to take on many facets, from using the stars to pitch tickets in a telethon, to posing the entire team and its coaches on the stage of the Grand Ole Opry for a promotional poster, to having known performers sing the national anthem before games. But the "Got Tickets?" advertising and billboard campaign captured most of the attention.

The campaign was developed to support the season ticket drive to sell twelve thousand seats. Some earlier franchises, such as Tampa Bay and Ottawa, were required to sell ten thousand, but this was the biggest challenge in hockey expansion history. As Predators Executive Vice President of Business Operations Tom Ward remembers, the challenge at the time seemed almost impossible: "We had no team, no logo, and no players. We had no one to pitch our product, a product that was unfamiliar to our market.

And as relative newcomers, we had no credibility to speak of. Barry Trotz's friendship with Garth Brooks, and Craig's increasing presence with people like Amy Grant and Vince Gill, gave us a basis to approach recognizable and believable spokespeople to support our cause. The Gaylord Entertainment connection [minority owners of the team] helped smooth the way all around."

The original connection between country music and the Predators had happened innocently enough in Portland, Maine, where Barry Trotz was coaching the American Hockey League Pirates. Garth Brooks was in town for a concert, and Barry arranged for some of Brooks's road crew to get some ice time for a pickup game following a concert. Trotz, Assistant Coach Paul Gardner, and Garth all played in the pickup game. Later, Trotz arranged for ice time for the crew at other places around the U.S. It started with personal friendships, but the links with country music have grown from there to include the hockey players and management. Barbara Mandrell threw a welcome party for the entire team at her home in October 1998.

Tom Ward, as top marketing minds usually do, recognized a rare opportunity to create a campaign that would capture the imagination of his audience, demonstrate the sense of fun and surprise that would characterize the franchise, and sell twelve thousand tickets at the same time. Little did he know that he would also win the attention of the entire sports community and solidify the growing friendship between Nashville's signature industry and "the coolest game on ice."

Ward, along with his staff and the Predators' ad agency, Dye Van Mol & Lawrence, conceived a campaign that would grab everyone's attention. They asked some of country music's biggest stars to pose for billboard and advertising pictures with big smiles and no front teeth. Each performer held a hockey stick, and a caption read simply GOT TICKETS? Among those adorning the ads were Garth Brooks, Lorrie Morgan, Martina McBride, Deana Carter, Vince Gill, and Amy Grant.

"One of the jokes making the rounds of the late-night talk

shows," says Ward, "was that Nashville would be the only hockey franchise in the country where the fans had fewer teeth than the players. We decided to use that, play on it, and turn it around to our advantage. We have to give full credit to those stars who agreed to be depicted without front teeth and support a new, unknown sport."

The "Got Tickets?" campaign, which was a takeoff on the "Got Milk?" ads, garnered national attention and eventually won advertising awards for the concept and execution. More important, however, it inserted an element of fun that told the community something very different was afoot. It was also a signal to the city that the country music industry had enthusiastically embraced the Predators. Tom Ward and the professionals around him didn't rest with "Got Tickets?" Already garnering a reputation as a shrewd, effective marketing strategist, Ward had tickets to sell, and he knew he had to be inventive.

"I was worried that we hadn't spent enough money to reach our goal. We believed it was more than anybody had ever spent on such a campaign, but our deadline was closing in, and we'd only get one shot to do this. There was a lot riding on it. The franchise, careers, reputations. The pressure was incredible. I thought we needed to do more, but there just wasn't enough time to do everything. That's when we get most creative. In sports terms, it was the big-game, high-pressure situation," Ward says.

"We had a number of good, solid programs in place, but I believe the area that accounted for 50 percent of our sales was our special event marketing. When we went into the program, my experience told me that we needed to have a spike in our communications effort every thirty days. We decided to use special events as our communication spike to keep fan interest piqued and to keep ourselves in the newspaper and on the six o'clock and ten o'clock news. Everything was timed to get live coverage on the 6:00 P.M. news. I really think that's what kept this thing going. Every time we started to hit a drought, *boom,* we hit the market with a special event. Everything for us became a sales event.

"In September [25, 1997] we introduced the logo with a big splash and got great attention and interest. Two days later we did the Ice Breaker Bash at the arena with twelve thousand people showing up. We followed that in November [13] with an event at the Wildhorse to announce the Predators name. The next spring [February 12, 1998], we unveiled the team jersey at Cool Springs Galleria [a huge suburban shopping center]. We had all the media out for these events. These were what I call our Phase I event programs.

"Then we went into Phase II. Phase I was the launch through December 31, and Phase II was December 31 to March 31, which was crunch time. It was the final drive to the goal," Ward explains.

"In Phase II we kicked off the 'Got Tickets?' campaign with our celebrities and their two missing teeth. Then we did the Hockey Tonk Jam at the Ryman, which was one of the most unique sports marketing events that's ever been done. We video-taped the Hockey Tonk Jam to use as the basis of a special TV event to launch that campaign. Getting the stars to blacken their teeth was easy compared to the effort that went into the made-for-TV event."

The event grew out of Ward's fertile and ever-active marketing mind: "It was just one of those things where we had the music community involvement in the 'Got Tickets?' campaign, and I was sitting down trying to think through how to use it as a sales tool. What we ended up with was a TV special that was a cross between a Farm Aid concert and a Jerry Lewis telethon. It was actually two events.

"We set up the concert and videotaped the material. We didn't sell a lot of tickets that night, although we had two thousand people crammed into the Ryman Auditorium [one of the historic Grand Ole Opry venues]. We had great support from performers like Tim McGraw and Faith Hill. And we'd commissioned famed Nashville songwriters Harlan Howard and Pat Alger to write and Delbert McClinton to debut the song 'Hockey Tonk: The Predators Song.' That made the event the Hockey Tonk Jam.

"What was most important about that was, we used the tape to produce a one-hour, made-for-TV special a few nights later on Channel 2 [ABC affiliate, WKRN], a local TV station. So the second event was our telethon. That was huge because it opened the doors for Channel 4 [NBC affiliate, WSMV] to do another telethon. Next, the cable company, Intermedia, got involved. TV stations don't usually do such things. I think this kind of cooperation is unique in this market. We were able to work with the media, especially Channels 2 and 4 and Intermedia, to in effect produce infomercials that must have run three hundred or four hundred times. We could never have afforded to buy that much TV time. Obviously we did have some very key entertainment and media partners here that leveraged our efforts two or three times."

And why did they do it? Deana Carter, one of the early and most vocal of the Predators' supporters, summed it up best. She told *Sports Illustrated* that "country music people are showing that we're supporting the team. There was a question of how much support there would be for hockey locally. I'm proud of my hometown, that it could cut the mustard."

It would take more than mustard, though, to ensure that Music City USA and the music industry fully understood the potential of the new hockey team. Behind the scenes, owner Craig Leipold and his senior advisers struggled with how to increase local involvement and believed that the music industry was a key. Craig set out personally to make people in the music industry financial partners of the team. Time and events would conspire to prevent him from accomplishing that, yet the effort set in place the enduring relationship between the two.

HOCKEY TONK

Early in the process of putting together Nashville's application for an NHL franchise it became apparent to Craig and the local people supporting him that they ought to engage the city's music industry in some way. The presence of the country music industry was, and is, Nashville's distinguishing characteristic. After all, it provided the nickname by which Nashville is known worldwide: Music City USA.

"It was at the point when we first started putting the NHL application together," says Craig, "that I really focused on getting other investors in Nashville, for community reasons, to be part of this franchise. For most of my professional life (and even now) my home has been in Wisconsin, but I'd always felt very close to Tennessee and the South. In fact, I was born in Memphis and lived there before my father, who was with Kimberly-Clark Corporation, was transferred to its headquarters in Neenah, Wisconsin. He was transferred again to Arkansas about the time I was applying to college, and I ended up at the University of Arkansas and Hendrix College.

"When I came to Nashville, though, my most important objective was to make this Nashville's team in every way. I wanted to tie in with a music artist, someone high profile like Amy Grant, Brooks & Dunn, Vince Gill, or Garth Brooks. I felt that we would benefit and that the community would like to see that type of person involved. The involvement of local artists would not only be popular with the community, but it also might help sell the tickets we needed to get the final commitment from the league for the franchise.

"So, we started talking with several of the artists in town— Amy Grant, Brooks & Dunn, Tim McGraw, Vince Gill, and since Garth Brooks was on tour, his people. We wanted to know what their interests would be in owning a piece of the team."

Craig adds, "For me, it was the first time I was able to meet any of them, and it began my personal love affair with country music. I was really surprised at their response. These people immediately returned phone calls. Then I met with all of them. I'd had some experience with other show business people, and some of them can be very hard to deal with. Not these people. As Nashvillians already knew—and I found out—country music people are wonderful, warm, genuine, and down to earth.

17

"At that point I felt the people in the music industry were going to be important to our success because they were so responsive. They were sure to play—and still do play—a big role in our success, with the now famous 'Got Tickets?' campaign, game promotions, and just being great fans. They've added an extra degree of fun and excitement to our business that any sports franchise would love to have."

One funny incident early in this process caught Craig off guard and helped to establish the mutual respect between the music industry and the Predators. It signaled to Craig that the fan base in Nashville was solid, and that the country music industry would help set the tone for the fan interest and fun spirit that have quickly come to typify the Predators' style.

"Amy Grant was number one on my list. My first meeting with Amy turned out to be a very interesting moment. First of all, I was a bit surprised when she suggested we meet at her favorite bagel shop in town. I was going to go alone, and she said that Chas Corzine, her manager, would join us. This wasn't going to be a stuffy meeting in a conference room full of staff people and advisers, but just a simple conversation, in a regular place, among the three of us.

"I got there first, and then, just a few seconds later, Amy arrived. She was wearing a sweat suit and a T-shirt. We said hello to each other, ordered bagels and coffee, and sat down to talk. My recollection of that meeting is that it lasted several hours when it was probably an hour-long meeting," Craig notes.

"For the first thirty minutes she talked about her kids and I talked about my kids. We were kind of connecting through the children. It was more of a 'get to know you' discussion than a business one. Then we started talking about hockey and ownership. She said she'd only been to a couple of hockey games in her life but found herself drawn to the game. She thought getting involved would be an exciting thing. 'My family would enjoy it,' she said, 'and I would enjoy coming to the games. I think this would be fun.'

"We talked a little bit about why I wanted to have local partners. At that time we were getting some good publicity in the media. What the political folks call 'spin.' I said that we were beginning to educate the city on the sport of hockey, and that participation by someone like her would be helpful."

Craig recalls, "The bagel shop was pretty full. I was immediately impressed because while Amy is very recognizable, and I could tell people did know who she was, everybody left her alone. I didn't know this at the time, but have since learned that this is pretty typical about the people in Nashville. They are very respectful of the country music performers' personal time and space.

"However, there was this one guy over in the corner of the shop who had been there for quite some time. When he got up to leave, he came over to our table and said, 'Excuse me, may I interrupt you for a moment please? You're Craig Leipold, aren't you?' I said, 'Yes, I am.' Then he said, 'I just want to tell you how much I appreciate what you're doing. People in this city don't have any idea what hockey's going to do for us. It's the most exciting sport. I am so thrilled. I'm originally from the North. We had a hockey team where I lived, and it embraced the whole city. I'm so excited we're going to get one in Nashville. I'm telling my friends how wonderful it's going to be. It's fantastic.'

"I thanked him and he started to leave, then he turned around and said, 'Oh, Amy, how are you?'

"That was a real telling moment for me! Here I am having bagels and coffee with Amy Grant, and a guy wants to stop to talk hockey. At that point I was telling Amy how exciting the game is going to be and this guy, totally unsolicited, stops by with a ringing endorsement. We had a good laugh about it, but the point was made. Amy's become a great fan and a real supporter of the Predators."

Eventually Craig met with many of the country music people who have come to support the Predators in many ways. The real goal was not to garner finances, but to increase the team's participation in the community. At the root of this was Craig's overriding

19

philosophy about community involvement. He has believed in this philosophy from the beginning of his career.

Despite his deep desire to have local people involved, time was running out to establish the ownership for the application to the NHL. It was beginning to look like a good idea, but there wasn't time to put it together. People grow to like and trust each other, as was happening as Craig met and talked to people in the country music industry, but in the end, the documentation, disclosures, and legal hurdles took over and ended up requiring an inordinate amount of time. They had to submit the final ownership position to the NHL before the franchise was granted. Craig and Gaylord Entertainment were the majority and minority owners, respectively.

Craig was perhaps a bit concerned about his not being from Nashville: "It was not financial. It was who we are—local owner-ship. It was community. It was profile. It was marketing. I wanted to tell the community from the outset that this team was as much theirs as mine. I may be the legal owner, but I wanted this to be Nashville's team. I really fell in love with Nashville from the very first day I came here.

"As for my family, my wife has her career, and my children are settled in their schools. It was obvious from the start that I would live here only part of the time. I was concerned about how people here might react to a family from Wisconsin owning 80 percent of the team, even if a local company, Gaylord Entertainment, owned the other 20 percent.

"Although the potential partnership with some of the country music people didn't work out, it was an interesting process to go through. And it set the stage for what was going to become one of the more colorful advertising campaigns in pro sports, and for a deep and abiding mutual respect between hockey and the country music industry."

More than anything else—more than creating toothless posters, writing songs, and making videos—the connection between hockey and some of country music's biggest stars became decidedly personal, with the owners, the staff, the coaches, and above all, the players.

CELEBRITY CAM

From the very beginning, the music industry and its stars embraced the game of hockey and made it their own. In turn, hockey players embraced country music, and the entire sports world took notice.

The players have to strain their necks sitting on the bench, trying to see who's at the game. But for the fans, stargazing in the arena is a bit easier. The Jumbotron's Celebrity Cam provides close-ups of many of the stars at the game. And Reba, Vince, Amy, Garth, Barbara, Deana, Brooks & Dunn, the Dixie Chicks, and others are never too shy to give everyone a wave.

Some players, like Predators winger Rob Valicevic, have been country music fans for a long time. He says, "My little sister started me on country music back in college, probably in my sophomore year, so I've been into it for six and a half years. It's a great style of music, I love it, and there are times I can't get enough of it. I definitely think there is a connection between hockey and country music. I had the chance to meet Garth Brooks. He is a great guy, very personable.

"I think, as far as professional athletes go, hockey players are very approachable. It just seems like in football or basketball the athletes are not as accessible. In our field of sports we like to talk to other people, and I think country music stars are the same way. They just like to have a good time, sit down, have a cup of coffee, and talk. I think we have that little bit in common."

For the players, the presence of such talented performers at games, appreciating the sport and the excitement, is a special incentive and has become a real interest of the Predators and their visiting opponents. From their warm-up skate to a little free time in the penalty box, the players, both the hometown boys and their rivals from across the continent, are sure to note the music stars in attendance.

"Playing in Nashville is somewhat like playing in LA," observes Predators Captain Tom Fitzgerald. "But I think we're luckier. LA's got the entertainment people backing them, but we not only have the music industry people backing us, they're true fans as well. They come out to the games to see us play. They stop by the dressing room [hockey players typically refer to the locker room as a dressing room] after the games to talk to us. They are really down-to-earth people. It's a special feeling when people who have devoted their lives to entertainment, who are real professionals, enjoy seeing us play. They have been so supportive.

"We don't consider ourselves entertainers. We consider ourselves athletes who are playing a game that we love. The country music people are true entertainers. But we've got to keep our fans happy, just as they do.

"It's funny. I've become a big fan of the Dixie Chicks, and then one night I saw them in the stands. It was great to see them there, enjoying the game. A lot of our guys, and the guys that come in to play against us, are really aware of who is at the game and who is coming down to the dressing room afterward," says Fitzgerald.

"And a lot of them come by after the game. It seems like Deana Carter is there all the time. I had a year-end party for the whole team and decided it would be a good gesture to invite some of these people who backed us all year. So Barbara Mandrell and her family showed up, so did Deana Carter, among others.

"I'm not putting a label on hockey players, but in general, I'd say we're pretty much down-to-earth people. Most of the guys are from blue-collar families where you learn early that you've got to work hard to get ahead. We make a great living at what we do now, but that doesn't mean that you forget your roots and values. To be successful in hockey, you have to work hard, and I think the country music industry has the same work ethic. The stars are often not from wealthy backgrounds. They've worked hard to get where they are, and they don't take their success for granted. They don't take their fans for granted, and neither do we. Look at Fan Fair [the country music event held for fans every summer in Nashville]. That's a big commitment for a performer. I think country music artists are the hardest working and the most fan-friendly of all entertainers."

Fitzgerald continues, "Hockey is the same way. I know this sounds biased, and it probably is, but I think hockey players are different from many other athletes. All professional athletes work hard, and I don't think you can really compare one sport to another, but hockey has a long season, with tremendous physical demands over many months.

"That's not to say that football, basketball, and baseball players don't work hard or that they take for granted where they are, but except for a very few markets, hockey has had to earn its way into the hearts of the fans. While country music has had a core following for a long time, its recent growth in popularity is with an entirely new fan base. Just like hockey.

"I think that's a large part of the connection between country music and hockey—why there's magic there, and why we seem to be so good for each other.

"And I think there is sort of a rural, small-town, workingman's ethic that pervades hockey. That lines up pretty closely with the kind of people that come into country music and the kind of people that country music appeals to. I think it's a great connection."

By the time the Predators opened their season on October 10, 1998, many around the country were saying that the marriage between Music City USA and hockey seemed made in heaven. But those in the know were very aware that, except for some twists of fate and a lot of hard work, there might not have been an engagement, let alone a marriage. The magic of the Nashville Predators' storybook season almost never happened.

Nashville Joins the Major Leagues

Expansion has been great for hockey. There's no question that places like Nashville and Dallas and some of the other cities were ready for this sport. In fact, it seems to be an ideal sport for some of the expansion locations. Obviously the fans in the other new cities such as San Jose, Phoenix, Anaheim, Miami, Raleigh, Tampa, and Denver have really taken to hockey!

On a personal level, for me, coming to the country music capital of the world is incredible. I'd always heard about it but had never been here. Hockey is an ideal sport to mix with country music. The fans here seem to really have a good time. They remind me of the fans at Lynah Rink, at my alma mater, Cornell University—loud, raucous, and really having a great time. For the home team, that's like getting some free goals. For the Predators, it has to be so much fun to play in that atmosphere.

The fans here seem to know how to enjoy themselves. They come for the kind of fast, exciting entertainment that only hockey can be. As a player, I find it entertaining too!

I think the fans are unique here. Although hockey is new to the city, they seem to understand and get involved with what's going on. They do some things differently here—such as with the PA system, for example—than anywhere else in the league, and at least from a player perspective, it seems to be working. The fans seem to really get into it.

Of course, the fans here really pull for the Predators. That's to be expected. As a player you focus on the game, but I've got to tell you that all the excitement in Nashville gets us charged up too. On the bench, you look around and everyone is just buzzing with excitement. We get excited too, and really want to play our best for such great fans.

—#25, JOE NIEUWENDYK,
CENTER, DALLAS STARS;
MVP 1999 STANLEY CUP

An old adage goes something like this: "If you don't know where you're going, any road will get you there." After a successful career in business, first as a salesman for one of the country's largest corporations, then as an entrepreneur building his own business from scratch, and finally as a turnaround specialist who rescued an ailing textile firm, Craig Leipold had a reputation of always knowing where he was going and how he was going to get there. When he stepped off the familiar roads of business, though, and entered the winding, twisting, unknown pathways of professional sports, he found, for the first time in his career, that neither the destination nor the journey was very clear. He did know, however, that his instincts and skills, honed over his twenty years in business, would eventually lead him to where he was destined to be. The surprising thing was, neither hockey nor Nashville was on his radar screen when he started his exploration into professional sports.

In early 1986, in the middle of his business career, Craig decided to do what many college students do before they go to work: see the world. He'd sold his highly successful telemarketing firm, Ameritel, and wanted to take some time off to sort out what he'd do next. He had just returned to Wisconsin from a series of trips around the world, and his thoughts turned to what he would do with the rest of his life. Although he didn't take any specific steps at that moment, it occurred to him that he might be successful in the sports business. The idea of being in sports had been around, deep in his subconscious for some time, perhaps since childhood.

"There isn't one specific moment when I can identify my first interest in the business of sports," he says. "I've tried to pinpoint it, but nothing jumps out at me. There is not a clear point at which

I said, 'That's what I want to do.' I remember I thought about it when I sold Ameritel and was trying to decide my next vocation. I kept asking myself, 'What do I want to do? Where do I want to go?' When I looked at my skills, my business background, it was general management, but heavily marketing oriented. Because of the noncompete agreement when I sold my company, I was blocked out of the telemarketing business for a number of years. I asked myself what I liked best. The answer: 'I really enjoy the marketing business. I'm good at sales. I want to stay in a business of my own. And I love sports.'"

A chance meeting moved Craig closer to making sports a bigger part of his life. Having founded Ameritel Corporation just two years earlier, Craig attended a national sales meeting for one of his clients, SC Johnson, at Doral Golf Club in Florida. Newly single, Craig was teamed for golf with Helen Johnson, who, it turns out, was quite an athlete in her own right. Although a high school athlete in several sports, Craig hadn't played any in college. Helen had captained the Cornell University tennis team, won the New York State Singles Championship, and was a member of the Cornell Sports Hall of Fame. The golf game, and Helen's interest in sports, was fortuitous as the couple eventually married.

"At the time I met Helen, I was reflecting about what I wanted to do. I would begin seriously thinking of one business or another, but I couldn't help drifting back to sports.

"I would say that my first real plan, my first real thought about how to get involved, was with baseball. I thought about buying some minor-league baseball team. At that point I was never really thinking of a major pro sport. My mind wouldn't let me take that leap.

"That's kind of where I was in that thought process—just daydreaming. I didn't really think sports was a possibility, so then I ended up buying another company, Rainfair. I never totally gave up the idea of being involved in sports. I wanted to do it; the idea just wouldn't go away."

SETTING A NEW COURSE

Sports stayed on the back burner of Craig's thoughts for some time after he acquired Rainfair, a business that was in need of attention. One of the oldest businesses in Racine, Wisconsin, it produced a variety of protective clothing items for industrial use. Stiff competition from around the world had put the company in a difficult business situation, and like many other U.S. firms in its industry, it needed a new direction and management dedicated to change. The turnaround at Rainfair became an all-consuming effort, requiring Craig's full attention.

Craig describes it this way: "There was a period of time after I purchased Rainfair that I was totally consumed in that business. It was such a business challenge to take this company and turn it around. And I could see that it wouldn't be done overnight. It would easily take five years. I figured that's all the time I had anyway. It was a make-or-break situation.

"It was a very tough business. The situation was at times unpleasant, but we turned it around. The company today is doing well. But the turnaround wore me out. At the first opportunity I got to sit back and reflect, I got to thinking again, this time more seriously, about sports. At this point the company was very stable, and I said to myself, 'Okay, Craig, it's time to get out of Rainfair. Where do you want to go?'

"And in my mind the answer was a lot clearer: it was sports. Now I let my thinking leap from minor-league sports to the big leagues. I decided to get some advice. I went to talk to U.S. Senator Herb Kohl, owner of the Milwaukee Bucks. He's a very interesting gentleman, with a keen understanding of politics and the sports business. We were meeting regularly, often once a month for breakfast or lunch. He had seen everything with the Bucks— the highs and lows—since he owned them. He showed me that being in the sports business is often a labor of love.

"Despite all the trials and tribulations that the Bucks and basketball have been through, he's still at it. And he has clearly retooled the team. The Bucks are a good team now. He has invested a lot of money with this team, and I learned early on that, financially, professional sports is not a business for the faint at heart!"

Craig admits, "Even knowing all that, I would have invested in basketball. There were a lot of rumors at the time, primarily because people saw us together, that I was buying the Bucks. That was not the case. But I was learning a lot just being around Senator Kohl and talking about sports ownership. I got an insider's look at the operation of the team.

"One thing I learned early on was that you could spend a couple of days a month on the financial side of the business. The rest of it is marketing, how you take the product to market. It's particularly true for a small-market team like the Bucks. It's a prototypical small-market team. In these types of market situations you need to generate revenue from a variety of sources that the big-market teams never have to be concerned about. Small-market teams are very sensitive to attendance. For example, they struggle with questions like how to take ticket sales from 85 percent capacity to 95 percent. Big-market teams usually don't have to worry that much. Since their population base is so great, they get a lot more walk-up attendance and, in most sports, big advertising revenues and other sponsorships," says Craig.

"In small markets you have to be more aggressive, more entrepreneurial. I began to think, *Hey, this is exactly what I'm good at. This is what I've done successfully all my professional life. Maybe professional sports is not out of the question.*

"And so, with a few trusted people around me, I began to develop a model and a philosophy of how I would market a sports product if I could acquire one. The beauty of doing it that way was that I didn't have a specific team. The group's thinking was not handicapped with existing marketing programs and philosophies.

"One of the most important perspectives of this thinking was to reach out to the community, something we had seen missing in many teams we looked at. Many did nothing at all in the community. Others seemed to be highly integrated in their communities and, consequently, highly successful. We believed that community outreach was not only a key to success, but it was also the *right* thing to do in a city. I decided it was central to what I would do if I got a team. And it's exactly what we are doing here in Nashville now. It's so fundamental. But many teams and many cities have never experienced it before. In some cities, and some of the more traditional sports, it would be a dramatic change. For an expansion city with a new sport, it was the critical element."

Craig emphasizes, "In Nashville, I think our community approach has been a lot of fun, but has also generated considerable interest. I think we've clearly added a new dimension to the city, not just in sports, but to the general community as well. We try hard to make a contribution through the Predators Foundation for children and people in need. I'm most proud of that. But it has also enticed people to go down to the arena to watch a game.

"So, what did we learn before we even thought about Nashville and hockey? Clearly a lot of the things we've been doing here. Not the specific strategy, but the overall strategy that integrating a team into the community can make a difference in ticket sales and the image of the team by the way you market the product.

"But up to this point it was still textbook learning, if you will, because I wasn't able to exercise the strategy. I didn't have a franchise, and, for the moment, I didn't have any real leads on one."

THE LURE OF BASKETBALL

Craig wanted to get into professional sports, but it wasn't hockey, at least originally, that had his attention. Still unaware of the opportunities in hockey, Craig pursued a number of sports activities, most notably basketball. He came to rely on and frequently consult a number of people in sports. Among the most important to him was sports agent Joe Sweeney, who represents, among others, Brett Favre of the Green Bay Packers. "Joe," says Craig, "helped me to understand the financial dynamics of sports today.

"Actually my first foray into professional sports was when I got involved with some people who were trying to put together a minor-league basketball league, the entire league. It never worked out or at least hasn't yet. It was one of those deals that didn't work for me, but eventually took an unusual turn and I ended up with something entirely different that does work—in this case, the Predators.

"I started out trying to get into pro sports with a bunch of people intent on starting a minor basketball league of ten to twelve teams and ended up owning the Predators. It was a strange twist of events. But one I wouldn't, in hindsight, trade for anything. Owning the Nashville Predators has turned out to be the highlight of my professional career," explains Craig.

"One of the people initially involved in trying to put the basketball league together was a close friend of mine, Jim Fitzgerald, who was the owner of the Golden State Warriors and who once owned the Milwaukee Bucks. If people have mentors in business, I would say Jim Fitzgerald is mine when it comes to sports. Everybody likes Jim. He is a wonderful man. He is the kind of person who will take your phone call not knowing who you are. Throughout the process of my trying to understand professional sports, I would call Jim and we would talk. Occasionally we would meet. I told him I had a dream of owning an NBA franchise somewhere in the country. His recommendations were very specific: 'Do this. Don't do that. Life is too short for this or that.' That sort of thing. Good advice for the future.

"He emphasized that it's hard to make money in sports, particularly basketball. He really discouraged me from buying an NBA team. 'Don't do it,' he said. Despite his advice, I pursued owning an NBA team. Sometime later he came to me and said, 'I'm putting together a plan to start a basketball minor league.' They had twelve cities targeted, and Nashville was one of them.

"In the end, the basketball league didn't get off the ground, but my involvement was fortuitous. It was my first real introduction to Nashville, and I immediately fell in love with the city. That positive impression stayed with me and would start the chain of events that led to the Predators."

Basketball was not going to just go away. Because Craig had let it be known that he was interested in a professional basketball franchise, the owners of the Sacramento Kings contacted him at the time he was in the thick of his hockey expansion try. Unsure of whether the NHL would expand, or if it did, whether Nashville would get a franchise, Craig made a bid to bring the Kings to Nashville. Although it got little attention in Nashville at the time, Craig was in serious contention for the Kings. The local Sacramento government had to decide whether to refinance the arena to keep the team. In what turned out to be a seesaw battle, the council, in the end, decided to refinance the arena, and the Kings stayed put.

"I felt I had to pursue both options," says Craig, "because neither was a sure bet. I wanted to see professional sports in Nashville, so I worked hard at both. By the time the Kings deal came up, though, I was solidly pulling for hockey. I loved basketball, still do, but what I'd learned about hockey had by then put it on top of my list." While it was basketball that first brought Craig to Nashville, it was hockey, and a meeting with Gaylord Entertainment's Dick Evans, that was to keep him here.

FALLING IN LOVE WITH NASHVILLE

Craig serves on the board of Levy Corporation (a restaurant and food service management company), which was entering into a joint venture in the Wildhorse Saloon with Gaylord Entertainment. Levy was to own half, and Gaylord the other half. To educate the board on the Wildhorse concept, Levy held a meeting in Nashville. The trip would turn out to be momentous, not because of the board meeting, but because it was Craig's first business visit to Nashville and the first time he would meet Dick Evans, then with Gaylord, who would eventually broach the subject of hockey with him.

"It was about 1995. I guess I'd been in Nashville before, but just passing through, never in the mode of looking for new opportunities," says Craig.

"The day I flew down was in the early spring. I'd left Wisconsin

33

with its snow and slush and sleet. It was awful. I'd worn my heavy coat. In Nashville there wasn't a cloud in the sky. I got off the airplane, and I could smell the air: clean, fresh. And it was warm, too, one of those great spring days that I found out later Nashville is famous for. And I thought, *Man, what a city.*

"I knew that Nashville was building an arena because I had heard about it. I purposely came early so I could go downtown and look around. At that point, the arena was about 50 percent complete. There wasn't much to see, but what really impressed me was where the arena was in relation to downtown. The location, and what it would mean for the vitality of the city's downtown, struck me immediately. My first impression of Nashville: 'Great city, great location for an arena, great vision for the future.' I remember thinking how well thought-out this was; someone had put some time and effort into this."

Craig adds, "I walked down the street, down Broadway, all the way to the river. I still had a couple of hours before the board meeting, and I took off my jacket and sat down by the river just soaking up the sun and thinking, *This is heaven. This is really a great place.*

"After a while, I got up and walked over to the Wildhorse Saloon where we had our board meeting. Later that night we had dinner with the Gaylord executives, and I met Dick Evans for the first time. It really was a meeting that changed my life."

Dick Evans had come to Nashville several years before to run various parts of the Gaylord Entertainment operations. A seasoned entertainment executive, he had started his career at the center of the entertainment world—Disney. Later he was to hone his skills at Madison Square Garden (where, coincidentally, he hired Jack Diller, who would later become the president of the Predators). Evans was known as a skilled operator who had his finger on the pulse of the entertainment world. He knew what would sell and what wouldn't. From Nashville's perspective, he also knew sports. He'd been intimately involved with the Rangers and the Knicks in New York and knew that Craig was interested in sports.

Earlier, one of the Levy brothers had indicated to Dick that a board member, Craig Leipold, was very serious about acquiring a professional sports franchise and wondered whether Dick would talk to him. Dick agreed and said he'd chat with him at the dinner following the board meeting. It was arranged that Craig and Dick would sit together at the dinner.

Craig recalls, "They sat Dick and me together, and we ended up talking for hours at the Wildhorse well past dinner. Dick obviously knew a lot about sports. I was very intrigued by his experience running sports teams. He was interested in what I wanted to do, so we just talked and talked. At the time I started talking to him, I was really asking about the minor-league basketball idea. I wanted his thoughts on whether it would work in Nashville. He was quite high on Nashville and said, 'This is a really great city with an untapped professional sports market. It is a great sports town. The people here are fantastic. They want professional sports and will support it. Your league could work.'

"He then told me the story of the arena. How it was built with the idea of attracting a professional team. He told me a lot about Nashville, the mayor, the council, the Sports Authority, the business community, the people, the fans, and how everyone in the community was working together to make Nashville a great city, a great place to live and work. He sold me on Nashville. He gave me all the details that confirmed my feeling about the city earlier in the day.

"Then he planted a seed in my mind, which was to eventually become the Nashville Predators: 'We need to get something in the arena. Maybe get an NHL team and minor-league basketball.' Dick knew Jim Fitzgerald, and he said he would like to bring Jim to Nashville.

"A couple of weeks later, Jim Fitzgerald, Ed Lang [an SC Johnson executive on loan to work with Craig], and I flew down and met with Dick Evans. We went through what we had already done and what we were thinking about doing. Dick was very interested and thought Gaylord might be serious about participating," Craig notes.

"We'd made a lot of progress on the league at that point, so I started spending more time in Nashville. I believed I could partner with Gaylord to put a franchise here. After a series of meetings, Ed Lang, who was helping me with the financials, and I came down for what we thought would be one of the conclusive meetings. We were starting to firm up the deal of how we would put a team in Nashville. Then, at one point, Dick turned to me and said, 'Before we get too far, let's talk about the National Hockey League.'

"The whole time we were talking about a minor-league basketball team, I was thinking, *Oh, boy, where is this going? I thought we were going to do the basketball league. Hey, I'm a salesman; I recognize the old bait-and-switch thing. Get 'em talking about minor-league basketball, then move 'em over to hockey!*

"And I thought, *Hockey? In Nashville? Come on!*

"He said, 'Listen, don't get excited. I just wanted to share with you guys my idea.' He started talking hockey, about his vision of how well an NHL hockey team would do here. Then he said we could complement hockey with the minor-league basketball team. He gave us an enthusiastic hour-and-a-half talk about hockey, and then we spent the last twenty minutes with him talking about the basketball league.

"At that point in time, I had never really looked at an NHL franchise, but I was intrigued. I'd played a little pickup hockey as a kid and really loved it. It wasn't a big sport where I grew up. I'd seen the Hawks [Chicago Blackhawks] play and always found it really exciting. But it hadn't been on my radar screen. All of a sudden Dick had introduced something that I felt I needed to find out about.

"Ed Lang must have been reading my mind or my body language. When we left the meeting, he turned to me and said, 'Well, okay, I feel like I've become an expert on the NBA and minor-league basketball, but I guess I need to figure out what's going on with the hockey league stuff.'"

A HOT SPORT

Ed Lang and Craig dug up everything they could on the National Hockey League: What were the hot issues? Where were the teams? The owners? Which teams were most successful? Why? Were they making money? To their surprise, they found that hockey was the place to be. It was hot. Everything was going up: attendance, sponsorships, TV viewership. A lot of national sponsors were turning to hockey as an alternative to an overcrowded NBA sponsorship market. Hockey was an upscale sport with an attractive fan base. People liked the speed and excitement. It seemed to perfectly capture the modern lifestyle. And hockey had what sponsors crave: great demographics. Its fans are young, educated, sophisticated, and family oriented.

"We were truly surprised at what we found," Ed Lang remembers. "Although hockey had been well established for many years, we felt it was at the start of a big upswing. We began to think hockey was the best thing happening in sports today and the growth sport of the future. We got real excited about the business of hockey. Couple that with where hockey is successful, in all these new markets, and with the type of owners hockey was attracting, and we knew we had a winner."

Craig acknowledges, "When I started looking at the big picture of what was happening with hockey, I just got more and more convinced. San Jose was shaking up Silicon Valley. The Dallas Stars were blowing away the [NBA] Mavericks. Tampa Bay had just started and, despite some difficulties, seemed positioned for big things. The Florida Panthers had been established just a few years before and were really doing well. Disney, with the Mighty Ducks, had recently come into the league, and Phoenix had just gotten a team from Winnipeg.

"And the players. Wow! What a great group of outstanding athletes. Gretzky, Lemieux, Jagr, Yzerman, Lindros, and Hasek! Great players and, from all accounts, great people too.

Wonderful role models. And the tradition. Orr, Hull, and Howe. And the Stanley Cup. The oldest and most contested championship in sports. I thought, *Man, it doesn't get any better than this!*

"I looked deep and hard. I found a traditionally northern sport that was finding a new and growing market in the South. NASCAR! It's the NASCAR of team sports. I was sold. I wanted to be part of it."

The idea for the basketball league was still there, but Craig decided he was going to put all his efforts into hockey.

"What an exciting time to be involved in this sport! So I called Dick up and said, 'Let's talk NHL hockey.' He said, 'I'm ready.' He knew he had my attention!"

Craig was learning about more than hockey. He and Ed Lang began learning everything they could about the Nashville market, its people, economics, culture, and approach to sports. And they liked what they saw. Craig was taking every opportunity to visit the city and understand its rhythms. He became a frequent visitor for business and pleasure.

"I came down one time to play in the pro-am BellSouth [Golf] Classic. That put me here for three or four days. I also brought some close and trusted friends down to play in the tournament. I wanted their advice. They said to me, 'Craig, you're right. This is a great city. We love the people. The people are great.'

"In those days I always stayed at the Renaissance Hotel. Nobody knew me particularly. My name hadn't surfaced yet in the press. But I'd walk into the hotel lobby, and the staff would say, 'Mr. Leipold, how are you today?' I figured out pretty quickly that this city is special. They didn't know anything about me or what I was doing there. They were just friendly, good people. The city sends that kind of message. My love for Nashville is why Dick and I always met here. To be fair, to save me the travel, Dick would offer to come to Wisconsin. But I'd say, 'No. I'll come down there. I don't mind. I'll come to Nashville.'

"And I did a lot. And Dick and I talked hockey. Then we made a trip to the National Hockey League, to the office in New York," Craig recalls.

"At the time, there were no expansion plans publicly announced. We had no idea whether they'd be interested in putting a team in Nashville or anywhere else for that matter. We decided to be proactive and make the first contact.

"Dick said, 'Let's fly to New York and meet the NHL people. Obviously they know me, but they don't know you. They need to meet you as an owner in this deal and see your interest firsthand. We need to take that first step.'

"We went to New York, and while we were waiting in the NHL lobby, the secretary said, 'He'll see you now.' We walked in, and Gary [NHL Commissioner Gary Bettman] was at his desk on the phone with his back to us. The exact words out of his mouth were, 'Just because you're an owner of a team doesn't give you a license to be stupid.' Those were the first words I heard out of the mouth of Gary Bettman. I thought, *Okay. I'll go with that.* I was surprised and impressed by the fact that they apparently mince no words in this league. It was a good sign. I got the immediate impression that this league is serious about its business.

"Dick and I sat down as the commissioner got off the phone. After Dick introduced me, the two of them started to talk. Dick and Gary knew each other and used the time to get caught up a little bit. The attorney for the NHL, Jeff Pash [now the attorney for the NFL], was in the room as well, and the two of us began talking about the league. I quizzed him: 'What's happening around the league? Are there teams that might be moving?' That sort of thing," says Craig.

"At that point Gary interrupted us. He said, 'We really like Nashville. I know New Jersey looked at Nashville, and we're unsure right now what's going to happen at Hartford. But you need to understand that if one of these teams moves, it already has its ownership in place. These teams aren't looking to sell. They're looking to move.'

"This was not what I wanted to hear. If that happened, obviously Dick and I were wasting our time. We were going to be out of the picture. So we changed the subject and started talking about expansion. Gary said the league had talked informally about expansion, but there was nothing specific on the table. He said, 'We've talked a little bit about expansion. We think there is some merit to it. We have twenty-six teams, the NFL has twenty-nine, and the NBA has thirty. We have talked about expansion in general terms and think there's room for several more teams in this league. I would suggest, if that is the route you want to go, you guys should start thinking about putting together an expansion application. Let us know your interest formally.'

"I was encouraged that they would at least listen to our proposal. And the meeting, although it didn't last all that long, was successful. At least we didn't get turned down before we even started."

Bettman closed the meeting by wishing Craig and Dick the best of luck. He told them that if they were serious about an expansion franchise, they should submit an application as soon as possible, and the league would consider it. He didn't make any promises, however. Bettman, of course, was unsure of what the league might do because expansion had been discussed only in the most general terms. The board of governors had taken no official stance on it. The board of governors rules the NHL and is made up of one representative from each team, usually the owner or team president. In addition, franchises often designate two other executives as alternate governors, in case the team's governor is unable to attend a meeting. If expansion did come, Bettman was sure Nashville would be given every consideration.

The commissioner was noncommittal about a team for Nashville, yet he and the powers that be in the NHL already knew Nashville well. It had been rumored as the site for a move by the New Jersey Devils and others. And Nashville Mayor Phil Bredesen had visited the commissioner early on to tell him the story of the city and its arena. Bettman had been impressed with the mayor, the city, and the arena plans. Expansion decisions were the province of the entire board of governors, but Bettman had concluded that he would support a Nashville destination.

"BIG APPLE" SUPPORT FOR NASHVILLE

NHL Commissioner Gary Bettman confides that Nashville was at least "on the list" for any future league expansion, even before the governors voted to add more teams. Nashville got on the list because Mayor Phil Bredesen visited Bettman in New York and told him about the city's plans to build a new arena.

Bettman comments, "I was immediately impressed with Mayor Bredesen. He was extremely likable. A smart, articulate, business-oriented mayor. He called me out of the blue and asked to visit me. When he got here, he unveiled an audacious plan and said, 'We're going to build an arena in Nashville for an NHL or NBA team. We don't have any professional sports in Nashville, but we want to. That is my vision. I believe it will work. Here is why you should bring the NHL to Nashville.'

"You know how somebody says something to you and it just rings in your head; it just seems right from the start. That was the beginning."

It may have started there, but the road to Nashville was anything but a straight shot from New York. At least three existing NHL clubs had looked at Nashville. The long, winding road would go first through New Jersey, then to Hartford, with an intervening stop (even if more speculative than real) in Edmonton. In the end, none of the potential moves were to prove viable, but the exposure proved Nashville met all the criteria for expansion.

According to Bettman, the NHL uses three criteria in expansion: ownership, market, and arena. He says, "We knew Nashville had built a great arena. Phil had done a very good job of prepping me and selling me on Nashville. After his visit, I knew Nashville had a vibrant economy that was growing and good employment but, at the time, no professional sports. Nashville also had a great global profile, with the country music recording industry, Gaylord Entertainment, the convention and tourist business, all combined as a superb 'brand' Music City USA."

While the market and economic numbers looked good to the

NHL, Bettman maintains it went beyond that when considering Nashville for an NHL franchise: "It was more than just a straight statistical thing. All the economic indicators were there, and I believed that it could sustain a franchise. But there were some intangibles too. My gut told me that this city could do it; all they needed was an owner. When we eventually headed down the path to expansion, we had a lot of initial interest. We worked the list down to four cities over three years. I believed that Nashville would come out positively in this process with the governors' selection committee. And obviously it did."

In the process of getting to the final four, Nashville faced stiff competition from larger cities. Bettman says, "Atlanta was quite formidable. Houston was on the list, but it couldn't satisfy all three criteria—there was no guarantee of a building in Houston. Columbus [Ohio] was like Nashville in many respects except, again, Nashville had the building. Initially Columbus lost the referendum to build an arena and then later won it. It took real guts on Phil Bredesen's part to build the arena with no guarantees. But that's what made Nashville an easy pick. We were comfortable with the market, and the building was there. Then, when they produced the owner, it met all three criteria. But for that, hockey in Nashville probably wouldn't have happened when it did."

Bettman observes that hockey fits well into the overall development of Nashville: "The fact is that the economy in Nashville has been growing and is strong. It has economic diversity: health care, the Saturn and Nissan plants, government, education, tourism, and entertainment. If you are going to have a viable economy in the new millennium, though, you've got to keep moving forward. That was Phil's vision. Phil focused on some things that are economic engines. Sports is one of those engines, but Phil also paid close attention to the intangibles. Cities that are emerging as great cities today have those intangibles—energy, spirit, and a commitment to break out of the mold."

As a former businessman and later as mayor, Phil Bredesen was well aware of what companies visiting Nashville would tell the Chamber of Commerce after looking around at what the city had to offer. It was apparent that the decision criteria for a lot of companies to relocate included professional sports. It was one of the check-off points that Nashville's competitor cities such as Tampa and Charlotte had, but Nashville didn't.

Bettman argues that hockey and the arena put Nashville among, and even beyond, some of the country's bigger cities: "There are plenty of big-time cities that have teams, but their downtown areas are small. Their sports facilities and arenas are in the suburbs. But the fact is, Nashville made a commitment not just to growth, but also to the economic vitality of its downtown. In Nashville, there are concerts, there is culture, there are museums, there is opera, symphony, and ballet, and now there is professional sports. It's all part of the package.

"Hockey has great fans. The best in all sports. Forget the old hockey stereotype. Our fan base has the best demographics. Hockey attracts people across a broader range than any other sport. But most of the hockey audience is what advertisers call 'upscale.'

"The market wasn't as big a question to me as it seemed to be for Nashville itself. I believed strongly that the Nashville economy was big enough for hockey, particularly since it wasn't full of other major-league teams. I believed that with the right support the market was big enough to do it."

With the arena in place and the NHL convinced that Nashville's economy and market demographics would support professional hockey, it all came down to ownership. As Bettman says, "Craig came along and filled in the missing piece. We got the owner. Even though he was a guy who had no sports experience, we knew immediately he was right for hockey, right for Nashville.

"It's interesting that many new owners, particularly if it's an expansion team, have no sports experience. Generally the prototype is a successful businessman with an interest in sports. Craig, from the outset, got it right because he understood the importance of being part of the community, which is sometimes easier for someone from out of town to overlook. But he understood that from the beginning, particularly in the context of hockey in Nashville."

According to Bettman, the reason for the quick success of the Predators in Nashville was their becoming part of the community. "I believe all of our owners try to do the right things in their market," he says. "Craig understood what needed to be done from the outset—make NHL hockey work in Nashville. He understood the need to be a part of the community. He understood there was the need for civic and corporate support. He understood the need to get the fans involved and feel a part of it. He understood the need to take a sport that people viewed as nontraditional and make it Nashville's team.

"He had the right vision. Phil had the vision about building a great city with sports being an integral part. Craig had the vision to do the things to make people feel ownership in this team. He brought something to Nashville to make it a part of the community that Nashville didn't have before. I think that's what helped make it work.

"He didn't come in and say, 'This is what you have to do.' It was, 'Together, this is what we can do.' That was his approach, and it succeeded."

THE NHL "GRAND DESIGN"

Perhaps unknown to those waiting anxiously in Nashville for word on the expansion, putting a franchise in cities like Nashville was part of the "grand design" Bettman and the NHL had been pursuing for more than a decade.

"We are the number four sport," Bettman says. "We spent the nineties going to new markets.

"Look at the NHL footprint. In 1990 we were in eleven U.S. markets. It made it very difficult for us to be competitive with the other national sports in terms of television, advertising, and promotion. Our footprint wasn't as prominent in the United States as the other big three sports. By the millennium, though, we'll be in twenty-one U.S. markets. The fact is, our new cities, Miami, Dallas, Tampa,

Phoenix, Denver, Anaheim, and now Nashville, are doing great. We are the number four sport but growing faster than anyone else.

"Hockey is where it is today not because of where we used to be, but because of where we are now, because of that larger footprint."

Lots of people were concerned not about professional sports per se, but about hockey. Tennessee is a football state, they said, and basketball is a close second. But hockey? No way, said the critics. Southerners will never respond; there is no hockey tradition to build on in Nashville; and an NHL team will never make it.

But building a hockey tradition right from the start was a prime goal. Tradition, NHL Commissioner Bettman argues, relates not to time, but to action: "I always knew, and Craig believed, that when you award a city a franchise, and it's done right, they come to the games even though they are not familiar initially. And with hockey, we knew they'd get pumped because the game is that good. We never had any doubt that the game would sell itself. People say, 'Well, gee, Nashville isn't a traditional hockey market.' Detroit is not a traditional hockey market because it has had a hockey team for a long time. Hockey is a 'tradition' in Detroit because of the way the team has related to its fans. Bring a hockey team and a first-class arena, provide quality services, get people interested and excited, they'll come, and they'll get hooked. That's what builds tradition. That's what accounts for the Predators' first-year fan frenzy. Nashville built tradition from the start. It got off to a great start, and it's going to get bigger and better."

NO SLAM DUNK

Despite support from the commissioner, a great new arena, and a highly motivated ownership team of Leipold and Gaylord Entertainment Corporation, Nashville was far from assured of an expansion franchise. There was an application to produce, presentations to make, an NHL Governors' visit to plan, and tickets to sell. And most of all, there were the competitors to worry about.

An impressive list of cities and potential owners like Ted

Turner, hungry for the NHL in Atlanta, were already lining up to get into the expansion hunt: Hampton Roads; St. Paul; Houston; Columbus, Ohio; Oklahoma City; Portland, Oregon; and in the middle of one of hockey's most historic areas, Hamilton, Ontario. Some had assembled outstanding ownership groups; others, such as St. Paul (in twin city Minneapolis), had previous hockey experience. Some—Columbus, Houston, and Hampton Roads—were larger markets, and still others, such as Portland (the NBA Trail Blazers), had professional sports experience. And one, Atlanta, had everything. But all of the competitor cities had one thing in common: they desperately wanted the NHL, and they didn't care that Nashville had built an arena or had staked its reputation on getting a professional sports team to occupy it. They all knew that Nashville was a great city, was frequently mentioned as an NHL destination, and had recently attracted the Oilers of the NFL, who moved from Houston. (At the time known as the Oilers, the team became the Tennessee Titans for the 1999 season.) They knew all that, but they had their own stories to tell, and they would do their best to oust Nashville or any of the others on the list to get a franchise.

The Nashville team had its work cut out for it. The "expansion application team" that Craig, Gaylord, and the mayor's office put together was to respond exceptionally well to the challenge. In record time, with huge constraints and against many odds, the team produced what an NHL official was to describe as a "first-class application" and gave the NHL Governors a very strong presentation.

It was all necessary, but not sufficient. Nashville faced one, almost unanswerable, question: Would the people of Nashville and Middle Tennessee support hockey? A decisive answer was to be delivered directly to the upper echelon of the NHL. But it was not to come in the form of an official report or even a consultant's market study.

The answer came from the people of Nashville themselves.

3

The Seventh Man

I'd never been in Nashville before playing the Predators, but I was anxious to come here. It's exciting playing here because every time we've been here it's been sold out. My first time here, I was really surprised. The fans were knowledgeable and really into the game. Just like Chicago. Hockey in Nashville is great entertainment for the fans and for the visiting players. And the noise pumps us up too!

—#10, TONY AMONTE,
CHICAGO BLACKHAWKS

The fans have become our secret weapon. Our seventh man. They are unbelievable. I've never seen anything like it. It gets our players going. It gets me fired up and I'm an old guy. I have a job to do on the bench, but I'd love to sit in the stands with these fans because they have a blast. I look around at everything going on, and I can see the crowd is really into it. I think the biggest indicator of our fan support is that no one ever leaves, no matter what the score is.

—ASSISTANT COACH PAUL GARDNER

After that first meeting with the commissioner, Craig was confident that, given an opportunity, Nashville could muster a good application for a team. He knew that Gaylord and, in particular, Dick Evans were very committed to putting together the expansion application. Even though he would play a central role in the ownership of the club, Craig gives Dick and his staff at Gaylord the credit for driving the application process. "Most of that application was done without my help," he says, "because the majority of the application was concerned with Nashville, its demographics, and market. Dick, the people at Gaylord, and the team of support people—local PR, legal people, and the staff from the mayor's office—deserve the real credit for what turned out to be a very successful application. They were highly motivated to produce a great application, and they were passionate about Nashville.

"Obviously the application was to sell Nashville. Dick and the team knew Nashville best, probably better than anybody. Plus, Gaylord had tremendous resources to put together the most incredible expansion application. Although my name was on it, probably 95 percent of the application was devoted to what Nashville has to offer.

"Since the NHL was not officially in an expansion mode, we didn't have a formal application, so we used what we had, an NBA model. Again, we were fortunate to have Dick. Because he knew the sport, he largely authored it. The previous two NHL expansion teams were Disney's in Anaheim and Wayne Huizenga's in Miami. Neither of those situations really fit what we needed to show.

"Without real guidelines, we put together our story. We first of all wanted to knock their socks off with the application. I later learned that we did. But again, Gaylord did most of the work. And Tom Sherrard's office [the law firm of Sherrard and Roe, attorney for Gaylord and eventually the Predators] coordinated the final proposal because, as much as anything, it's a legal document."

Gaylord Entertainment's participation in the franchise was not automatic. The commitment, like nearly everything else connected with getting the franchise here, almost never happened. Gaylord supported the arena building project and the NHL application. However, Gaylord's Terry London admits, "Our participation was keyed to Nashville getting the franchise in '98. If we'd had to wait, we probably would not have joined." At the same time, the NHL had told Craig that Nashville would probably get a franchise, but the league wanted to expand by only two teams in 1999.

According to NHL Commissioner Gary Bettman, if Nashville pushed for '98, it might not get it. "What do you want," Bettman asked Craig, "a sure bet in '99 or take your chances on '98?"

Craig told him in no uncertain terms that it had to be '98, and Bettman told him to take the weekend to think about it. Craig talked it over with Terry London, who had recently been appointed CEO at Gaylord Entertainment. London was adamant—it had to be 1998. "He was unequivocal, tough-minded, but absolutely correct," says Craig. "So I told Gary Bettman of our decision and then held my breath. Fortunately the NHL agreed. Otherwise, there would be no Predators in Nashville."

DELIVERING THE APPLICATION

After a solid month of work, the team completed the expansion application, and Craig and the team decided to personally deliver it to the NHL offices in New York in August 1996. Mayor Bredesen, Tom Sherrard, Craig, and Dick Evans made the trip. In the course of the conversations, the mayor reminded Commissioner Bettman that other NHL teams had mentioned Nashville as a great location. "Whenever an NHL owner called," said Bredesen, "the city invited him in and was very accommodating. We'd been a bridesmaid a lot. Now we were ready for a franchise." Bredesen also reminded him that one of the most important things he'd heard in discussions with hockey people around the league was the need for a great facility: "Don't forget Nashville's already got one. We've got *the* state-of-the-art arena in North America. We've got a city that's very receptive and positive, anxious for pro sports. Now we've got a great ownership group. Please give this application serious consideration."

At the time Nashville asked to be considered for an expansion franchise and to join the National Hockey League, the league had not officially decided to expand. The league hadn't adopted a formal application process. Nor did it have a formal application. Therefore, the Nashville group decided to submit a lengthy and detailed application. The narrative part of the application, which was thirty-two pages in length, also included more than one hundred pages of additional exhibits.

The application that Nashville filed with the NHL had thirteen sections generally divided into three major areas. The Nashville team of Craig Leipold and Gaylord Entertainment, supported by the staff of Mayor Phil Bredesen, the PR firm Atkinson Public Relations, and the law firm of Sherrard and Roe, provided the league with what NHL officials were later to describe as a "first-class" application. The application included the following information.

Nashville and Middle Tennessee
- Middle Tennessee offered a growing population with a rising income (87 percent with income greater than $25,000).

- A strong business community with more than twenty-five corporate headquarters.
- More than twenty newspapers and publications, and several radio and television stations servicing the area.
- An international airport that is one of the busiest in the U.S.—busier in 1994 than Charlotte and Jacksonville, both of which had major-league sports teams.
- One of only six U.S. cities intersected by three interstate highways—in addition to several federal and state highways.

The Arena Facilities
- The Nashville Arena (now the Gaylord Entertainment Center) was a brand-new, state-of-the-art facility, with broadcasting and locker room facilities.
- The ice rink met NHL standards.
- Seating capacity for hockey at the arena would be over 17,100, including 2,000 premium seats and 74 luxury boxes (16 seats each).
- The city of Nashville had committed to providing a training facility within Metro Nashville.

Ownership/Financial Information
- The owners of the team, Craig and Helen Leipold and Gaylord Entertainment Corporation, offered impressive business experience and financial resources to successfully launch and maintain an NHL team.

In conjunction with the application process, in 1995, the applicant had an extensive survey conducted to determine the community's interest in an NHL team. The results were overwhelmingly positive:

- 72 percent indicated that they wanted to attend an NHL game.
- 46 percent said they had a "high interest" in the NHL.
- 62 percent thought an NHL team would improve the quality of life in Nashville.

When they gave copies of the application to Bettman and the other NHL officials in the room, they felt the initial reaction was positive. Craig literally held his breath while Bettman and his staff thumbed through it. It was either the beginning or the end of a dream he'd had for many years. Either the start of a new phase of his business career, or the end of the road in a long and difficult period of trying to get into pro sports. Bettman gave the group from Nashville the first indication that they'd done their job. "It's all here, guys. Good job." After thanks all around for the effort and the traditional "we'll be in touch," the Nashville group left Bettman's office.

When walking them to the door, Jeff Pash, the league's attorney, invited them into his office. He looked at the group and said, "This is unbelievable, really incredible. A great job, guys. It's a first-class proposal. You've got a great start on the expansion process."

Later that night, the NHL made the official announcement that Nashville had formally applied for an expansion franchise. The Nashville representatives were pleased and excited. After getting such a positive reaction, they went into a monitoring mode, watching what other cities might do.

Within days, Ted Turner announced he'd seek a franchise for

Atlanta. The Nashville group had always suspected that Turner and Atlanta were going to throw their hat in the ring. Then a group in Houston announced they were going to apply for a franchise. Fairly soon after that announcement, two rival groups in Houston announced that they would seek a team. All three of the Houston applications had solid ownership groups. Then George Shinn, owner of the NBA's Charlotte Hornets, said he was applying for a franchise for Hampton Roads. He announced that the person he had designated from his organization to head up his bid was the Hornets' vice president of marketing, Tom Ward. (In a strange twist of fate, Ward ended up working exclusively on the Hampton Roads bid, to be called the Rhinos, for the next six months, before being recruited to come to Nashville.) Then a steady succession of cities announced their intentions: St. Paul, Columbus, Oklahoma City, and Hamilton, Ontario.

After the initial exhilaration, the Nashville group grew increasingly worried as the number of announced intentions grew to nine cities and eleven applications. Their private bet was that the NHL would award just two franchises. It would be a tight race for the two spots.

Craig recalls that the group would periodically get together and go through a kind of competitive runoff: "We'd go through the pecking order and make our predictions. Atlanta—guaranteed. You put the Turner bid in the same category as Disney. That leaves eight other cities. How do you not give Houston one? Three bids from credible people, assuming they can get their arena done? Hockey is king in Minnesota. Then you've got Columbus, a great city. Can we beat Columbus? Oklahoma City? What about Hampton Roads? It's got a huge TV market, bigger than ours, and a good ownership group. They've got NBA experience.

"We were worried, really worried," says Craig. "Clearly we knew if there were two, we were going to be on the bubble. How do you beat Houston? We figured Atlanta and Houston, and then everybody else. I just didn't know where Nashville would fit in. It was a long, exhausting process that went on for months and months. It was like an emotional roller-coaster ride with no end in sight. They never gave a deadline for the expansion application. We'd start feeling pretty good, then another application would come in, and then another, and we're thinking, *When will this end?*

"In some ways we didn't want it to end. While the application process was still open, we still had a shot. When the process closed, then a decision would be announced, and if we didn't make it, we would have been devastated. And we thought it was going to be close for us, really close. Did we really have a chance with all the great competition?

"From the league's perspective, it was probably very smart. They kept it open to see how much interest was out there. They seemed to be saying: 'Anybody else want to apply for a franchise?' Finally they cut it off and announced that all the applications were in. Then they said they would cut the list of eleven applications down to six cities vying for two, *or four,* expansion franchises.

"We were shocked, but exhilarated. All of a sudden, it went from two to possibly four franchises. If there were four, we stood a much better chance of getting one."

In the meantime, one incident almost caused a major problem for the Nashville bid. Both Dick and Craig were inclined toward action rather than sitting back and waiting for something to happen. Both were decisive leaders, and so far in the process of getting a franchise for Nashville, action had worked over waiting.

"There was one incident through this process, between the application and the board of governors' visit, that created a small problem for us," Craig recalls. "Dick Evans and I decided to visit various members of the board of governors. We picked four key people. We went to meet with the [then] Pittsburgh Penguins owner Howard Baldwin. We sat down with him and shared what we were thinking about doing. Howard said he would support Nashville. He thought Nashville would be a great place for a team. After that, we headed out to see John McMullen, then owner of the New Jersey Devils.

"On the way there, Dick checked his voice-mail messages. There was a message to call the NHL immediately. It was a 'cease and desist' message. It said, in effect, do not visit other members of the board of governors. When he got the message, we were on the final approach coming into the airport. Dick said, 'John McMullen is a close friend of mine, and we are going to see him.' We went ahead because we were already there. But after that, we didn't visit the other two governors. We just came back to Nashville.

"The next day, I spoke to Gary Bettman, who made it clear that personal visits were outside the rules. But he also said he wouldn't hold it against me personally. Fortunately it never got in the way of getting the franchise."

PRESENTATION TO THE GOVERNORS

With four cities possibly getting franchises, the Nashville group believed they had a good shot. The next step, a critical event, was a trip to New York on January 14, 1997, to make a presentation to the governors. With eleven presentations (three from Houston), it would take the governors nearly three days to hear everybody out. Nashville drew the short straw. The team would present second to last, on Friday afternoon, following the Atlanta/Turner presentation on Friday morning. The team felt particularly hard-pressed because, in the meantime, a vital member of the group, Dick Evans, had left Gaylord to go to south Florida to work for Wayne Huizenga's sports operation.

"We'd lost our most experienced member, a guy well known to the governors," says Craig. "It was like going into the Stanley Cup final game, all tied up, and losing one of your top scorers. We didn't know quite what to expect. To me, it seemed that we were down to one make-or-break hour after literally years of work. And we were thinking, *We're second to last, Friday after lunch. We'll be lucky to keep their attention.* Right before us was Ted Turner. Actually right before us was lunch, and these folks had been at it for a couple of days and a bunch of applications! How could they remember anything after all that? We were not happy with when we got to present."

To get ready for the presentation, the team assembled in New York the night before. They were going to practice until the presentation was down pat and airtight. The core presentation team included Craig, Mayor Phil Bredesen, Bud Wendell (then CEO of Gaylord, there to replace Dick Evans), and Sue Atkinson, who was doing the PR on the application.

Craig describes the situation: "We did a dry run at the hotel that night. We all thought it was pretty good, but Bud Wendell had a lot of distractions he couldn't get away from. I found out later that Gaylord was trying to sell TNN [one of its cable networks] to CBS. He couldn't participate in the dry run because he was too busy on the phone. We were a little worried about that, but we got through the dry run without him and hoped he'd rise to the occasion the next day. And he did.

"On Friday we went into the meeting and did our thing. And if I do say myself, it was a great presentation. We did it with computer-generated slides. I brought an audiovisual professional with me from SC Johnson. We went through the whole slide show without a hitch. We ended the presentation with a video featuring Amy Grant saying, "If you want me to play at your building, play at mine." The governors asked some questions, and we were right there with the correct answers. It felt just right. We hit all the hot buttons. I'm a salesman by inclination and training, and I know when it's going well. I looked around and could tell by the smiles that it had gone well. We shook hands with the governors, thanked them, and left as the last group came into the room," Craig remembers.

"Following the presentation, we went into a conference room to review what we'd say to the press. The New York press and the media from Nashville were there waiting to talk to us. Everybody agreed that it was an absolutely fantastic presentation.

"A couple of weeks later we learned that the NHL had cut the applications down to six cities, and we knew immediately that we were going to be one of those six." The Nashville group was now feeling very confident about the bid.

VISITING DIGNITARIES

Then the NHL Governors' Expansion Committee decided to visit each of the cities in contention for a franchise. They'd start in St. Paul, then go to Columbus, Atlanta, Nashville, Houston, and finally Oklahoma City. They'd spend the better part of a day in each city to gauge the community's commitment to hockey, meet local dignitaries, and evaluate the arenas or review plans for building facilities.

Thus, Nashville was to face one last hurdle in the quest for the franchise, the board of governors' visit.

Despite all the hard work the Nashville group had put in, the board of governors' visit would clearly be the single most important event of the application process. It had to be well planned and executed flawlessly. The team knew the mayor's office would cooperate and had every indication that the business community was behind them. This time, Nashville fared a little better in terms of where it fit in the process. The NHL Governors were going to visit Nashville on the afternoon of their second day of visits.

Craig says the team kept a close watch on the progress of the other visits: "We were monitoring, via the media, each one of those visits. We watched the press stories of the progress in St. Paul, Columbus, and Atlanta. We read things like 350 people showed up for a rally, 25 business leaders met with the governors, and the mayor of the city hosted a reception. Things like that.

"Then it was our turn. We had the entire afternoon planned and scripted. The board members arrived, and DeWitt Ezell, president of BellSouth of Tennessee, was to immediately host a CEO reception in a room that overlooked downtown Nashville, but particularly the arena. More than two hundred CEOs in town showed up. They took time away from their busy schedules and came out to support us. Mayor Bredesen came, as did many members of the Metro Council. Even Don Sundquist, the governor of Tennessee, came to lend support.

"Everybody in the business community was there—a virtual 'Who's Who' of Nashville business. It was spectacular. At that point I didn't know most of those people. I was personally over-whelmed that they came out to support us. There is no question that their show of support was critical in helping us get the fran-chise. It was important for everybody to see we were going to have the business community behind this team.

"When the reception was over, we walked as a group to the arena for the tour. The arena was to be our biggest selling point. No other city had an arena built and ready to go. On the way over, I was thinking, *This should be the clincher. We have ice. No one else does. Everybody else has dreams, but we have ice!* The board of governors toured the arena. They were in awe. They said the arena was great," reports Craig.

"I believe it was the defining moment for Nashville getting the franchise the following year.

"I felt confident we'd get a franchise. But by then we'd heard that the franchises would probably be staggered over time. So the big question became, Who would be first? For us, the decision was critical. The economics of what we were trying to do, combined with the long hours and hard work we'd invested, and the antici-pation and excitement in Nashville, all led to the need for us to enter the NHL in the 1998–99 season."

Craig says, "We'd been inside the arena for probably an hour and a half, and it was really going well. I think the arena just blew these guys away. It is so classy, so well done. Many of the owners were saying to me that they wished they had a building like this. They were impressed with how it was constructed, the seating, sight lines, acoustics, everything. One owner said to me that this would be *the* premier building in the league if we got the franchise. I was feeling pretty good. The day we'd put together—the various groups involved really outdid themselves.

"Nearly everything that happened up to that point had been picture perfect. The arena tour was to be the crowning moment. But I had no idea what was to come.

"Everything the league and the Governors' Committee had heard from us had been more or less official. What the committee hadn't heard was what the people of Nashville had to say—the folks who'd buy tickets, watch TV games, and the like. It was the big unknown for us and for the league.

"When the committee got to Nashville, they'd been on the road for a couple of days. Apparently they had seen some crowds before in the other cities. We got word there'd been about three hundred people in St. Paul and about six hundred in Atlanta. I was hoping to do better than St. Paul and a bit better than Atlanta."

HOCKEY HEAVEN

What went on inside the arena was nothing compared to what greeted them outside. Craig remembers the surprise and the electricity of the moment.

"As we were wrapping up the tour inside the arena, I was pretty satisfied with the day. We'd done everything we could. We'd showcased Nashville and had a great meeting with the business community. Some of the CEOs we'd met with were hockey players from high school, college, or old-timers' leagues up north and even here in Nashville. And a lot of them had kids in Nashville youth hockey. I think Bettman and the owners were impressed.

"While I was optimistic about our chances, I knew we'd need a great finale to send the governors off. We'd done all the right things, but we needed something emotional. We were saying our good-byes inside the arena, but no one was aware of what was waiting for us outside.

"We'd planned a rally, but I was nervous about who'd actually show up. We sensed the support was there, but we needed a good way of showing this to the league in something other than a report. A good crowd outside the arena would do it.

"I realized that it was a tough time. The arena tour, the last stop of the day, was near the end of work. People would be anxious to beat the traffic and get home. We hoped they'd come to support us, but you can't make people do that. We just had to rely on the deep sense of desire in the community for hockey."

Craig describes the scene: "When we stepped outside the arena, it was like stepping into another world—hockey heaven! The radio stations were there. A band was going, and nearly three thousand screaming fans were having a party. You could tell they could almost taste the new team. They wanted to take time out of their schedules to show the NHL how much they wanted hockey. There were kids and adults. Some people held posters, and nearly everybody had a hockey jersey on—mostly old jerseys from teams they'd supported before coming to Nashville.

"I was overcome with emotion. I thought, *They've got to give us the first franchise now!*

"In hockey they often talk about how really supportive hometown fans can become the seventh man on the ice. An extra attacker, just by the support they give the team. That day we had a seventh man. I truly believe that then, as now, the fans became the heart and soul of this franchise. At that point I believe we jumped to number one over Atlanta. We didn't have the TV market that Atlanta had, but we had everything else.

"When those owners walked out of our arena to hear the roar of that crowd, some of them experienced something they had never had a chance to experience in their own cities, in their own arenas. Many of them bought existing franchises in cities that had had hockey for years. They have great support from their fans, but those fans have had hockey for years. The pent-up desire of the fans in Nashville for hockey came rushing out in a spontaneous burst of emotion," Craig notes.

"Our fans lined the red carpet that led to the van for the officials, and everybody—fans, owners, NHL officials—started high-fiving each other. People had on these old jerseys. Some of them looked at least twenty, thirty years old. Some of them were maybe older than that.

"It was like an NHL old-timers' convention with hockey jerseys from cities all over the U.S. and Canada. I think all the owners were looking to see their cities and teams represented. I was thinking: *Wow, look at the history, the tradition—the New York*

Rangers, Toronto, Chicago, and the Flyers. Oh, yes, and Detroit, a lot of Detroit! The jerseys did it. We didn't ask people to wear them. They did it on their own. You can fake a crowd as they do so often at political rallies. Get out the voters, so to speak. But you couldn't fake those jerseys!

"I think we were all caught up in it. Somebody yelled, 'Thank you, board of governors. We appreciate you being here.'

"It was a special moment to be in the crowd that day. I was surprised by the size of the crowd, but even more by the emotion. The Nashville fans didn't have a team, a name, or a logo; they had only the sheer love of hockey and the pent-up desire to have a sports team in Nashville. Any lingering doubts I had disappeared that day! The fans won us the franchise for the following year.

"I was really pumped up! To this day, I can still feel the emotion of that special moment when we came out of the arena."

"WE'RE GOING TO GET IT"

The moment wasn't quite over. The committee still had to go to Houston and Oklahoma City for their final day of visits. As they loaded into the van for the ride to the airport and started pulling away, the fans kept cheering and yelling to the owners that they wanted a team.

Craig recalls the discussion inside the van on the way to the airport: "Everyone was charged up, and the owners started talking among themselves about what a great day it had been, particularly the crowd at the arena. Then a couple of them started joking and kidding each other.

"One owner said to another, 'Hey, look at all the people with your team's jersey.' And another owner chimed in, 'Yeah, that's more than you see at your own games.'

"I looked over to Steve Solomon [then executive vice president and chief operating officer of the NHL], and he gave me a look that said, 'You did it!' I don't know if he would remember that moment, but for me, that was the signal. Solomon was in the inner circle, and I was silently saying to myself, 'We're going to get it. We're going to get it.' It was like everything clicked. It was meant to be.

"The trip to the airport is a blur in my memory. Everything seemed to be happening so fast. There were so many conversations going on that it was impossible to keep track. What I remember most was body language."

But some in the van remember that one of their group said, "Hey, Gary, can we go home now? We've seen enough. We don't need to go to Texas."

Craig remembers that by the end of the ride to the airport, he knew that a positive decision was near, if not already made: "That's all part of it, you know, the kidding and the laughter, the emotion, and the kind of statements that were being made. We took them to the airport, and we were all shaking hands as they were getting ready to go to Texas. However, certain owners were shaking my hand, and it wasn't 'good-bye' or 'thank you.' It was more like 'welcome.'

"Then they flew off. Those of us left in Nashville, the core team, thought, *Hey, we did it.*

"We all came back to the arena, exhausted, but exhilarated. It was a tremendous feeling. Of course, we had to wait quite a while to find out for sure, but we believed we'd done our best and deserved to get the franchise for the next year."

At that point, the Predators had virtually no staff. In addition to Craig and his chief financial assistant, Ed Lang from Racine, the core team that brought the franchise to Nashville consisted of Russ Simons and the arena staff, Mike Rollins of the Chamber of Commerce, Butch Spyridon from the Nashville Convention and Visitors Bureau, the Gaylord people assigned to help, the mayor's office, Sue Atkinson and Kevin Phillips of Atkinson Public Relations, lawyer Tom Sherrard, and from the Nashville Sports Council, Executive Director Jenny Hannon and Ellie Westman.

"Sue, Tom, and Kevin and the people at Gaylord really made up the management team," says Craig. "The Gaylord people were particularly critical from an organizational perspective. I didn't know Bud [Wendell, then Gaylord president], Dick Evans was already gone, and Terry [London, now Gaylord president] had not been appointed yet. But their people really helped out. For me personally, I came to rely heavily on Ed Lang, Russ Simons, Kevin Phillips, Tom Sherrard, Jenny Hannon, and Sue Atkinson and her people. They coordinated the whole thing. We didn't have any of the Predators organization yet."

THANKS, FANS!

Craig and the team were elated to find out that they had a franchise—and the first one at that. But the seventh man had clearly scored the winning goal for Nashville. Over the course of the next year, the seventh man was to play an increasing role for Craig and the team. The Predators would erect a banner in honor of all the contributions the fans were to make to founding the team. They had played a decisive role in the visit of the NHL Governors, but more lay ahead.

The franchise was conditional on achieving a record number of season ticket sales. Thus, in getting the franchise, Nashville was presented with an even larger challenge—one that had never been faced by any expansion team in any sport. To get the franchise, they'd need to sell twelve thousand season tickets in record time. Craig knew he needed to turn his attention to building a management team and to do it fast.

Work Hard; Play Hard

Work Hard. Play Hard. And Provide Outrageous Customer and Community Service.

—TEAM MISSION STATEMENT
ADOPTED BY THE NASHVILLE PREDATORS,
JUNE 1998

We had a deadline [to sell 12,000 season tickets], and if we didn't meet it, we were extinct, just like that saber-toothed tiger.

—TOM WARD,
EXECUTIVE VICE PRESIDENT OF BUSINESS OPERATIONS,
NASHVILLE PREDATORS

War Is Hell. Expansion Is Worse!
—SIGN OVER TOM WARD'S DESK

Craig is a fan. In the end, we wanted this team for ourselves and our city, but there was a part of us that wanted it for this fair-haired guy that walks to the arena along with the rest of us. I'll admit it. Here in Nashville, we kind of like it when the good guy wins.

—NELSON EDDY,
DYE VAN MOL & LAWRENCE

Nobody works or plays harder than Jack Diller. And nobody was less likely to end up in the Predators organization. A Yale University–educated lawyer, born and raised just outside New York City, Jack Diller had devoted his entire life to professional sports. He served first as team attorney and then president of one of the world's biggest and most successful sports organizations, Madison Square Garden's combined New York Rangers and NBA New York Knickerbockers. He broadened his experience as executive vice president of operations for the New York Mets of Major League Baseball and served on the board of directors. More recently he was president and part owner of the NBA San Antonio Spurs.

ACCEPTING THE CHALLENGE

In many ways, Jack sat atop the professional sports world and could have easily stayed in San Antonio or commanded virtually any job in sports. Why, then, would an accomplished, successful, well-known sports executive, used to the upper echelons of big-time sports, put his career and reputation at risk? Why would he come to a midsize southern city with no real track record in professional sports? Why would he agree to head an unlikely hockey expansion franchise that had no name, no logo, no team, and no staff, and the biggest season ticket challenge in sports history? Because, like the big-game players of the many teams he'd run so successfully in the past, Jack rises to the challenge. The bigger the stakes, the greater the challenge, the better Jack Diller performs.

Jack explains, "I've been asked that question many times, particularly in the beginning. 'Why put everything at risk at this point in your career?' was the gist of what many of the people in professional sports would ask me when it was first announced I was coming to Nashville. I can understand the sentiment behind the question because it really didn't make much sense in a lot of ways. If it had been any other time in my career, I probably wouldn't have come.

"In the final analysis, though, it was hard to resist. I'm here because I'm at that stage where I've done a whole lot of different things, but never an expansion team. I started a cable television company in the early days of cable, but had never been involved in the creation of a sports franchise. That, and Craig. I'd come to know Craig pretty well, and he said to me early on in his effort to get this team, 'If I get this franchise, join me and lead the effort to put it together.'

"I've always been attracted to a big challenge, a big opportunity. And to me this was it. It was the challenge and the combination of a great owner, being at a stage in my career where I was looking for something I'd never attempted, and the fact that Nashville was a community that was on the move."

As was the case with Craig Leipold, Jack's first introduction to the city was very positive, and he, too, was particularly struck with the hole in the ground that was to become the Nashville Arena and, in 1999, the Gaylord Entertainment Center. And Jack Diller's first visit to Nashville was to make a lasting impression on him.

"Nashville was an area that I didn't know well before the idea of the Predators came up. I brought the Spurs here to play basketball in 1994, about the time they were building the arena. I remember quite vividly driving down Broadway in our team bus, seeing this tremendous hole in the rock, and thinking, *What's that?* So I arranged a little free time and came to talk to a few people who were around the site. Workmen actually. They filled me in on what was happening. They told me the story of the arena. I was immensely impressed because most cities that build new sports facilities today already have a team and typically build in suburban locales," Jack says.

"Nashville as an expansion opportunity never entered my mind again until I got a call from Craig. We'd never met, but a mutual friend had made the introduction. This was very early on in Craig's drive to get the franchise.

"I was really having a great time in San Antonio when I got my first call from Craig. I don't remember exactly when the call came, but he was doing the right things. He was talking to lots of people in the sports business, trying to find out who's who in the business. He wanted to know who he could get to make an introduction and who he could talk to. Being the dynamic but thorough guy he is, he was trying to learn everything he could and meet as many people as he could.

"We conversed frequently over a long, long period of time about the business of sports in general, then the business of hockey, and then the way in which you start a franchise. And as time went on, and as he became focused on Nashville, there would be even more concrete things to talk about—whether there were opinions on individuals, opinions on how you handle this or that situation. I didn't know Nashville as a market, so under cover of night, I came to Nashville for the second time and tried to get a better feel for the market. I was trying to get into a better position to give Craig some advice. I probably didn't do a very good job, though. I don't think I recognized how steep the hill was to sell those twelve thousand season tickets!"

Jack Diller joined Craig just days after the franchise was awarded to Nashville. He took charge and got into full swing for the season ticket challenge. Fortunately for Jack and Craig, the courtship period that led Jack to Nashville had gone on for some time. When Jack finally arrived in Nashville, there was to be none of that awkward adjustment period between owner and president to slow the process down. They had done their due diligence on each other and found that they were ideally compatible for the roles they would play. Jack worked inside, putting the teams—on the ice and off—together, while Craig focused externally, primarily on building essential community relationships. The many hours they'd spent talking started to pay off because they knew their respective business philosophies meshed perfectly.

CRAIG'S MANAGEMENT PHILOSOPHY

If community involvement formed the basis of Craig's developing philosophy on how to operate a sports team, his overall management philosophy was firmly rooted in his leadership style at Ameritel and Rainfair. He worked for a big company, started a new company, and took over an ailing company and turned it around. Thus, while his thinking about the marketing strategy of sports management was still in the evolutionary stage, Craig's approach to management was well formed. If a sports franchise ever did come his way, he'd know exactly how to deal internally with staff and organize it, how to motivate and control the operation as well. Craig knew that management is management. He would take what had always worked for him in business in the past and apply it to any sports organization he was able to acquire. When he won the NHL franchise for Nashville, he didn't have to think twice about how to organize it.

"My management philosophy at the Predators is the same as it was with Rainfair and Ameritel Corporation. And interestingly enough, the makeup of the people was very different. Ameritel had all young, very ambitious kids [twenty-four to thirty years old] who were ready to make their mark on the world. Rainfair Corporation, when I purchased it, was a very old company with longtime employees. It had been around forever in a neglected old building. It had a very negative atmosphere. Each organization had its own style and culture. But one thing remained the same for me: you need to get close to your employees, know them personally, get to know their families, do things with them, go to lunch and see what's on their minds, personally and professionally.

"Simply going out to lunch has always been a very important time for connecting with the employees of the companies I've been involved with. And that's true of this one, the Predators. But it was also true at Ameritel and true of my time at Rainfair. About 11:30 or so I usually gather up three to five people, and we go to lunch. Each time it is a different group. I usually don't plan anything special, just kind of connect as we're going out and then we talk at lunch. We don't always talk about business, but if there is a business issue that comes up, we can deal with it on the spot, informally," Craig says.

"At Rainfair, our management team traveled quite a bit, so lunches were a way of helping me connect with people I hadn't seen in a while. For example, I'd go to lunch with one of the managers who had just returned from China. He'd tell me about the trip, how the business was doing over there, how the factory was doing. Then you kind of go on to other things that the person is interested in, like his kid's basketball game the night before. In order to have a good business relationship, I believe you need to have a personal relationship with people. They need to trust you both from a business and a personal standpoint.

"In a nutshell, my management style is really pretty simple: be concerned about people as individuals, develop an atmosphere of trust in the organization, and help each person succeed so that the overall organization succeeds.

"There was no question in my mind where that style came from. I've been deeply touched by my father's management style. My style is absolutely his approach. He used to run plants for Kimberly-Clark Corporation. When I was young, I worked in the summer in those plants, and the employees just loved my dad. The people in his plants never had a union because they trusted him. 'Lefty,' they called him. He knew all of them personally and looked out for them. That's the style I saw that was successful. You don't have to dominate people. You don't have to pound your fist to get people to listen. The best way is to help each individual be successful, and ultimately the company is successful. People treated as individuals, in a trusting environment, want to succeed for themselves, for their boss, and for the business. For me it's a simple philosophy.

"This doesn't work for everyone. You need to have the right personality to do that, but it works for me because I don't particularly like to be a dominant person. I can be, and there are times when as the one ultimately in charge, I have to do that. But it's not my typical style. So I inherited my basic business philosophy from my dad, and I hope I am passing this on to my kids.

"I am pleased when my children are around to see how this team is operated. When they come to the games and see that people obviously like the Predators, I hope they get the message that you can be successful while helping those around you to be successful too. I know it's a cliché, but I believe the Predators are successful not because of me, but because we work as a team, both on the ice and off. In the end, that's a better feeling, more satisfying, than trying to do everything yourself."

Craig's management style proved critical in the early stages of the Predators organization, particularly the trust between management and employees. As he created the new management team, he brought together a lot of people who had never worked with each other before. He had to set the stage, to quickly create a common culture and approach that would guide the actions of a diverse group of people and activities. And there was little time to lose.

PRIORITY: A TEAM PRESIDENT

The schedule for hitting the season ticket milestone was short. Getting the first of the four expansion franchises was a big win, but it also meant that he had to get a large group of people moving very quickly as a unified team. Putting a team president in place was his first priority. He already had one key spot filled, Chief Financial Officer Ed Lang, his financial assistant, who had been with him from the beginning of his exploration into the sports business. For the head of the new organization, Craig knew he needed a seasoned sports professional. He had been talking in general terms for some time to Jack Diller, a lifelong sports executive.

Although he was loath to admit it publicly, hockey had been Jack Diller's first love, and he would welcome a chance to get back to it. He had done just about everything a manager could do in sports; however, he had not started an expansion team. He craved the opportunity to do everything with a clean slate. Craig had been informally talking to Diller for some time, picking his brain about how to set up a franchise operation should he get it: "How would you get started? How would you go about bringing the necessary people together? Not just the hockey people, the ones who would pick the players and put a team on the ice, but the other team, the team behind the scenes?" When the dream of getting the franchise approached reality, the talks between Craig and Jack took on urgency. Craig hoped he could attract Jack. He knew it was his most important draft pick.

"I knew," says Craig, "that the person who was hired to be the president, the person who was going to run the business on a daily basis, was going to be the most important hire. Without question, without really any other names seriously in my mind, I knew ultimately that the person I wanted was Jack Diller. Obviously I spoke with other people. But I knew in my gut that Jack was right for Nashville and for this team.

"The first time I met Jack he was the president of the San Antonio Spurs, and they were playing the Milwaukee Bucks. He flew into Milwaukee and came down to Racine and met me at my home. We had a really comfortable, informal, sit-down, Sunday afternoon conversation. I was very impressed with Jack right off the bat. He had this air of confidence about him that suggested to me that this job [president of the Predators] was perfect for him. He was the perfect complement for me. I loved sports and had learned a lot in the past months, but he'd done just about everything.

"Frankly I was a bit worried that he'd see the job as a step down. I guess in some ways I thought, *Who am I, a real newcomer, going out to approach Jack Diller, knowing what his experience has been throughout the last twenty-five years in the business of sports?* He was clearly well established in his current position as CEO and part owner, running the San Antonio Spurs," Craig admits.

"He really should not have been a target for me. But here's a guy basically saying, 'Listen, I love what I do. I've done almost everything in sports there is to do. I'm even part owner of the

Spurs. But there are a couple of things that I haven't done in my life. I've never started a pro team, and I would like to do that.'

"So he had an inner challenge that he wanted to fulfill. I understand that urge, the desire to be deeply involved in something new, to create something from the beginning. I'd done that at Ameritel, and it was the most exciting thing I'd done in my life, up to the Predators.

"Best of all, Jack loved hockey. He wanted to get back into hockey. He loved the speed and the culture of the game. It was the sport he grew up with. He personally loved it more than any other sport. And fortunately for me, he wanted to do an expansion franchise. That's kind of what got the whole thing started. I was singularly impressed with Jack, his experience, his philosophy of management that matched mine completely, and his deep love and knowledge of hockey, a game I was just learning about.

"I was really encouraged by his interest in what I was doing, so I arranged to meet him again in Wisconsin. We met and just talked. There was nothing firm on the table, which was, in the long run, very good because we were always talking about how to do things, how they're supposed to work. It gave us a chance to really get to know each other without having a specific agenda," Craig observes.

"Eventually I shared with him some of the things we were thinking about in Nashville, numbers we were looking at. I asked his opinion of the plans, and he said, 'Yeah, these are doable.' I knew we were in sync on the basics. Mostly though, in the preliminary stages, we talked about our philosophies of business. And he was very interested.

"At one point, he asked me, 'Craig, how involved do you want to be in the day-to-day operation of the franchise?' I really didn't know. I was so excited about getting the team that I wanted to do it all. In my previous ventures I'd been totally involved. But professional sports was something new, and I had little practical experience. Also, since I wasn't going to be in Nashville full-time, it was impractical to think I could run the club on a daily basis. But it was also obvious from our conversations that Jack was not ever going to feel intimidated by my getting too involved. He was never going to feel threatened by my occasionally getting into the guts of the organization. I could tell from our many conversations that he had the confidence not to be turf oriented. I thought our personalities blended well.

"The other thing we talked a lot about was how to start a franchise. Jack was not a business executive who'd been doing the same thing for his entire career and refused to change. His management philosophies were up to date. He was talking cutting-edge management philosophies. He would say things like: 'This is how it has always been done in the business, but this is how I would like to do it this time.' It was never: 'We'll take the model of the Rangers or the model of the Knicks or the Spurs, and we'll put it in here.' He was always teaching me how other teams do it and how it *should* be done."

Craig says, "I liked his professional approach, but most important, I liked him as a person. It was obvious that we hit it off really well. In short, he was a very confident executive and a very solid business guy. I believed that he would make a strong connection in Nashville. And he has.

"We've now been together since 1997, and we've never had a serious disagreement. I'm not the type of manager who draws a line in the sand. We don't always agree on everything, and that's good. I believe the Predators have an advantage because we have some different experiences. But in matters of real importance, we are pretty much in tune.

"I will also say, I defer to Jack a lot. I'll sit down in a meeting and listen to a proposal from one of the staff, and I'll think, *I'm not too sure about that one.* But if Jack is for it, I'll say 'Okay, let's give it a shot.' To be honest, there were a couple of times when I wasn't in agreement about how we were doing something, but I didn't object. In hindsight, when I think back, his decision was the right decision.

"So you learn by that as well. If there is something I'm not in total agreement with, I often keep quiet. When the decision turns out to be the right one, I've learned something new. Sometimes that's a tough thing for a boss to do, but I've found it's the right thing for me and for the Predators."

JACK DILLER ON THE TEAM

The NHL awarded Nashville a conditional franchise on June 25, 1997. Jack Diller joined the team as president on July 1. To get the rest of the Predators marketing and hockey staff together, Craig turned the recruiting largely over to Jack.

According to Craig, "As part of his process to bring in everybody in a key role, he always made me part of the decision. Obviously Ed Lang, who came from Wisconsin and became CFO [and the Predators' first employee], was a given, but the rest of the senior hires, like Tom Ward, were the result of Jack's efforts. He gets the lion's share of the credit for the great, well-oiled machine that we put together so quickly and, in my opinion, has done such a terrific job."

But this was nothing new for Craig. He'd made his success in his previous companies by finding the best people, building a climate of trust, and empowering people to get the job done. In Jack Diller, he'd found a true partner, someone in whom he could entrust the vital job of building the franchise from the ground up. Although Jack was to be one of the few senior people in the Predators organization with no expansion experience, his entire career seemed to lead him to this time and place.

Jack Diller was born in the farm country in eastern Long Island. His father was a potato farmer in the days when Long Island was still an active agricultural area. The closest town, with 734 people, was eighty miles from New York City. The school he attended had seven grades in three rooms. It was extremely rural in those days, without highly developed communications. He didn't even get New York City television. But because the city was so close, his parents took him there a couple of times a year. For reasons he can't clearly remember, his parents became very interested in ice hockey. As a young boy, he went with his family to see the Rangers and a New York minor-league team in the same day.

"In those days the minor-league team would always play at the old Gardens in the afternoon, and the Rangers would play at night. So here is this small, rural family from Long Island, that had no connection with hockey, none of us could skate a lick, but we were really captivated by the game."

After college and law school Jack began practicing law with a large firm in Manhattan. As luck would have it, Madison Square Garden was a client. Although he never worked on the account, he knew several senior partners who did. They encouraged his interest in sports law and eventually became his mentors, introducing him to the people at the Garden. Before long, he decided that he wanted to become more closely associated with some aspect of business.

"It just so happened that as I was thinking more of a business career, the new Madison Square Garden had opened. It was a much more complicated building and operation than the previous one. They were bringing in people from various disciplines, such as Manny Azenberg from Broadway theater. Another new recruit to the Garden was Alvin Cooperman from NBC, who wanted a lawyer on the staff. They talked to me, and I was very attracted to the job, but not necessarily because it was a sports business. I didn't begin my business career with that mission in mind. It was attractive because it was an organization undergoing change. There was a lot happening. They didn't compartmentalize me as the lawyer. I could get involved in whatever I wanted to.

"Cable television was in its infancy, and I was fascinated with its potential. Perhaps my interest was related to growing up without the opportunity to see much TV. At that point in time cable was simply a retransmission device for folks who lived on the other side of the mountain or in rural Long Island, so they could watch the network stations.

"We created the first package of programming ever done for cable. It was the Knickerbockers basketball games and the Rangers hockey games. It was a tremendous leap of faith because you were saying that you were going to give away free, within fifty feet of the arena, something that you were charging people $3.50 to buy a ticket for. At that time it was a high-priced ticket. We wouldn't have been so brave if we had not had a strong Rangers team in those days. And that package of programming really drove the development of cable television in New York and became the template that drove many other markets. We had to deliver something to the customers they couldn't get somewhere else," Jack explains.

"After a few years I had significant experience in cable, so I left the Garden for a while to work with companies that were heavily involved in creating cable television programming. I came back to the Garden in 1987 at a point in time in which the Garden had changed drastically. It had gone from being an independent company to being a subsidiary of Paramount (then Gulf & Western). That was my first and only experience with a major corporation. I learned I wasn't a big-company guy, but it was an exciting time at the Garden. It was more of a turnaround situation.

"When I went back, the Knicks had been out of the play-offs for a while. I went in and was first involved in a restructuring of the overall company. We created three operating lines of business: the building itself, an entertainment segment, and professional sports. Professional sports was named the MSG sports group, and I became the president of that. MSG was comprised of the Knicks and the Rangers. So I was head of both basketball and hockey at the same time. One or the other of the teams played at home a couple of days a week, so I didn't have a lot of time off. You never do in sports. We took a Knicks team that had only won twenty-four games the year before and turned them around to thirty-eight wins the next year and fifty-four wins the year after that.

"Hockey and basketball in New York have very distinct experiences. The Garden was always packed for the Rangers, and nobody ever knew whether that meant there was a tremendous market for hockey in New York or whether there were only 17,250 hockey fans and they all went to every Rangers game at the Garden. The Knicks, on the other hand, were only drawing 8,000 people if they were playing poorly. If they caught fire, they became the hottest game in town. So they had the highs and lows."

THERE REALLY ARE TEAMS
OUTSIDE NEW YORK

"Eventually I left the Garden and joined the New York Mets in 1991."

Jack continues, "I'd moved into sports and changed jobs several times, but I'd never really thought about leaving the city. I'd been with the Mets for a while when one day I got a call from San Antonio. I almost had to get the map out and figure out exactly where it was. I was a typical New Yorker by then. I knew San Antonio was west of the Hudson, but I couldn't really place it.

"It was one of those classic dialogues where you say, 'Thanks, I'm honored you called, but I'm really not interested.' They insisted on talking, though, and it turned out to be an offer I couldn't refuse. It involved some ownership in the franchise and involved something of a turnaround situation. That really got my juices going. One of the great things about sports is that people do keep score, and at the same time it is the thing that makes life difficult—but it always makes it exciting one way or the other.

"So I went to San Antonio in 1994 as president and CEO of the Spurs. A local group had bought the franchise but didn't really know the business. They tried to run it for a year and then decided they wanted somebody to run it for them. That was my first experience with a small city about the size of Nashville. And in many ways it was my training ground for what we've done here," Jack says.

"In New York, as big as the Knicks or the Rangers franchises are, neither of them has a direct involvement with their community. And neither of them has the ability to affect their community the way the Spurs do in San Antonio. It is the only professional franchise in a city of one million people. The Spurs became a vital part of the community.

"We think that the Predators can do that here in Nashville

with a million-plus-person marketplace. In New York, we didn't advertise. Our advertising budget was one ad a year to tell people that tickets were on sale. The exciting thing about a small or new market, whether in San Antonio or here, is that you have to develop the market with advertising and community activities. In the end, if you are successful, you have a relationship with your community that is very intense, very intimate.

"I remember that when I first got to San Antonio, the coach of the basketball team, John Lucas, told me that even though he had more years in his contract, he was going to quit. I sat down with him and tried to talk him out of it. But he insisted. So, finally I decided to accept his resignation. Now I was used to going out and picking up the *New York Times* or the *New York Post* and looking somewhere toward the back of the paper to find out what happened in New York sports. But the next morning I pick up the *San Antonio Express News,* and on the front page, above the fold, there I am in my rumpled old suit announcing that John Lucas has resigned as coach. And I suddenly realized, hey, the franchises and these markets have totally different dynamics.

"Clearly managing in a smaller market is quite different than running the Rangers and the Knicks. I enjoy this assignment much more, and I find that from a personal standpoint, my lifestyle in this community is a lot more satisfying. Nashville is a great place to live. I'm not knocking New York. But on a personal basis I feel that I'm in the right place. On a professional basis it's the most fun I've had because the relationships, the contact, and the intimacy of the franchise with the community are so much greater here than my other sports experiences."

SETTING THE EARLY STRATEGY

Craig's wife, Helen, an expert in brand management and advertising, helped the Predators' marketing effort immeasurably in the early stages. As chairman and CEO of Johnson Worldwide Associates, and onetime head of worldwide advertising for SC

Johnson, her family's company, she had years of experience in establishing a solid and lasting image for products. She knew what it took to get people's attention and to convey a positive story about something she believed in. She brought a passion for knowing the audience and for customer communication to the early discussions about the team's name and positioning. Prior to joining SC Johnson, she worked in advertising for Foote Cone & Belding for five years where she was involved in several accounts, such as Kraft Foods. Of the early group that assembled periodically to plot team strategy, Helen was uniquely qualified to influence the discussions on the name, brand, and communication approach.

"When we first got started," Craig remembers, "there really was not a strategy mapped out of what we needed to do here, in the first month, second month, third month, and so on. We were going on instinct more than anything. Things were moving so fast; instinct was all we had. It was absolutely a moving target. We would try something, and if it worked, we would expand it and do more. And if it didn't, we'd move on to something else. This was before we had a marketing director, and Jack was still in San Antonio. I knew we needed to start running some ads and billboards and other communications programs, but I couldn't do it all. We needed an advertising agency, and we needed professional direction.

"I called on Helen. As it happens, she is the best person I know in advertising. There is nobody in consumer package goods who has more or better experience than Helen. She literally grew up with it. So she came into town and set up interviews with all the top agencies. I trusted her judgment absolutely. I trusted her so much that I didn't even go to the meetings. I had too many other things going on. She interviewed all the major ad agencies and ended up hiring Dye Van Mol & Lawrence. I had never even talked to the people there. I didn't know who they were. She came away from her interviews saying, 'There are great agencies in Nashville. But we've got to pick one, and I believe these guys from Dye Van Mol & Lawrence are pretty creative.'

"Helen hired them to do the bulk of the marketing promotion

81

and advertising. She set the initial strategy in place and got the ball rolling for us. Dye Van Mol & Lawrence was ultracreative and passionate about doing this project. We are not their biggest client by far, but I am convinced we are their most fun client. I know they take a lot of pride in their efforts for us because they did such superior work. They lived the magic of the first year with us.

"Having set the early marketing strategy, Helen had to return to her full-time job. Jack turned his attention to attracting a top-notch professional to run the business side of the club. We felt we needed nothing less than the best sports marketing professional in the country, and we got him."

ENTER TOM WARD

If Jack Diller was Craig's first and most important pick, and with David Poile on board, then Tom Ward was Jack's most important on the business side. Picking the rest of "the hockey people" would come later. Craig and Jack realized that they desperately needed a top marketing and sales professional. Craig had been for- tunate that he had a helping hand, at least temporarily, to get the vision of the marketing program in place.

When the question of who would take on the task of selling twelve thousand season tickets first came on the table for discus- sion with Craig, Jack already knew who he wanted. Jack's choice was a renowned sports marketer, but he had no substantial hockey experience and didn't know the Nashville market. Neither mat- tered, however. They were not on Jack's list of important criteria. He wanted the best sports marketing talent in the country. And from his basketball days, Jack knew that it was Tom Ward, head of marketing for the NBA Charlotte Hornets. Although he didn't know him personally, Ward had established an impressive track record in Charlotte.

Born in Connecticut but raised in D.C., Tom Ward knew he always wanted to be in sports. When a couple of injuries ended his high school football career, he knew it wouldn't be as a player.

Like Craig, though, Ward had been a longtime basketball fan. After completing his university studies in marketing, he knocked on doors in Washington until he landed an entry-level sales job with the NBA Bullets (now the Wizards). After several years of rising through the ranks there but watching a revolving door of people in senior management, he took a chance on running the marketing and sales for an NBA expansion franchise in Charlotte, North Carolina. For the next ten years he was to establish an unbelievable series of records for marketing, sales, and service. In Jack Diller's mind there was simply nobody better in sports.

"By this time," says Jack, "Craig and I were in the final negotiations to bring David Poile in as the head of hockey operations, but we needed to move quickly on the top business hire. I knew it might be more difficult to get somebody who didn't know either Nashville or hockey, but I wanted someone of equal stature to David Poile to handle the sales and marketing.

"The reason I wanted somebody of that stature was, I'd seen a terrible tendency in other professional franchises not to give sufficient weight to the top business position. I think a lot of that comes from a lack of understanding that this is first and foremost a business. I wanted to form a strong team of two top lieutenants who would buy into the proposition that the business side and the hockey side are equally important if the franchise is going to succeed. Obviously David Poile is the best in the hockey business, and I wanted the best in the other top position. Fortunately we got him.

"From my NBA days I had respect for what Tom Ward did in marketing the NBA in Charlotte. Given the best of all worlds, for the top marketing job here, you hope to attract someone of that caliber with hockey experience. Although not an experienced hockey pro, during the time of the 'gold rush' for the expansion franchises, Tom spent six months in Hampton Road putting together a bid for a team. So, although he didn't know it at the time, he was really training for his job with the Predators," Jack observes.

"As it turned out, a lot of things happened that fell into place for us to attract Tom. He'd gotten a taste for hockey and was, like

83

me, anxious for a new challenge. So we met on Father's Day of '97. I remember it well because we are both fathers, and while we were anxious to talk, we both wanted to get back to our families. We met at Dallas–Fort Worth Airport at some ungodly early hour because each of us wanted to be back with our families. It was not very glamorous for a job interview, but we sat in one of the open food courts and talked. I could tell immediately that the fit was really good. Tom had that same fire I could feel in myself. He wanted to do a hockey expansion franchise. He participated in one in basketball, but he wanted to run his own show and to start with a clean piece of paper.

"Well, he almost got his wish, but not for a clean sheet of paper. When he got to Nashville, he found we literally didn't have any paper or a pen or a copy machine. When you start with an expansion franchise, you don't have anything. You've got to really have fire in the belly to do expansion because you have none of the support systems you find being in an established organization.

"I have fun being in there when the marketing people are presenting some of their strategy. If anything, we've made a mark in the sports world because of our marketing. I think it's attention getting, creative, fun, community oriented, and best of all, it works. Helen conceived the overall approach in the beginning, got it started, and Tom and the folks at Dye Van Mol & Lawrence have enhanced it and executed it with precision," explains Jack.

"Of course, we filled out the senior team with two other key people, Gerry Helper, a consummate communications professional, and a 'sleeper' with Ed Lang. I say Ed was a 'sleeper' because when I first met him, he looked like a big-company finance guy. And that is what he was. Now he's a casual dresser, and he's playing old-timers' hockey. I expect to see him come in with a guitar one of these days.

"In both cases, Ed and Gerry play more vital roles for us than those in similar positions in many other franchises. Although Ed is the CFO, he does more than look after the financial side. He has human resource responsibilities as well, and handled the entire office construction project. He is also responsible for looking at other sports opportunities for us. He makes the contact and the initial appraisal of what's there.

"It's the same with Gerry Helper. In Gerry's case, in addition to running the communications program, he's responsible for our youth hockey development and community relations activities. That is a critical function because community relations comes first with us."

Community relations was key to the Predators' success in selling the season tickets and suites and winning the franchise. As Tom Ward explains, few people had any time to settle in: "I came here August 19, 1997, my first day. We had no employees, no staff. We had a couple of coaches out scouting. Craig said we were going to launch in September, and 'by the way, we'll have six months to reach a goal of twelve thousand season tickets.' I thought, *What have I gotten myself into?*"

"DON'T GET LEFT OUT OF THE COLD"

Although they still had no name, the Predators' striking logo (a saber-toothed tiger in blue, silver, orange, steel, and gold) was a great asset as the months went on, reinforcing the team's image through a series of advertising and awareness campaigns. The management team spent some time talking with other nontraditional hockey markets around the country that had success early on, cities in other warm climates such as Florida, Phoenix, and San Jose. Everyone had tried different approaches, but all of them recognized that the team would have to come out of the starting gate with a bang. They would have to "really rattle the cage so people would know we were here," says Tom.

As a result, they ended up spending close to $100,000 in local promotions within a seven- to ten-day period, just to come in with the "Ice Age Returns" campaign. "That was the theme we used because it tied back to the Ice Age with the saber-toothed tiger," Tom explains. "It was a natural tie-in to hockey, and we had some great graphics that depicted the arena in an Ice Age surreal setting." The tag line was "Don't Get Left Out of the Cold."

Tom adds, "That first event was a make-or-break time for us. Nothing was sweeter to our eyes than when twelve thousand people showed up on that first day. We sold close to three thousand season tickets in one shot. At that point, we all said to ourselves, 'This thing may work after all.'"

It was still an uphill battle from there, however. "After that first day it was a struggle," says Tom. They had planned to go after three segments of the market: the big business market, the small and midsize businesses, and the portion of the public that fit the demographic of a typical hockey fan.

The key players knew they needed some help. Tom notes, "Craig was from Wisconsin; Jack was just coming from San Antonio; I was coming from Charlotte. We only knew a few people in this market. I would say from a management standpoint that probably 80 to 90 percent of the people came from somewhere else." So the Predators staff put together a task force of the power brokers in the community who could utilize their network to get in and open doors to the major industries and major companies, those with more than five hundred employees.

In total, some thirty business and community leaders formed a team under the leadership of DeWitt Ezell, president of BellSouth, Tennessee, and Doyle Rippee, president of Bank of America Tennessee, to call on some four hundred local businesses. In what was to become typical of the Predators' style, they reached out to the community for help, but they backed their request with superb professional support. Motivating the team with an initial sales meeting at the arena, the Predators senior staff described the task at hand, their promotion support, and Craig's aggressive agenda of personal calls to the top businesses in town. Each member of the team received a sales binder and selling aids worthy of the most professional sales organization in the country.

Following a new NFL team into town, however, proved to be a big obstacle for the hockey upstarts. Many of the targeted companies had already budgeted tickets or sponsorships with the Titans and had "given at the office" for corporate boxes and Personal Seat Licenses (PSLs) for the new stadium. In addition, some of Nashville's largest headquarter companies were struggling financially. "This first phase didn't work as well as we had hoped," Tom admits, "but it did get us in doors that otherwise would have been hard to open because we were a foreign subject as far as they were concerned.

"The medium-size business segment, approached by direct mail, was probably the most successful segment of the whole campaign. The Chamber of Commerce loaned us their mailing list and helped subsidize a shipment of around five thousand hockey pucks to small and medium-size businesses within a fifty-mile radius of Nashville. The campaign focused on the tag line, 'The puck travels at the speed of 100 miles per hour, season tickets are going just as fast.'"

HOCKEY STICKS AT THEIR DOORS

With the taste of success from this unconventional campaign, the Predators again approached the big-league companies—with sticks in hand. Predators employees, some dressed as hockey goalies, hand-delivered hockey sticks with the brochure attached. It got them in the doors of a lot of offices that they would have never gotten into otherwise.

"When a goalie with a hockey stick shows up on your doorstep, you either throw him out or invite him in. We got a lot of people in just because of the curiosity factor," says Tom. They got a little publicity as well, including the incident of one employee in a goalie mask being turned away from a bank. "The guy at the bank said, 'I'm not letting a masked man in here. This guy is going to rob us!'" After the situation was straightened out, though, the goalie was able to deliver his promotional package.

For the last market, they targeted men, primarily twenty-five to forty-nine years old, making a substantial income. More direct mail was aimed at them and supported by an ongoing mass market program. In all, they quickly spent close to $1 million. "And I was scared at the end that it wasn't enough," Tom acknowledges.

The team also had success through telemarketing follow-up and traditional salesmanship. All this had to be done, even though there was almost no time to get a staff together. "Just putting together that whole staff was a fire drill. We had three weeks to get it up and running," explains Tom. "That was probably the most difficult thing, assembling the team in a short time and turning it around in really about three to four weeks. Then immediately launching the campaign. How many businesses are really up and running with a month's preparation? Ideally we'd have liked time for research and hiring and training staff. What we got was on-the-job training. You got in there, and you were in the trenches. You either did it, or you didn't last."

Despite the evident enthusiasm for the sport, when it got down to making a commitment for 41 home games, the people on the sales side had a tough job convincing Nashvillians that they would want to see that much hockey. "Why should I buy something that I don't know, that I don't understand?" was a typical response. Also, according to Tom Ward, "the number of games shellshocked the community. They're used to 10 games in a college basketball or football schedule."

Special event marketing ended up saving the day, accounting for nearly 50 percent of the season ticket sales. "When we started, we figured we had to have a spike on the radar screen every thirty days to keep the interests piqued, to keep ourselves in the newspaper, on the 6:00 and 10:00 P.M. news, and I think that's what kept this thing going," Ward says. "Every time we started to slow down a bit, boom, there was a special event. We used special events to introduce the logo, the name, and the uniform, and the media showed up for everything. Everything for us became an event to raise awareness."

In Phase II in December 1997, Ward and the marketing team kicked off the "Got Tickets?" campaign, a takeoff on the "Got

Milk?" ad campaign. The marketing team parlayed their music business contacts into another successful special event, a Hockey Tonk Jam on March 4, 1998, with Faith Hill and Tim McGraw, at the famous Ryman Auditorium. They turned the event into a prime-time TV special, a cross between a Jerry Lewis telethon and a Farm Aid concert, with Hill, McGraw, and Delbert McClinton, which aired on Channel 2 (WKRN), the ABC affiliate in Nashville.

"All of a sudden we had created some momentum after the Ryman event by showing the made-for-TV special. We ended it on March 28. That was three days before our sales deadline. We finished with our special event, the Bring It Home Bash. Then Denny Bottorff, CEO of First American, helped push us over the top. We signed First American as our official bank, and they said whatever was purchased that day by the fans at the event, they'd match," says Ward.

The team was in its last days before the deadline, still three or four hundred season tickets short. "That may not sound like a lot, but it's a huge amount. When First American made that commitment, we knew we were going to make it. But it was scary right up to the last minute. The NHL was going to hold the line for ticket sales. They were not going to do anything special for us because they had three other expansion teams behind us. I don't know what they would have done if we hadn't made our numbers. There was talk of a several-million-dollar financial assessment or perhaps delaying our entrance into the league by a year."

MEETING THE GOALS

The NHL had set ambitious goals for the team to meet, especially within a six-month time frame. They had to sell 12,000 season tickets, 75 percent of the suites, 75 percent of the 1,800 club seats, and all of the dasherboard ads around the ice. In addition, the team had to have all the TV, radio, and cable broadcast agreements finalized. Ward explains, "They wanted to make sure the market was going to succeed. They didn't realize that what they were asking us to do in our situation, in a six-month period, was really unrealistic. They held us to our goals. We had a deadline, and if we didn't meet it, we were extinct, just like that saber-toothed tiger."

If the essence of sports is score-keeping, then undertaking the season ticket campaign and corporate suite sale was the granddaddy of all sports. The team maintained a visible chart of sales for everyone to keep track of daily progress. It was a tough discipline, but at the end of a campaign, the drama and hard-bitten reality of keeping score attract players to play and sports management people to fill arenas. Despite a lifelong career in the sports/entertainment business, the Predators' communications czar, Gerry Helper, typifies the single-minded devotion to winning that attracts people to the sports business. He ignores much of the rest of the entertainment world where there is no visible competition. "I seldom go to the movies," he says, "because they don't keep score on the screen."

That twelve thousand season ticket goal, the ultimate franchise score-keeping, drove the whole organization. From the telemarketing reps to the highest level of management, little else mattered. The goal meant different things to different people, however. For Tom Phillips, in charge of suite sales, it meant preselling some fifty-four suites. For Ed Lang, it was a matter of succeeding at a job he loved or facing a big unknown. If they didn't get the franchise, he still would have had a job with SC Johnson, but that's not what kept him going, putting in long days, brutal weeks, month after month. "Everybody was on the firing line," says Lang. "We'd all bet reputations, careers, and many of us had uprooted our families and moved them to Nashville. For everyone involved, it was tense, but it was also exhilarating. I was surrounded by highly skilled sports management professionals who were driven to succeed. The thing that kept me motivated was that I wanted it to be successful. I didn't want it to be a flop."

The pressure took its toll on some of the key players in the organization. "It was crazy," Tom Ward explains. "We were working eighteen hours a day, six or seven days a week, and I tell you, we're lucky we survived those days. Some days you just thought you were going to go into cardiac arrest. We had a lot of pressure on us with so many people relocating here, with lives, careers, the entire franchise at stake."

Not during the ticket campaign, but immediately following their first season, Predators President Jack Diller made two trips to the hospital, one planned and the other unscheduled. The planned trip was to fix a longtime nagging back problem. The other was for an emergency heart bypass. Fortunately for Jack, and the Predators, both fixes left him in better shape than before.

While Jack's heart was to cause the entire Predators team to collectively hold its breath, on the ice, the Predators players provided some breathtaking, heart-pounding excitement for the Nashville faithful. Despite the difficulties of putting together an NHL hockey team from scratch, the players, General Manager David Poile, Head Coach Barry Trotz, and the hockey people with whom they surrounded themselves created a magical first season for the fans. Even though they had suffered an unusually high number of injuries, a situation that would have taxed even a long-established team with solid bench strength, the Nashville Predators skated to the third best season in expansion history. The team scoured the world for on-ice talent. But Jack Diller and Craig Leipold didn't have to look far for a seasoned pro to build their first team and its future.

5

They Shoot . . . They Score!

We have no egos in this room.

—#21, CAPTAIN TOM FITZGERALD,
NASHVILLE PREDATORS

The players talk about the difference in the teams they've
played for in terms of the management, the owners and
their attitude. All the players like it here. Craig is younger
than most owners and is the kind of guy who's always in
the dressing room after the game. Win or lose, he's the
same. And it's not just "Hey, how are you doing?" Craig
wants to know about how your family's doing. He knows
my kids' names. I'm not used to an owner like that. I think
he's just as excited as we are about being involved in a new
franchise. It makes it much easier and much more fun for
the players.

—#6, DEFENSEMAN BOB BOUGHNER,
NASHVILLE PREDATORS*

---

*Bob Boughner joined the Predators in their first season. He was traded to the
Pittsburgh Penguins during the second season.

We're a little lean, but that's not an excuse. Everyone we
had really stepped up and played.

> —PREDATORS HEAD COACH BARRY TROTZ,
> ON THE INJURIES THAT HAD PLAGUED THE PREDATORS

I've been to the play-offs every year, so this is a little new to
me. But you try to dwell on pride and commitment.

> —HEAD COACH BARRY TROTZ

When we get on the bench for the start of a game and hear
our crowd roar, we know it's show time. We're fired up, and
we know we have to perform.

> —ASSISTANT COACH PAUL GARDNER

Many owners get into professional sports and can't resist becoming involved in what's happening on the ice, the court, or the field. New to hockey, and sticking closely with his management philosophy of hiring the best and leaving them alone to do their jobs, Craig defers entirely to his sports professionals about on-ice matters. He gives David Poile, the head of hockey operations, full credit for hiring the coaching staff and putting a team on the ice.

The entire senior hockey staff—general manager, coaches, and scouts—along with Craig and Jack, spent a lot of time together talking philosophy, such as, What kind of a team do we want? What style of play? Should we go for experience or build for the future with youth? Fast and aggressive offensively? Big and strong defensively? Once they decided on the big-picture approach, Craig stepped back and let David and the hockey people do their thing. "It's David's team," says Craig. "My input was minimal."

David Poile is perhaps the consummate hockey professional. Although he never played or coached in the NHL, he is one of the league's most respected managers. Renowned for his skills at drafting and trades, he has been one of the league's most successful general managers for nearly two decades. If the oft-repeated source of Wayne Gretzky's success, "I don't skate to where the puck is; I skate to where it's going to be," was applied to David Poile, it would be, "He doesn't pick players for what they are; he picks them for what they're going to be." If ever there was a general manager who best balanced current success with a commitment to long-term success, it is David Poile.

SEARCHING FOR A GENERAL MANAGER

Craig gave Jack Diller the ultimate responsibility to hire David Poile. However, despite Craig's lack of in-depth experience in hockey operations, it turned out that he was a knowledgeable participant in this critical selection process. But like the establishment of the team itself, David Poile's arrival in Nashville almost never happened.

When the NHL's decision on which cities would get franchises was getting close, Craig had begun to think about putting together a staff of both business and professional hockey people. He'd watched a lot of hockey and enjoyed it as a spectator, but over time he had not really paid much attention to the people behind the sport. He was missing information in his understanding of "who's who" in hockey.

Noted in other business circles as a quick study, Craig had spent much more of his time working on getting the franchise than worrying about how he would manage it if he won it. Consequently he was short on details about the various hockey people available. To fill in some of the blanks, he relied on his friend Mark Pacchini, not a hockey professional, but a longtime fan with an almost encyclopedic memory about hockey. Although he can laugh about it now, Craig still shudders to think that he almost missed hiring David Poile.

"We were still going through the franchise application process," he says, "when I first heard David's name. I felt the NHL was down to the six or eight cities that were to be the finalists. I still didn't know if they were talking about two or four cities, and I wasn't really sure what our situation would be. One day I got a call from Howard Baldwin, who at the time was the governor and owner of the Pittsburgh Penguins. I immediately took the phone call in my office, and Howard said, 'You should talk to a guy I know who has just become available, and who is well respected throughout hockey. His name is David Poile. If you get the franchise, David would be a great addition to your staff. He worked for the Washington Capitals for fifteen years and has just left them. He is top notch. He is one of the top five in the league.' Then he said, 'I've talked to David, and David would like to talk with you. Would that be okay?' And I said, 'Absolutely.'

"I was still in the franchise hunt, and I didn't want to let on to one of the owners, one of the decision makers, that I didn't know who he was talking about. But I was thinking to myself, *Who is David Poile? How will I find out?* Then it hit me. *I'd better call Mark [Pacchini].* Mark was with me just a couple of days before, talking hockey, and he knows everything about hockey. I called him, but he wasn't in his office. I told his office staff that it was important I speak to him. They assured me they'd get him to call me back as soon as possible," Craig explains.

"I hung up the phone, and within a minute my line rang. *Great,* I thought, *they found Mark.* But it wasn't Mark. It was David Poile. 'David,' I said, 'how are you doing?'

"David said to me, 'I've heard a lot about Nashville, the potential franchise. It really sounds great.' I ended up talking to David for thirty minutes and had no idea what job he was looking for. *Was it the president of the team? Was it the GM? The head coach? The marketing guy?* So I asked questions that would give me a clue without tipping my hand.

"As an example, I started off, 'David, tell me a little bit about your experience.' Now here's a guy who, I later came to find out, is almost a hockey institution, who's been the highly successful general manager of the Washington Capitals for the past fifteen years. He said, 'I was with the Capitals for fifteen years. And before that I was with the Calgary Flames for a couple of years. I went with the Flames right out of college. Then I joined the Capitals. I had some great years with the Caps. I felt good about what we accomplished.'

"Now I know he's spent his entire professional career in hockey, but I'm not sure whether he's a player or a coach or what. I still don't know what his job is. No idea what job he might be looking for.

"All I could think was, *Craig, don't ask a dumb question*. He could have been the head coach of a Stanley Cup winner for five years in a row for all I knew.

"I decided to try another tack and said, 'Well, tell me about your family.' He talked about his family, his background. David's got a great family. His father had been in hockey all his life. 'Family and hockey are everything to me,' he said. We went through the whole family discussion. I asked things like, 'Have you ever been to Nashville?' 'No,' he said, 'I haven't.' Nothing is working. No hint!" Craig says.

"Then I started getting back to hockey, roaming around looking for something that would come up and tip me off to what it is the guy does. I asked, 'Well, tell me, what do you consider the biggest challenges on the ice for a new franchise?'

"He gave me a list of challenges. I was impressed with his answers, but still mystified about the job. Finally we hung up, and I wondered if the guy knew I hadn't a clue what he was looking for.

"Throughout this entire phone call I didn't have any idea about the position we were talking about. It just never came up, and I couldn't coax it out of him. He sounded great, but I was worried that if he was somebody special, I may have blown it.

"Later in the day, Mark Pacchini finally called me back, and I said, 'Hey, Mark, David Poile called.' Mark almost jumped through the phone. 'David Poile called you! He's great! One of the best general managers in hockey! He only missed the play-offs one time in his career with the Caps. He has a fantastic reputation for always being prepared, very well prepared. You must have had a great conversation.'

"I never let on to Mark about my not knowing about David, but I probed him for more details. Mark's hockey knowledge proved invaluable. He knew a lot about David and his family. He took me through David's career. Everything. How David was a star player and captain of his college team at Northeastern University in Boston. How he joined the [then Atlanta] Flames as an administrative assistant and worked his way up to being assistant GM. Then he was named GM of the Washington Capitals and built a team that made fourteen trips to the postseason, winning nearly 60 percent of its games over that period. *Mark really knows his stuff,* I was thinking, *Too bad I didn't know all this before! I hope David Poile doesn't think I'm totally out of it.*"

Craig recalls, "Then Mark told me about David's father, Bud, who played seven seasons in the NHL and was GM for both the Philadelphia Flyers and the Vancouver Canucks when both teams joined the league. Later his father was president of the Central Hockey League (CHL) and the International Hockey League and won the Lester Patrick Award for outstanding service to hockey in the United States. His father is in the Hockey Hall of Fame. He just walked me through the whole shooting match. After that phone call I knew more about David Poile than about any other person I'd heard about in hockey!"

SOLD ON DAVID

Just about a month later, Nashville had the franchise, and Craig had already hired Jack Diller. Jack's style is to keep Craig apprised of his key moves. Jack is known as a decisive manager, but also a manager who is not afraid to seek other people's input as well. He likes open decision-making, with no surprises. Confident in his experience and approach, Jack likes everyone around him to understand what he plans to do and why.

He and Craig were meeting in Nashville's Renaissance Hotel downtown, just blocks from the arena. They'd covered a lot of ground in planning for the new team, but were at the point of discussing the critical general manager slot. Of course, Jack knew that Craig was still learning the details of hockey. He also remembers their long talks about philosophies of management, about how Craig was going to take a hands-off approach.

Jack began this part of their meeting by saying that, in his opinion, there were only two people the Predators should really be interested in as general manager. He named one individual and gave a short résumé of his hockey experience. "The other," he said, "is David Poile."

Before Jack could say anything else, Craig interrupted him. "Oh, I know David Poile," Craig said, "general manager of the Washington Capitals for fifteen years. Nearly a 60 percent win record, with fourteen postseason appearances. Finished first or second in the Atlantic Division eight times and had 90 or more points in seven seasons. Won the Patrick Division title in '89 and went to the Stanley Cup Finals in '90. Drafted Peter Bondra [50-goal scorer] and Jim Carey [Vezina Trophy winner as best goalie in the NHL] and traded for Dale Hunter, Larry Murphy, and Dino Ciccarelli. Before that he was with the Calgary Flames. Now, who was this other guy again?"

Craig remembers, "Jack just looked at me, speechless at first, and then said, 'Man, you are really studying this stuff.'"

Craig and Jack felt it prudent to interview both candidates, but Jack later conceded it was a foregone conclusion. Both were really sold on David Poile.

"In large part," says Jack, "David's reputation, experience, and success speak for themselves. There just isn't anyone better. But his selection also fit perfectly with our strategy in terms of the general manager and coach relationship. And it fit most closely with our philosophy of building for the future. Our early discussions really considered both of those jobs together. Our thinking was that if we were lucky enough to get David Poile, we could get a rookie coach. However, if we couldn't get David and had to go with a rookie GM, then we would really need a coach with experience. Either approach would work, but we knew that David was our best bet. I obviously didn't need to convince Craig!"

Despite his first telephone interview, Craig supported the decision wholeheartedly. "I didn't need to know hockey to know quality when I saw it," he says. "Never mind that I didn't know the background on David during that first call. When you meet him, you know. My real success in business has always been finding the right people, and I knew that David was right for us. A general manager is the leader. He is the one who carries the responsibility for our on-ice performance today and into the future. I'm in this for the long term, and that's David's goal too.

"David was involved with an expansion team [Atlanta Flames] before he went to the Capitals. Also, he'd learned a lot from his father, who had done two expansions [Philadelphia and Vancouver]. We needed to have a GM who knew how expansion worked and knew every other GM in the league. We needed a guy who was absolutely trusted throughout the league. With expansion, you need to do a lot of horse trading, and a lot of it depends on trust. David is one of the most respected and trusted managers in the league. I was extremely pleased that he was available and that we could attract him to Nashville."

On July 9, 1997, David Poile was named executive vice president of hockey operations and the first general manager of the Nashville Predators. From Jack and Craig, David got a clear signal about what kind of franchise they wanted to build. It fit his perspective as well. Once the overall approach was agreed upon, though, David was free to do what he does best: pick hockey talent, from assistants, coaches, and scouts to the guys who carry the puck on the ice.

IT'S A HIGH-SPEED SPORT

Craig readily admits that at the beginning, his hockey knowledge just about began and ended with what he'd learned about David Poile. He felt comfortable leaving the job of putting the team together to the professionals he'd hired: "In terms of the hockey team, the only conversations that I was part of were almost totally strategic. 'How do we want to set up our team? What options do we have?' Even then, I was more of a listening participant. I would give minor input, particularly when I thought that the makeup of the team was going to have an impact on the business of the team.

"Clearly we discussed the teams and players in the league. There were big, strong, defensive teams that focused on keeping the other team from scoring. At the time, a philosophy called 'the trap,' a relatively new style, had become a big thing. A lot of teams were going to the trap. It's a defensive strategy and not very popular in terms of the fans. All you are trying to do is trap the other team and knock the puck back into the neutral zone or through it. It doesn't produce a very exciting game. We discussed the defensive teams and the teams that emphasize speed and offense.

"I listened to the debate, the pluses and minuses of each approach, and I finally said, 'You guys need to decide what's best, but let me give you my input. This is a new city for hockey, one that doesn't know a whole lot about the sport. We've been telling them that hockey is fast, with high-speed, high-impact players skating up and down the ice at thirty miles per hour, and a puck traveling one hundred miles an hour. Speed is what hockey is all about. It's what we're trying to sell in Nashville. Defense is great, but speed would be my pick.'"

Craig asserts, "I'm absolutely certain that we didn't go for speed as a result of that minor piece of input from me because I told the guys that in the end, it was their decision and theirs alone. But I'm glad that we did go for speed and offense. It creates a very exciting game. With a young club, though, you can make defensive mistakes when you're out there and thinking of scoring a goal.

"Other than that, my input was purely from a financial standpoint. David Poile understands that part too. When we first started our discussions, we established our budget. David never exceeded it and, in fact, got us right where we wanted to be. Actually David is very long-term oriented. He kept a little money in his back pocket, waiting for that special player who might become available.

"David also drafts for character, something Jack Diller and I both believe in. I think the reason we did as well as we did our first year is that we were strong as a team, with everybody playing as a team, not as individuals. At the trade deadline some 'name' players were available, but David declined to go after them. Most of them were nearing the end of their careers and had been considered stars for a long time. They'd developed reputations as being very individualistic too. I agreed with David's approach. It would have created a problem with the cohesive team structure that he and Barry Trotz and the other coaches had worked so hard to create."

"I think a great franchise starts with the owner," says Predators Captain Tom Fitzgerald, "and the people that are hired from day one. In our case, it's obvious Craig didn't hire staff for the short term. He went out and hired the best, and he hired them for the long run. First, Jack Diller, whose background and success speak for themselves. He's a consummate sports management professional.

"And then there's David Poile. He's been a general manager for sixteen, seventeen years. Everybody around the league, players and management alike, respects David," says Fitzgerald. "I don't pretend to know much about managing a sports team. But I've been around professional hockey for a dozen years. I've seen all kinds of management. At twenty-five I was one of the younger guys on the Panthers. I learned a lot. I have a pretty good idea about what it takes to win, on and off the ice."

"There is one other thing about David that has always impressed me," adds Craig. "A lot of the sports people that I have seen over the years on TV and now close up, firsthand, seem somewhat emotional. I don't mean just hockey people, but in other sports as well. Sports can bring out a lot of emotion. I'm thinking about people such as Mike Ditka. Certainly hockey can bring that emotion out. Anybody who has ever seen me at a Predators game knows that I get very excited. But you need to keep levelheaded and unemotional when thinking about the big picture. David seems to be especially good at that. I don't know anybody who has spent more time in hockey, from the time he was a kid, than David. He would have every right to get emotional. It's his whole life. But he is able to keep his cool under trying circumstances. I like that. It's good for the Predators. I'm sure at times that, inwardly, he is dying, but he never, ever, lets it show."

THE ASSISTANT GM

David Poile isn't the only one in the Predators operation to literally grow up in a hockey family. Assistant General Manager Ray Shero grew up all over North America as his father, Fred, coached minor and professional teams. He was still at home in the early 1970s when his father coached the Philadelphia Flyers to two Stanley Cups. That was a special time to be around hockey, Ray remembers, because all of Philadelphia's sports teams had suffered a long championship drought. When the Flyers won, he says, "It captivated the entire city."

Allowed in dressing rooms, scouting meetings, and coaching conferences of his father's teams from the time he could walk, Ray knew hockey inside and out. A college star at St. Lawrence College (captain and leading scorer), Ray was drafted by the Los Angeles Kings. After his playing career ended, Ray became a players' agent for several years before joining the NHL Ottawa Senators expansion franchise in the 1992–93 season as assistant general manager.

Totally comfortable with the Predators' philosophy of growing with youth over time, Ray watched the Senators grow from a 10-win season that first year to a Stanley Cup contender today. His philosophy on expansion, shared by many in the Predators organization, is that "expansion is not an excuse; it's an opportunity." Because he was no stranger to expansion and the tough growing period that accompanies it, he was in no hurry to leave Ottawa just as it began showing real success. But David Poile called him with an opportunity. "I was not looking to move [from Ottawa]," Ray says. After listening to David, however, he was anxious to bring his talents to Nashville. "If it wasn't for David Poile and Nashville, I'd still be in Ottawa."

Ray joined the Predators hockey staff in December 1998, and he oversees the vital minor-league and scouting operations—the future of the club. But Ray Shero is equally involved in the Predators' success today. When not scouting new talent, he is often found beside David Poile during games in the GM's box perched high up at the south end of the Gaylord Entertainment Center. "Nashville is a new market and an exciting place to play," he explains. "The organization has worked hard on and off the ice, and we've been able to establish credibility in the city and around the league."

Poile and Shero assembled a team of almost as many people behind the scenes as they did with Head Coach Barry Trotz and Assistant Coaches Paul Gardner and Brent Peterson on the ice.

THE VIEW FROM THE BENCH

While the view from the GM's box may be the best the arena has to offer, the view from the bench is somewhat mixed. (Between their on-ice shifts, the players sit together on a wooden bench. That, and the entire area behind it where the coaches stand, is traditionally referred to simply as 'the bench.') Although it provides a perfect view of the on-ice action, the coaches behind the bench see little more than half the fans. In Gaylord Entertainment Center, their backs are to the east side of the arena. But that limited view doesn't stop them from absorbing the energy generated throughout the entire place.

Assistant Coach Paul Gardner comments, "When we get on the bench for the start of a game and hear our crowd roar, we know it's show time. We're fired up, and we know we have to perform. As we come out to the ice and hear that noise, I've said to Barry many times, 'Well, if we can't get fired up for this, nothing will get us going.'"

Barry, of course, is Head Coach Barry Trotz, who at age thirty-six in his first season with the Predators, was the second-youngest coach in the NHL. On opening night, October 10, he admitted that he, like some of his players, had the jitters. He told a reporter for the *Tennessean* the day before that he was pacing and kind of zoned out on his wife and family: "But when I finally went to sleep, it was a good one. I woke up Saturday and was ready to go." Barry doesn't remember any dreams that night, but if he did dream, it's unlikely that he could have foreseen the magic of that first season.

Early in the season he was unsure of what to make of the crowd and its response to the Predators. But as the year wore on, the reality that the Predators might just have the best fans in hockey started to sink in. Everybody thought that opening night was special. The coaches and players arrived in limousines and Humvees and entered the arena on a red carpet. Dignitaries from the city, state, and around the NHL were on hand to participate in the inaugural ceremonies. No one, most of all Barry Trotz, was prepared for the fan excitement to continue to build rather than diminish over the long season.

"It was still pretty early in the season [October 23], against Calgary, a Friday night, and it was nearly sold out," Barry remembers. "Calgary's coach, Brian Sutter, approached me after the game and said, 'Barry, what gives? We beat you [4-3], but the fans are going crazy!' I said, 'Isn't it great? It's been like this since the opening game.' He said, 'You've got to be kidding. It's unbelievable, just unbelievable! I've never seen anything like it. I'd heard it was loud here but I had no idea. We don't have any home games like this even when we win!'"

Barry recalls, "By Christmas I knew there was something special happening here. I didn't know whether it would keep growing, but by the end of the season I knew it was for real. We were out of the play-offs, but the arena was still rockin' and the fans were going crazy, having a blast. I've been in some great and storied arenas in my time, but this is the best. The excitement of our last game, where the players got a standing ovation and gave their jerseys and sticks to the fans in appreciation for their support over the year, capped off my most memorable hockey season ever. The fact that it was my first as an NHL head coach makes it particularly sweet."

CANADIAN PLAY

Calling it his most memorable season was quite a statement for a man who has collected a lot of memories in his young life. A native of Winnipeg, Manitoba, Barry Trotz has devoted almost all of the last fifteen years to hockey. Like many youngsters growing up in Canada, he had skates on shortly after he mastered walking. In the bitter cold and long winters of western Canada, he became a standout player at every level. By the time he was a teen, he was playing junior hockey in the Western Hockey League in Regina. He had to live away from home in those days, and he learned to balance playing hockey and doing schoolwork. Much of his fierce determination to win and his commitment to hard work come from those early days on the prairies. It is an ethic that reflects hockey's early, rural Canadian roots.

"The complexion of today's game is changing from that rural Canadian ethic because there are now lots of American and international players. But the Americans, Czechs, Finns, Swedes, and Russians are all very hardworking players. They come from good families, and much of hockey is still family oriented. That rural, hardworking ethic still pervades hockey."

Barry adds, "A lot of guys like myself grew up in small towns, but in order to play, we'd have to leave home fairly young and live with a family in another town. You're away from home and make real sacrifices for a life in hockey. They pay you fifty dollars a month for incidentals. Your parents are giving you all your spending money and you go to school and you're expected to keep your grades up.

"Several times a week you ride the buses for hours to play a game. You play your heart out, you may even get beaten up, then you drive eight hours back home, get back at 4:00 in the morning, and you are expected to be at school at 8:30. My parents said I could play junior hockey, but if I ever failed in terms of my marks in school, then they would not allow me to play."

Trotz's career has taken him a long way from those tough, lonely days in western Canada, but there he learned first to play and then to coach. He became an assistant coach in 1984 and three years later head coach at the University of Manitoba. At that point, too, he made his first connection with the pros, scouting for the Spokane Chiefs of the Western Hockey League. It wasn't long, though, before his hockey skills won him the attention of David Poile, and he became the chief western scout for the Washington Capitals in 1988. A year later he was appointed an assistant coach of the Capitals' AHL team in Baltimore, and head coach the following year. One of his key appointments there was Paul Gardner as his assistant.

When the team moved to Portland, Maine, Trotz began a sparkling performance as an AHL coach, leading his team to the Calder Cup (the Stanley Cup equivalent in the AHL) and winning the league's Coach of the Year honors. He then led the team to a second appearance in the Calder Cup Finals, established a record 17-game unbeaten streak, and was named to coach in the league's All-Star Game.

A ROOKIE COACH

Coming to Nashville with the Predators was Trotz's first step to the big league. He spent a year scouting and then took his place behind the bench as head coach in the team's inaugural season. Fortunately for Nashville, he brought his winning ways with him. Although many might have considered a rookie coach too big a risk for an expansion team, the people in management knew they had a winner in Trotz. He overcame odds that would have daunted even the most experienced coach, putting together a team in just four weeks. Then forced to use some forty different players over the season (the Predators were second in the league in injuries with 398 game days lost), he guided the team to 28 wins, the third best in expansion history.

Despite the injuries, despite the fact that seven of his players, like him, were NHL rookies, he recorded wins over powerhouse teams such as the Dallas Stars, the two-time NHL Stanley Cup champion Detroit Red Wings, the Phoenix Coyotes, the Colorado Avalanche, the Buffalo Sabres, and the New Jersey Devils. Some considered that choosing Trotz was a risk, but taking educated risks had become a trademark of the franchise before there was even an arena.

"It was a bold move for the people of Nashville to build the arena," says Trotz, "and Mayor Bredesen's decision to put it in the heart of the city and rejuvenate the downtown, I think, was a very smart idea. With games and scouting, I go all over North America, talk to a lot of people, and visit a lot of arenas. Most other cities don't have the commitment we have to the downtown.

"Then there were some bold moves from other people to make this thing work. Craig Leipold and Gaylord Entertainment took a chance on bringing hockey to an untried market, and then David Poile picks me, a rookie coach and the second youngest one in the league at that! I just think the people in Nashville and the people in our organization all took a chance, and it has worked. We all wanted it to work, and it has. I think the Predators and now the Titans have put Nashville in the spotlight as a big-league city."

Although steeped in hockey tradition and lore, Trotz thinks that the entertainment aspects of today's game have found a real home in Nashville: "I've been in pretty fortunate situations. When I coached in Portland, Maine, the owner, just like Craig here, was a fan. He just loved hockey. He said that he wanted to make it fun for the fans. So we added all kinds of entertainment. And we broke all the traditions in American League Hockey. The AHL is very traditional, and people said, 'You can't do that in the American Hockey League.' But we did it, and the fans loved it. By this time teams in the NHL, like the Mighty Ducks and San Jose, started doing it too.

"Traditionalists say, 'You're not supposed to have fun. You're supposed to watch the game. There's not supposed to be any hoopla.' Well, that's crazy. You have to provide value during the entire evening. Kids and adults want to be entertained. If not, they can take their money and go elsewhere. The hockey part takes about two hours, but we have the fans in the arena for nearly three hours. There is the time after the warmups, and two fifteen-minute intermissions between periods, so there's thirty to thirty-five minutes that we have to fill. Then with a couple of TV time-outs and

109

what have you, there's probably forty to sixty minutes that we have an opportunity to entertain."

LIVE ACTION

His role as coach keeps him away from many of the entertainment aspects of the game; however, the head coach's job provides the best view of hockey's ice-level action. The bench is a great place to watch, and according to Trotz, hockey is the best of any sport to watch live, no matter where you're sitting.

"I love watching NFL on TV. I go to Titans games when I can. But I love what they do on TV for football. You get the same play three or four times. There are only a few minutes of action in the game, but they do a great job of showing you what happened. But live, there is an excitement about hockey that gets you on the edge of your seat. And you can have ten minutes of sustained action when it opens up and both teams are taking chances and there are big hits. It really charges you up.

"The primary focus should always be on the game," he says, "but I really think the addition of the other things has helped people in Nashville to learn and enjoy the game. I think we are very fortunate in Nashville because we've got the most unique city in the world. The country music industry really adds an exciting dimension to the city. The industry is full of down-to-earth people. I think there is a really good connection between the music industry and hockey players. Our players are pretty down-to-earth too. Nashville is one of the entertainment capitals of the world. How could we not be entertaining? The other teams love to come here and be part of it."

If the fans in the Gaylord Entertainment Center are having a good time, though, win or lose, you can't tell it from the expression on Barry Trotz's face. Occasionally he'll celebrate a big goal, but Trotz usually remains unsmiling, transfixed on the action. While he lets Paul Gardner run the offense and Brent Peterson run the defense, Trotz never relinquishes overall control of the game. And he brings great concentration and focus to his duties. In the

The Ice Breaker Bash on September 27, 1997, attracted 12,000 hockey fans and launched the inaugural season ticket campaign.

NHL Breakout, a street and in-line hockey tournament, visited Opryland in May 1998 and involved 40-plus area teams and 5,000 attendees.

Craig Leipold welcomes Jack Diller as team president on July 1, 1997.

Passionate hockey fans roll out the red carpet for NHL dignitaries
during an April 1, 1997, visit.

Amy Grant was among the music artists
who helped the Predators' marketing efforts.

Head Coach Barry Trotz helps introduce
the team name at the Wildhorse Saloon
on November 13, 1997.

Head Coach Barry Trotz,
Assistant Coach Paul Gardner, and
Nashville Youth Hockey League
members unveiled the team jerseys on
February 12, 1998.

General Manager David Poile and goaltender
Mike Dunham at the NHL expansion draft in
Buffalo on June 26, 1998.

General Manager David Poile (left) welcomes the team's first-ever entry draft selection eighteen-year-old David Legwand, on June 27, 1998.

Craig Leipold enjoys the red carpet treatment on October 10, 1998 (opening night).

The Predators' dressing room before the players' arrival for the opening game.

The ceremonial face-off on opening night involving Craig Leipold, NHL Commissioner Gary Bettman, Mayor Phil Bredesen, and Gaylord Entertainment CEO Terry London.

General Manager David Poile, President Jack Diller, and Executive VP/Business Operations Tom Ward raise the opening game banner.

GNASH, the Predators mascot,
is a fixture at games and in the
community, making more than
150 annual appearances.

Garth Brooks obliges fans with
an autograph while taking in a
Predators game.

Predators players and coaches celebrate the franchise's first win,
a 3-2 decision over Carolina on October 13, 1998.

Predators fans brought their own special look
to the Gaylord Entertainment Center.

Pam Tillis performed the national anthem before a game
and later sang at the Predators second-year Gala Ball.

Assistant Coach Brent Peterson (left), Head Coach Barry Trotz,
and Assistant Coach Paul Gardner monitor the action and plan their next move.

Predators surround and congratulate goaltender Tomas Vokoun
after a 50-save effort that led the way to a 5-3 win over the
Detroit Red Wings on December 23, 1998.

The Dixie Chicks became Predators fans
during the first season.

The players brought their fathers on a
two-game winning road trip to
Buffalo and New Jersey.

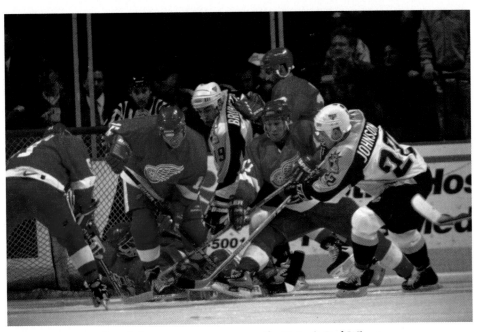

Greg Johnson puts pressure on the Detroit Red Wings
in a Gaylord Entertainment Center matchup.

Wayne Gretzky salutes Nashville fans after recording five assists
and being named the game's first star in his only Music City performance.

The Predators and Music City come together for the 1998–99 team poster taken on the stage of the Grand Ole Opry.

One of the more popular in-game promotions,
the "Windex on the Glass Seat Upgrade," brings lucky fans to seats at ice level.

Involving youngsters at the grassroots
level has been an integral part
of the Predators launch.

The Predators raised a banner in tribute
to their fans.

Greg Johnson, picked in the expansion
draft, provided speed to the
Predators lineup.

Carson Johnson, daughter of Greg
and Kristin Johnson.

Sebastien Bordeleau and Denny Lambert celebrate
a Predators score vs. St. Louis.

One fan's hand-made sign spoke on behalf
of the 17,113 at the Fangtastic Fanale on April 17, 1999.

Predators players literally gave the shirts off their backs
to fans following the final game of the 1998–99 season.

Craig Leipold and Terry London celebrate the naming
of the Gaylord Entertainment Center.

The Predators Foundation has donated more than $400,000 in grants to Nashville and Middle Tennessee charitable and community service organizations in just two years.

hours and days of preparation he puts into every game, he has worked extremely hard on a game plan, and he is determined to see it work.

Trotz explains, "On the bench I am intense and into the game. I think that is a reflection of my focus and preparation. My philosophy is that if a coach is not intense during the game, then it would be hard for the players to be intense. In the dressing room, I'm not hard-nosed or loud, nor am I a kicker and screamer. I understand that you can't be wound up tight all the time. At practice we work very hard, but we also know it's good to laugh. I try to keep things in balance.

"I think I am able to lighten up off the bench. People who know me say I'm a pretty easygoing guy. When something negative happens, I'll say there's nothing you can do about it. I don't go off the deep end when everything is not perfect. I think that you have a responsibility to come to work with professionalism and balance. People will say you have responsibility to the fans to come out and perform well because they are paying your salary. That's true, but I think the coaches' and players' first responsibility is to themselves.

"We expect professional hockey players to give a consistently good effort and not go through a lot of peaks and valleys. Even the most talented guys have two responsibilities. One is to themselves, to perform at a high level and give everything they have all the time. And the other is to the passion of competition and the responsibility they have to their teammates. Not so much for the coach, but for their teammates. They are on the ice together making it happen. Understanding those responsibilities is really important because in the NHL, when you play eighty-two games, you go to war."

Trotz is always on the lookout for talent, but he places equal value on consistency. It is one of the defining differences between coaching in the NHL and in the minors. Trotz comments, "You hear coaches talk about a player. He wasn't consistent enough to keep him in the lineup, or we have to send him down to the minors so he gets his game back on track. I think that's the difference between pros and minor leaguers. A minor leaguer can play really well for a while but can't sustain it. With a good pro, there are peaks and valleys, but they sort of even out. I think the good pros focus better, and they are able to sustain that. It's part of the mental conditioning process. Some of the best pros are the guys who have spent one or two years in the minors, get a couple of games in the NHL, go down for a couple of games, and come back. They gradually learn to sustain their focus, and it stays with them."

If talent and consistency make a great player, Trotz thinks these are the same attributes of a great coach. While players demonstrate these qualities on the ice, a coach does so in a thousand different ways: at practice, in scouting, in preparation for games, in the dressing room between periods and for pregame pep talks. He regards coaching as an educational process: "I think a great coach is a consummate teacher. I try to teach players how to play the game, individually, and within a team system. I've tried to create a system that I think can win games. It's my job to adjust the system so players can win games, be flexible for individual players, and get them on track when they start falling out of the system. You can't survive without being true to yourself, to your teammates, and to the system."

According to Trotz, all the effort is for naught if the team doesn't come together with the almost imperceptible magic that makes a team. He says the Predators were lucky to find it early on: "Our guys stick up for each other. There's pretty good bonding on this team. There's closeness. Some of it comes from our early success and the very close games we've played, but a lot comes from the travel. We're probably away eighty-two to ninety nights a year. There are a lot of nights where guys are just hanging out together. You talk to players who have retired and ask what they miss the most about hockey, and they'll say it is the relationships that they had with other players, the companionship, the friendships that are part of that hockey environment."

Trotz, Gardner, and Peterson command a close-knit Predators team from behind the bench. The on-ice leadership duties have fallen on the broad shoulders of Tom Fitzgerald, and he has amply demonstrated that he is very much up to the task.

CAPTAIN ON ICE

Acquired as a free agent on July 6, 1998, Tom Fitzgerald was immediately appointed captain. It was unusual for Poile to sign Fitzgerald in the off-season and immediately appoint him captain. But for Poile and Trotz, there was never any question. Both agree that Fitzgerald is a stand-up guy. "You only need to speak to Tom for a couple of minutes to know he's solid, a real pro, and a stand-out leader," says Trotz.

Captain of a professional hockey team is one of the most unique jobs in sports and a much-coveted position among hockey players. More important, however, is the role he plays away from the game—at practice, in the dressing room, and in a social setting with the players. He is basically the liaison between the coaches and the team as a group. He is often the inspirational head of the team, leading, cajoling, and motivating them. The captain will often call a team meeting when things are not going well. He aims to improve team play without involving the coaches or management.

Professional hockey teams often have from one to several assistant captains to substitute for the captain when he is not on the ice. The captain wears a C on his jersey while the assistant captain wears an A. During their first season, the Predators had three assistant captains: Darren Turcotte, Bob Boughner, and Greg Johnson.

The captain is often the first player sought out by the media to comment on the team's play, since he is thought to be the most knowledgeable about the team's attitudes and concerns. The job of looking out for the well-being of new and younger players, and counseling individual players not only about their game but also about outside influences that might impact their game, often falls to the captain as well.

Over the history of the NHL, some of hockey's most celebrated players have been the captains of their teams: Paul Kariya, Wayne Gretzky, Jaromir Jagr, and many others. Tom Fitzgerald fit the bill perfectly for the Predators. Considered one of the better defensive forwards in the league, Fitzgerald has always gone about his job off the ice as quietly and effectively as his work on the ice. On the ice, he leads with dogged determination to win and a "give no quarter" attitude. Perhaps he derived his attitude on the ice from his boyhood idol, Boston Bruins great Bobby Orr.

Fitzgerald, a native of Billerica, Massachusetts, near Boston, was selected as the New York Islanders' first-round pick in the 1986 Entry Draft. After two years at Providence College, he joined the Islanders in the 1988–89 season and played much of the next four seasons with the Islanders, appearing in 77 games for them in 1992–93. One of the first players selected by the Florida Panthers as part of their expansion franchise in 1993, he learned firsthand what it took to start an NHL team in a nontraditional market and was with the team during their quest for the Stanley Cup in only their third season. Traded to Colorado late in the 1997–98 season, he was acquired by Nashville as a free agent on July 6 and immediately appointed captain. Fitzgerald's experience in Florida would prove invaluable when he got to Nashville.

"I can say without hesitation that the entire Predators organization has done a great job," declares Fitzgerald. "Many of the acquisitions that we have made have helped us now but, most important, will be around a long time into the future. Hockey is a business. We all know that. And today's performance is what you get paid for. Getting the job done—and getting it done from day one—is what we're all paid for. That's professionalism. Being part of a great organization that believes it has a future and invests its money and acts that way consistently, that's something really special. I'm grateful that I have the chance to be part of it."

6

Outrageous Community and Customer Service

Off the ice, the management and support staff, from
the owners to the vendors selling hot dogs, showed
they were every bit as professional as the players. From
hockey clinics to teach young fans about the game, to the
Predators Foundation that provides financial grants and
other contributions to local causes, they demonstrated a
true appreciation of what makes this city great, and made
themselves an integral part of it.

—OP-ED PIECE, *TENNESSEAN*

BUILDING A TEAM WITH CHARACTER

When Craig Leipold established a home in Nashville, he didn't buy a house in the suburbs, far away from the fans and the arena. He couldn't get much closer to the arena without actually putting a bed in one of the corporate suites. He and his family chose a townhouse downtown, one where he and his wife can look out and see the fans approaching the arena, where his children can watch the bullet elevators go up and down at the Renaissance Hotel. When they worked with local Nashville interior designer Dana Sherrard, Craig and Helen put their children first, making it a place that the kids would want to come to, even bringing their friends. It needed to be suitable for entertaining, but not so stuffy that the children wouldn't enjoy themselves.

Craig and his management team have also tried to make the Gaylord Entertainment Center a kid-friendly place. Their concept of "Outrageous Customer Service" has always been as much about what happens outside the rink as what happens on game night.

"As an organization, we know our limitations. We are not the NFL," explains Gerry Helper, vice president of communications and development. "We don't have a huge national television contract. As a result, our efforts are far more grassroots oriented, such as our youth hockey effort headed by Marc Spigel. I think fans see that bottom-up effort through our community relations, communications, and development efforts. We do an awful lot out in the community. One thing that we did well was a pretty quick and effective job of learning the market and learning what you would consider the hot buttons. Connecting with the community was certainly a big point. I'm a believer that regardless of where you are, the grassroots effort is critical to the success of this game."

"Actually we put two Predators teams together, on the ice and off the ice," says Craig Leipold, "very much with Nashville in mind. Jack Diller, David Poile, and Tom Ward made decisions about the character of our staff and players with consideration about the community. That was a key strategy for us right from the start.

"We knew what we were looking for," Craig explains. "An organization that we and Nashville could be proud of. The team needed to be more than just an on-ice experience. We had to be sure that we had the total package in terms of the players, staff, and management. The players had to be as good as they could be on the ice, but they also had to be involved in the community. As a team, we talk a lot about community, community, community."

"I think we really make character a priority in terms of selecting new players," agrees Jack. "We did as much study of the players as possible under the tight circumstances, trying to do research on the kind of guys we were bringing in because in some cases we only knew five minutes before which players were going to be available.

"You have to have a group of guys who will not get frustrated if they don't win every night or if they lose five or six in a row. You have to have the right group of players, the right leadership both from your coach and from your captains, and I think that was why one person we went out and signed as a free agent was Tom Fitzgerald, the guy whom we selected to be our captain. We selected him because he had been through expansion, he was known as a stand-up guy, a guy who could lead his teammates. That has proved to be very true."

QUICK DECISIONS

"When we went into the draft, we knew a lot about the players' abilities on the ice. David is a master of that," says Craig. "What we didn't have as much information about was how they'd fit in the community. In the draft, you just don't have the time to discover how a player might be in a community role. In the expansion draft, we got something like three days' notice of which players would be available to us. Each team was required to let us know who was going to be unprotected on its list. Some teams would leave 10 players, 12 players, unprotected. With 26 teams, that's 260 players. So you can't do a lot of due diligence on these guys, other than their hockey ability.

"What you do, therefore, is spend quality time on the players such as the captain. Obviously Tom Fitzgerald is a guy we spent a fair amount of time looking at. And Mike Dunham, our goalie, was another.

"We really focused on Mike Dunham. We checked with his team, the New Jersey Devils. Everything that came back to us confirmed that Mike Dunham was not only a good goaltender, but also a good person, a solid guy. He's from a fine family. His father, Ron, is a golf pro. We went to meet Mike personally. We could sense immediately that this guy is a class individual. He'd contribute to the team on and off the ice," Craig recalls.

"We knew that in the Nashville market, community and family are important. So we asked around about players' views on community involvement.

"In the end, we couldn't check all the players, but some of the guys we did check—we thought they were good players, and they were going to be our point people for community activities in the city. They could go out and present themselves very well. So Tom Fitzgerald, Mike Dunham, and Bob Boughner are among those we look to on the ice and off. Of course, there were some other guys who have really come through for us. In fact, one of my real areas of satisfaction with the first year is how well the guys on the entire team represented themselves in the community. I'm proud of them."

Management also made sure that the players really wanted to be here. Gerry Helper says, "We spent a lot of time selling the market to our new players because they were going to be our ambassadors around the league and in the community. They've been wonderful. We have a terrific group of guys in terms of their character, their chemistry, and they understand what this is all about in terms of building and growing a new sport."

"As I've always said," Craig continues, "I'll leave the judgments about hockey ability to David and his staff. I have complete confidence in them. What I look for, though, is the whole person, his character, integrity, interest in his family and our community. When I meet a player, I'll say, 'Tell me about yourself. What is it about the game you like? Don't like?' What I don't want to hear is, 'I'm a hockey player. I don't care about anything else. This game is my life. I just want to play the game. That's all I want to do.'

"That isn't the kind of player we want. We need the commitment to hockey, but we need a whole lot more than that. We need the kind of guy who will go when the hospitals call. When a school needs somebody, he will do it. We wanted people like Tom Fitzgerald. We didn't have to go far to find out about Tom. We talked to people in Florida about him.

"Tom Fitzgerald has the exact kind of personal characteristics we were looking for. You know, we didn't really have to ask him to get involved. We knew that he would. Same thing with Joel Bouchard,* Drake Berehowsky, and Patrick Cote. In fact, all the others. Our guys are very involved in the community, particularly with children. We were fortunate that we got a team with exactly the kind of personality that we could market in this community.

"When we first talked with these players, the hockey guys were all talking with them about this type of offense and that type of defense. You know, things like, 'Would you be willing to play this style? Can you fit into this type of defense?' And I was saying, 'Tell me about your family. What do you like to do off the ice?'"

Craig adds, "I was pushing the soft buttons. When I'd hear the answers I was looking for, I'd say to myself, 'Okay, I hope the hockey guys choose him because he is going to fit well into the community.'

"I'm not suggesting that I personally was involved in the drafting process. I wasn't. I didn't say, 'Let's take this guy or not take

---

*Joel Bouchard was picked up on waivers by the Dallas Stars in the 1999–2000 season.

this guy,' but David and his staff knew exactly the quality of player we wanted. We believe that players have great influence on the community and the marketing success of our team. If we aren't successful in marketing, in the community, putting people in the seats, we aren't going to have funds to finance a team year after year."

PLAYERS OFF THE ICE

As Gerry Helper states, "To a certain extent, other sports can afford the luxury of sitting back and not making as much effort in their own market because they have so much national television revenue. They make money regardless of how many people come through the turnstiles. It's not the case with hockey. Hockey generates some 70 percent of its revenues in tickets." And according to Gerry, if the fans don't feel that the players are a part of the community, those tickets become much harder to sell.

"David Poile understands that," Craig says, "and helps us put fans in seats by making sure we get players who are solid hockey players, but also willing to do things in the community. We don't have anything contractual that requires the players to do things in the community. Our guys do it because they really want to.

"Here's a typical example. One of our staff, Frank Buonomo, had the job of coordinating all community requests. Near the start of the season, he went down to the dressing room with a community activity sign-up sheet, and all the players were there. He was nervous because everyone was new, and he was unsure what response he'd get. So he said, 'All right, I've got twenty-five requests here that cover the next two months. If you can each please sign up for one of the requests, I won't bother you again for two months. I just need one player for each request. If everybody signs up for one, we're going to be in good shape.'

"He circulated the sheet and was really surprised at what came back to him. He said by the time it got halfway through the room, it was overbooked. Everybody signed up for something. Most players signed up for two or more events. Drake Berehowsky signed five different times. At events where the organization was looking for two players, four signed up. Frank, who'd worked for the New York Rangers, said he couldn't believe it. When I heard about it, I couldn't believe it either. We have the best bunch of players, so much fun to work with.

"You need to understand your market if you are going to be successful. We don't need a 'Broadway Joe'–type player here. We need somebody who's caring, who's going to be involved."

Craig continues, "Another example. One of our players, I won't embarrass him by saying who, had just come into town. He had a phone interview scheduled with one of the radio talk shows at 6:30 in the morning. He made the call to the show as planned, and the show host said, 'Hey, this is great, but what is all that noise in the background?' The player said, 'I'm calling from a pay phone.' The host laughed and asked, 'What, the Predators don't pay you enough money to get your own phone?' The player said, 'Oh, yes, but my wife and I just moved into the house, and my phones aren't working yet. We're not hooked up, and I had to drive around to find a pay phone.'

"The guy actually got up and left his house at 6:30 in the morning to call from a pay phone. You can't plan that. You can't buy that kind of character. The player absolutely realized the importance of connecting to the community. He didn't know any of the strategy of the team. He had just moved to town and didn't know any of our community strategy and, just moving into a new house, probably couldn't care less about that. He just knew his responsibility. He made a commitment to call the show. I guess what I'm saying is that we consciously decided that community was a big part of the team, and in both the staff and the player selection it became a criterion for them."

COURTING THE FANS

Responsibility to the community pervades the entire Predators organization—management, staff, players, and coaches. Assistant

Coach Paul Gardner knew exactly what the team was looking for, and he played a key role in drafting quality players who were also committed to their broader role in the community. Gardner, a seasoned coaching professional who had an illustrious playing career (ten years and nearly 500 NHL games, scoring 402 points), learned from his own experience and also from his father. Like GM David Poile and Assistant GM Ray Shero, Gardner grew up in a hockey family. His father, Cal, played twelve seasons in the NHL and won two Stanley Cups. Cal coached in the AHL and was a broadcaster for the Toronto Maple Leafs. Paul's brother, David, played seven seasons in the NHL as well.

Paul Gardner's father taught both his sons that hockey players carried a special responsibility. "My brother and I each played for five different teams," Paul says. "My dad taught us that you are always responsible to the fans wherever you go. It didn't matter that you were traded and found yourself in a strange new environment. I was taught that as a twenty-year-old pro, you had to live up to your responsibilities. Dad would say, 'Lots of kids are looking up to you. Remember what you were like when you were a kid and walked into the dressing room, how excited you were? So remember all that.'

"In Nashville, there is no question that players are responsible to the community. We're a small-market team that needs the community. But the love affair between the community and the Predators makes it easy. It's different if you are going out in a big market and most of what you do is sign autographs. Here they know you are playing your best, and they love you for it. Our fans make you want to be out there.

"When Barry and I first got to Nashville, they wanted us to do a lot of events and be around for all the community involvement, so David Poile asked us if we could move here quickly. We searched the Internet, and my wife made about a thousand phone calls and got us down here right away. We've just fallen in love with it. We love our home. We love the people," says Paul.

"The opening of the season was such a whirlwind. Everything

123

was happening so fast. Now that I can sit back, I realize that Craig Leipold has charisma with the fans. Everything that we seemed to do involved the fans, and they seemed to just catch on to it. Everybody wanted hockey in Nashville, and they were excited about it. I've never seen anything like it in any other city in all the years I've played. I've played in some great minor-league places and some big-league cities, but I've never seen anything quite like the bond between the fans and the players here."

An important part of a professional athlete's role is dealing with the media. Gardner notes that hockey players are the most sensitive to the needs of the media: "I talk to a lot of the media around the country, and they will say hockey players are the best in dealing with the media. I give the NHL credit through the teaching they do. I guess we're the ones that need the media the most because we don't have the big TV contracts that football, baseball, and basketball do. So I give our communications people and the communications people throughout the league a lot of credit."

MIAMI TO NASHVILLE

Tom Fitzgerald has fielded his share of media questions about what it was like to move from a major market to Nashville. He has only positive things to say about his time with the Florida Panthers, but he draws a contrast between his time there and his joining the Predators. He went from a huge metropolitan area where the fans were spread out over quite a bit of territory to a much smaller, more intimate area.

Tom explains, "I think a big difference between the two clubs and their markets is the city size. Here in Nashville we are drawing from a smaller area than Florida. While I was there, the Panthers played in Miami [in 1999, the Panthers moved to a new arena in Sunrise, Florida, just outside Fort Lauderdale], but we also drew from the huge surrounding area, such as Dade County, and as far north as Palm Beach County. We attracted fans from all over the south Florida area.

"One of the things I find similar between the two areas, however, is the strong hockey knowledge in what people call nontraditional hockey markets. In south Florida, there are a lot of northerners and Canadians living in the area. The northerners that I met were largely from the Midwest, the Northeast, and the New York–New Jersey area—transplants who had moved down to Florida. That was really our original backbone of fan support.

"Interestingly I found it was somewhat the same thing when I came here to Nashville. Just look at the number of our fans here from Detroit, Chicago, and New York. And the Canadians too. You really need that initial, core fan base, and then you need to make it grow from there. Although hockey was new to south Florida, the market was already pretty knowledgeable. Actually I was surprised that it's not too much different in Nashville. I've been surprised at how well the fans here know and appreciate the subtler points of hockey.

"With the Panthers, most of us lived north of Miami, some as far as Palm Beach County. As it turned out, that was where most of the fans came from, north of Miami, particularly the Fort Lauderdale area. But we had to drive across three counties to get to the arena. Obviously you didn't get that same close, community feeling you get in Nashville. It's really terrific for a player to feel part of the community. It has been a great experience to see us get so quickly established here and to have the fans be so knowledgeable and supportive," Tom adds.

"I'd say another big difference between the Predators and the Panthers is that not only is the population base smaller, but the geography is much more compact as well. There in Florida, things were so spread out that it was tough to feel like part of the community. In Nashville, one of the things our players mention is that if they go to the grocery store, to Kroger, they bump into fans. They recognize you. They didn't do that so much in Miami. Yeah, they recognized some of our big stars, but most of us were fairly anonymous. Nashville is a small, compact area, and a very close, supportive, community-oriented place. The team draws a lot of support from that. I think it's the reason we did so well so early. We feel like we're playing for people we know and like. And they seem to know and like us."

PUTTING DOWN ROOTS

What did the players think when they first heard they would be playing in Nashville? First and foremost, the players were concerned about hockey, about getting a chance to play. For some, it was their first chance in the NHL; for others, it was a better chance than they'd ever had before to show what they could do. After that was a concern about what kind of place Nashville would be in which to live and work: What's the community like? Will the family like it? Will it be a good atmosphere for the kids? What about the fans?

Captain Tom Fitzgerald's attitude was a typical one for the players coming here: "Well, obviously being a free agent and deciding to sign with Nashville, a place I knew literally nothing about, was a big step. But the most important thing was, the team really seemed to want me. And I liked the 'build for the future' philosophy of the Predators. It's very important to me. It sounded like a good fit for me as a player.

"But then I thought to myself: *I don't know. This is a place I know nothing about. The only thing I know about the place, the only thing I can think of, is country music.* At that point I was not a country music fan. At least, I didn't think I was. Yeah, I liked Garth Brooks, Shania Twain. You know, the Top Forty–type people. I decided I'd better have a closer look at Nashville before I made any final decisions.

"I came to Nashville and I met Coach Barry Trotz. He introduced me to the kind of diverse community Nashville is. He talked about what a great place it is to live. Then he casually told me that a lot of the country music people, like Garth Brooks, are really supporting the team in a big way. He explained that Garth was doing commercials for us, along with Amy Grant, Vince Gill, and others. *Hey,* I think, *I've heard of all these people.* Then I heard about all the other great family- and community-oriented aspects of living in Nashville. I got excited about what I'd heard about living here because my family is very, very important to me. The country music angle was like icing on the cake."

SUPPORTING THE SEVENTH MAN

Tom Fitzgerald has always felt a keen responsibility to the fans: "Although the Predators organization wants to be close to the community professionally, it was my own decision to be one of the guys in the forefront of the team with the fans. I have always believed it was important for me to be up front, reaching out to the fans, speaking to the fans, going out and signing autographs.

"In Florida, with the Panthers, I was a young player then, and I didn't have those responsibilities. If you ask Brian Skrudland what he went through that first year as captain in Florida, compared to what I experienced my first year with the Predators, I would say they would be pretty much the same.

"I've been taught one thing. You just don't play hockey for a living. Players don't just go out and play a game and think the work stops once the sixty minutes are up. Our job goes beyond that. Our job also includes the responsibility to reach out to the fans, to sign autographs, to listen to what they have to say. They pay our salaries after all. The organization just passes the money through. Being open and available to the fans is part of a hockey player's job description, not just to play hockey.

"Often signing autographs after a game is tough if you have people waiting for you or the team lost or you played poorly. But you sign. Often it takes only ten minutes of your time. I think we've done a pretty good job of that here."

Gerry Helper adds that it's not always easy for players to face the fans or the media people after the game: "You sometimes have to remind them of that because they go about their job just like everyone else. They have ups; they have downs; they have great moments; they have slumps. At the same time, we go through our workday, and at the end of the day if people like you or me have a bad day, we go home and deal with it ourselves. When the players have a 'bad day at the office,' they no sooner come off the ice and there are twenty media people coming up asking, 'What happened? Why did you play so poorly?'"

Fitzgerald tries to keep the responsibility in view, however. He says, "We've been pretty lucky with the type of fans we have, so it's important to be responsive to them. When I was in Florida, the players parked in the same lot as the fans because of the way the Miami rink was set up. We had to walk through some two hundred to three hundred people every night. Fans would be behind barricades on each side, and it was like rolling out the red carpet. It would take forever to get to your car.

"It got to the point where nobody would go out alone, always with two people, and go through the gauntlet. You'd hope it would only take ten minutes to sign, but ten minutes would turn into thirty minutes, and then thirty minutes turns into an hour. It would be 11:30 or 12:00, and guys would want to go home, or be hungry and need to go out and get something to eat. Some would say, 'Why can't we just skip the autographs?' But I always felt it was part of my job.

"Here in Nashville we don't have to walk through a large group of fans to get to our cars. There is a place for fans to wait for us, however. At first, they were not going to let fans come down to that area.

"But I told the players: 'It's part of our job description to take time because our fans are our most important asset.' I also told them about the situation in Florida. 'We've got it lucky here. We don't have two hundred to three hundred people waiting outside for us after a game.' So we all agreed that we would take time and sign autographs. It doesn't matter what you feel like, or if you've had a bad game and would just as soon slip out the back door. You go in front of these people, and you let them see you."

Community involvement means more to Fitzgerald and the

Predators players than just signing autographs. It means putting in real quality time in the community, in activities that make a difference in people's lives.

According to Fitzgerald, every hockey team puts something into the community, but the Predators do a better job of it than any team he's been on. He says, "You try to reach out and really touch people's lives. I guess because I have kids of my own, I am really touched by visiting sick kids who are in the hospitals.

"But Nashville's been different. In Florida we'd have two guys going to Palm Beach Medical, and another two guys going to visit children in a hospital in Miami. Those hospitals are ninety, maybe one hundred miles apart. Here in Nashville, we are right in the same area. We can often take the whole team to a hospital, like we do at Christmas at the Vanderbilt Children's Hospital. We have a tough schedule in December, so instead of having four or five guys go at different times, the whole team went together. We sat down and did arts and crafts with the kids.

"I think almost all the players agree that doing things like that, being with kids and their families, is really important. Our players are not just putting in time. Our guys are really genuine and sincere when we go and do stuff with kids, especially those kids that are ill or have problems."

Fitzgerald continues, "I know how lucky I am, having healthy children. I find it hard to imagine what these families go through. I feel best when I can go put a smile on a child's face, or even a smile on Mom's and Dad's faces, or a brother or sister who doesn't smile all that often because someone in the family is sick. That makes my year.

"I don't do it because it makes me feel better or even for the Predators organization, but because it's important to me personally. I honestly believe that the players do it because they believe they can make a real difference. We know how it makes kids feel with a little attention because we were young once ourselves. We had our own heroes, guys we wanted to be like. For me, it was Bobby Orr, one of the greatest players of all time and a wonderful person.

"I often think about my childhood when I get a chance to sign autographs or go to a school. I love teaching kids who don't even know how to hold a hockey stick. I meet some great kids, and it's just fun to be around them. I think the whole Predators organization has done a great job that way, getting out into the community. All these schools ask us to come. And the Predators organization wants us to go. So in some ways it's part of our job, but in the end, it's just a great feeling to be able to make a difference in someone's life."

FROM THE ARENA TO THE STREETS

The visits to teach budding hockey players at schools and community centers give the Predators players a feeling of accomplishment. They also hope the visits bring in some new fans. "You know, if we send a couple of players to a school and do a program or a clinic," Gerry Helper says, "it's likely that the students are going to go home and say, 'Boy, so-and-so from the Predators came to our school. I want to go see them play!'"

Here in the South, it's not like Canada where kids are learning to play hockey barely after learning to walk. But as Gerry notes, "I think you find whatever games you play as a youngster, you kind of follow those even more avidly as you grow up." The team members do their part to build up the players and fans of tomorrow by sponsoring street hockey, in-line skate hockey, and ultimately ice hockey in the region.

"Marc Spigel is our amateur and youth hockey coordinator, and his mission is to get the word out and get more youngsters playing," Gerry continues. "A good portion of his time is spent going to the schools, doing clinics, taking players, taking our mascot. We have invested in a 'border patrol.' It's a portable rink, basically, that we can set up in a parking lot somewhere, and in fifteen minutes we've got a street hockey rink. Street and in-line hockey are two of the fastest-growing sports across the country. The more people that play the game, the more that are going to be long-term fans."

Team members go on summer jaunts to more outlying areas,

such as Bowling Green, Kentucky; Huntsville, Alabama; Knoxville; and Memphis. They ride in the Predators Prowler, a bright, thirty-foot RV with the team's colors and logo. Helper explains, "The idea was, if we can't get you in the arena, we're coming to you to show you the game—whether it's getting you into the vehicle and passing out some literature, showing you a video, or doing a street hockey clinic outside."

Sometimes a special guest from the community is along for the ride when the players travel to a game. In keeping with the family focus, the Predators were the first team to sponsor a "Fathers' Trip." Players' dads are taken on an all-expenses-paid trip to an away game with the team. The trip builds a significant rapport with the players' families. As Greg Johnson's father told Craig Leipold, "I'm proud that my son plays on your team."

MEETING COMMUNITY NEEDS

The Predators organization and the players have given back to the community financially, distributing more than $170,000 to area charities after the first season through the Predators Foundation. Instead of making one or two high-profile gifts, the organization reviewed a series of grants and made targeted donations to thirty-seven organizations. When Jack Diller announced the gifts, he stressed the importance of having a positive impact on the people in the region and estimated that the selected programs would assist and reach more than twenty thousand individuals. The donations, which will take place again in following years, strive to meet the educational, social, health, and cultural needs of the community, especially among children.

One recipient was the Youth Encouragement Services Center. "This grant literally is going to change lives," Executive Director Chris Barnhill told a reporter for the *Tennessean* upon receiving a check from the foundation. "This money will allow us to buy materials and computers that will help these kids get out of poverty and out of the welfare trap."

These donations were not just checks written by an executive. Most of the money was raised through charity events that brought players and the public together. There were celebrity auctions, a golf tournament, a Halloween haunted house, and a gala Unmasked Ball. The latter raised the most money, giving the city's movers and shakers in the business and civic communities a chance to rub shoulders with the movers and shakers on the ice. Anyone who missed these events the first season will have another chance; some have already become highly anticipated yearly traditions.

The emphasis on helping area youth was reinforced throughout the first season, with team participation in many local charity and development activities. The players' wives also got involved. They collected literally tons of food for Second Harvest Food Bank and gathered donations of thousands of toys to be distributed by Toys for Tots.

The team tries to enable a Predators on-the-ice experience for children who can't come on their own. Both the team and the arena's catering company, Levy, donate game tickets to area charities. Predators sponsor Kroger split up fifteen hundred tickets among forty-one charities (one for each game) to sit in the Kroger Ice Box during the inaugural season. Management encourages season ticket holders who will be missing a game to donate their unused extras to charities. Captain Tom Fitzgerald and his wife, Kerry, sponsor Fitzi's Friends—a program that brings twenty troubled children from the Dede Wallace Center to one game each month. The team's Officer of the Month program awards four tickets and dinner at the Wildhorse Saloon to a police officer who has gone above and beyond the call of duty.

As Gerry Helper sees it, the team members, both on and off the ice, have a duty to be good corporate citizens and to connect with the people who make Middle Tennessee their home: "Much as we all like to think we are a necessity in people's lives, we're not. An electric company can be as cold and calculating as it wants to be. You can't survive without the electricity. We're a hockey team. No one is going to live or die based on whether he goes to see a Predators game. Because we are a luxury, we need to connect emotionally. We hope that it's not based solely on whether we are winning or losing. We hope we've done a good enough job at the grassroots level so that people are going to be fans through thick and thin."

While grassroots activities fill the days of much of the Predators staff during the year, 41 game days bring their attention to fans into sharp focus. Game day is special. It creates an intensity level for players, staff, and fans alike.

Hundreds of players, people in management, and full- and part-time staff spend frantic hours of preparation that build to a noisy crescendo of excitement with the opening face-off. Literally hundreds of thousands of man-hours are devoted to assuring the maximum enjoyment possible during the 180 minutes that some seventeen thousand fans take over the Gaylord Entertainment Center on game day.

Game Day

Ice hockey is really a game for Southern sports tastes: speed, blocking and fighting. It's a good ol' boy's dream, and not so bad for the rest of us either. It's demolition derby with a stick. And, the speed of the NHL ice is awesome. Just you wait. Nashville fans . . . will rival the angst and friction of mixing UT fans and all those folks from Tuscaloosa, Ala., dressed up in crimson and yelling "Roll Tide." It's a whole new ball game coming to town, with action, body contact and fan delirium.

   That's an old Southern recipe for success.

—JIMMY DAVY, *TENNESSEAN*,
JUNE 1997

From my perspective, when I heard an expansion was going on I just thought that, just maybe, for a guy in my position it was a possibility to play in the NHL. I was happy, not just happy for myself, but for all the other guys that I knew were good enough to play here, but just have been overlooked. From my standpoint, it was good to see the opportunity.

—#12, ROB VALICEVIC,
NASHVILLE PREDATORS

Barry Trotz, head coach of the Nashville Predators, is making coffee. It's the beginning of a long day of planning, preparations, and meetings. It will be punctuated at the end by a game and then a plane trip to Dallas, Texas, for a rematch against tonight's opponent, the Dallas Stars. Barry needs coffee to get the day going, and since he is the first one in the office, he gets the chore of making it. He'd love a little time to savor the Predators' win three nights ago against the St. Louis Blues in St. Louis, but this is the NHL. In this league, he thinks, there's not much time to celebrate, only to play. The win, number 20 (versus 32 losses and 6 ties), has them on a near record pace for an expansion team and brings the team nearly three-quarters of the way through the grueling 82-game season.

Tonight is the first of one of the Predators' rare back-to-back, home-and-home series. Unfortunately it's against the best team in the league. The Stars are in first place and tearing up opponents. As he mechanically works through the task of getting water and opening the coffee bag, Trotz is running the Stars lineup through his mind. Just seconds later, if someone asks him whether he made coffee, he probably won't know, so intent are his thoughts about the Stars and his personal opponent tonight, Stars Head Coach Ken Hitchcock.

Like Trotz, Hitchcock is an intense coach whose focus and hard work and love of the game's intricacies have brought him to the NHL. *Hitchcock will probably stick with his established lines tonight*, thinks Trotz. And then adds silently, *He can well afford to. He's been unbeatable at home this year and is better than .500 on the road.*

Hitchcock directs one of the league's most powerful offenses with supersnipers: Mike Modano (the Stars' leading scorer); Joe Nieuwendyk (former rookie of the year, and one of the league's premier playmakers, who will go on to win the Conn Smythe Award as the most valuable player in the play-offs); and perennial all-star Brett Hull (son of NHL great Bobby Hull, and already one of the top ten point-getters of all time). Hitchcock also commands a defense led by goalie Ed Belfour (with a goals-against record that's one of the best in the league) and tough, mobile defensemen Sergei Zubov and Derian Hatcher.

The Stars are loaded, tough at every position, thinks Trotz, *with great players sitting on the bench; deep, deep bench strength.* The Stars GM, Bob Gainey (and one of the league's most respected defensive wingers when he won several Stanley Cups with the Montreal Canadiens), has put together a team that can score almost at will and really understands defense. *Let 'em get a goal ahead, and they'll just about close us down offensively.*

And if that's not enough, thinks Trotz, *we'll have to pay particular attention to Lehtinen [Finnish star Jere Lehtinen, who won the league's Selke Trophy in 1998 as top defensive forward, and who went on to win it again in 1999] and Carbonneau [Guy Carbonneau, one of the league's most respected veteran centers and former teammate of Gainey with the Canadiens]. Lehtinen will probably end up checking Ronning.*

Trotz doesn't know it at the time, but the Stars will go on to win the Stanley Cup in 1999 for the first time in franchise history. Relocated from Minnesota, the Stars have taken Dallas by storm, with regular sellouts and wildly enthusiastic crowds. As a franchise, they have been one of the most successful teams of the NHL's southern strategy; their excellence on the ice is matched by superb marketing off the ice. Everyone in the NHL expects them to make a run for the Cup in 1999, but Trotz is determined not to lie down for them: *If they want the Cup we'll make them earn their time with us.*

Trotz is already building his line-by-line matchups in his head. He'll test his ideas in an hour or so with his assistant coaches. Matching lines is one of the most important but complicated decisions for a coach in the NHL today. It's far more complex than the lineup decisions made by coaches in the NBA, the NFL, or major league baseball. With injuries, differing size, speed, skill sets, and specialties (scoring, checking, face-offs, special teams, etc.), individual player and line combinations in recent years have become as big a decision for coaches as which goalie to put in the net.

For the Predators, January and February have been a demanding period in a very demanding season. Since the day after Christmas, with a home game against the Washington Capitals, the Predators have played some 26 games in 59 days going into tonight's contest. Slightly more than half (15) have been at home, but the schedule has included trips to Carolina, Philadelphia, Detroit, Boston, Buffalo, New Jersey, Long Island, and St. Louis, with a long but comparatively fast trip out to western Canada to play Calgary and Edmonton. Their home schedule has included the Capitals, Bruins, Blues, Mighty Ducks, Sharks, Blackhawks, Coyotes, Canucks, Red Wings (twice), Penguins, Rangers, and Avalanche.

A highlight for this stretch—and the entire season—was the only game Wayne Gretzky will ever play in Nashville (he put on a dramatic show with five assists and got a standing ovation from the fans despite a losing effort for the Predators). With the exception of just five teams, all those that the Predators have faced during this stretch will go into the Stanley Cup play-offs this year, several will go late into the final rounds, and two (Buffalo and Dallas) will play in the finals for the Cup (the Predators will beat both teams this season). There were no easy ones during this stretch for the Predators, but for an expansion team, there rarely is.

The extended travel to play teams on the opposite coast is a tough part of any NHL schedule today. For the Predators, their baptism came earlier with the longest trip of the season, a two-week trip to the West Coast in November. They played the Edmonton Oilers, Calgary Flames, Vancouver Canucks, San Jose Sharks, Los Angeles Kings, and St. Louis Blues. It was a long trip for so early in the season, but they broke even with wins against the Flames, Sharks, and Kings. The wins left the Predators well positioned in the standings and alerted the rest of the league that they should not be taken lightly. Success brings tougher, more prepared competition.

Despite the experienced competition, the punishing schedule, the continuation of nagging minor injuries to several players, and another couple of regulars permanently out of action, the Predators are 10-14-2 over this January-February period, representing more than one-third of the wins they'll record all season (28-47-7). Not bad for an expansion team, particularly one that's been virtually hobbled by injuries.

Trotz is not wasting any time feeling sorry for himself. A hard-nosed realist, he knows that injuries are a fact of life in the NHL, and he'll make no excuses for them. Shuttling players between Nashville and the team's IHL affiliate in Milwaukee has given him a chance to look at some of the younger players in the organization, especially the surprising young goalie Tomas Vokoun.

Vokoun has become the starting goalie for the Predators, replacing injured backup goalie Eric Fichaud. *We are blessed with goalies,* thinks Trotz. *At least I don't have to worry about which goalie we'll go with tonight.*

The concern about the injuries to Dunham and Fichaud is balanced by the good news that the Predators have the outstanding play of Vokoun. Vokoun was left unprotected in the draft by Montreal, and many in the league were unsure whether he had what it takes to play regularly in the NHL. The Predators, however, have taken a chance on the young goalie from the Czech Republic, and he has become one of the bright spots of the season for the Predators. Mike Dunham started the season in net for the Predators and had played exceptionally well for the team. By the time he was injured in October (a recurring groin injury), Dunham had already become a hometown favorite. Shortly before Dunham's injury, backup goalie Fichaud was also injured. On October 26, Vokoun was recalled from Milwaukee.

Although he'd played just one period of hockey in the NHL (for the Canadiens in the 1996–97 season), Vokoun was thrust into the starting lineup for the Predators and performed remarkably well, registering his and the team's first shutout (at home against the Phoenix Coyotes on January 15). He beat the Red Wings on December 23 (facing a career-high 50 shots) and had a 3-game winning streak (December 19–27) with 2.14 goals-against average and a .943 save percentage. Even Vokoun is not 100 percent healthy, but the team is impressed with the young goalie's grit and determination. As Assistant Coach Peterson told the newspaper reporters near the end of the season, "Vokoun has played with a sore shoulder. He's played through a lot of things this season."

Right now, despite his shoulder, Vokoun is on top of his game. He was named the runner-up NHL Rookie of the Month in January. In total, Vokoun was to play 37 games for the Predators (tied for first in the league for a rookie goaltender that season) with 12 wins (second in the league). In addition to line matchups, picking a goalie is one of a coach's most critical decisions. Usually one goalie plays the bulk of the games, but coaches sometimes rotate him with the backup to provide the starter with some rest, allow the backup playing time, or occasionally shake things up emotionally.

With one of the hottest goalies in the league, there were no doubts in Trotz's mind that Vokoun would start tonight for the Predators: *It'll give Hitchcock something to think about.* Trotz sips his coffee and manages a rare smile.

7:20 A.M.
West Nashville

GM David Poile hasn't yet left for the arena, although he's been up for a couple of hours working the phones. He's talked to his scout Alexei Dementiev in Russia and had three different conversations with his counterparts in the East. With Alexei, he's been discussing a prospect in the Czech Republic that interests the Predators, and with the other GMs, he's been talking about their respective positions on a major rule change the league will vote on in its upcoming winter meetings. In between his hockey calls, he squeezed in breakfast with his wife, Elizabeth, and had one phone conversation with son Brian who, along with daughter Lauren, is studying at Boston College. Like Trotz, Poile likes to be at the arena early on game day, but the calls have caught him at home and kept him unusually late. In less than fifteen minutes, he leaves for his half-hour trip downtown to the Gaylord Entertainment Center.

Just a few blocks away, ten-year-old Mike Lewis has finished getting ready for school. He has a test today, and he stayed up a little later than usual studying for it. He's moving a little slower because of the late night, but he doesn't seem to notice or care. His mind is on the upcoming Predators contest against the Stars. An excellent student, Mike took time out from his studies last night to check the Stars' Web site to get his own scouting report on the team.

An avid sports fan, Mike closely watches both the Predators and the Titans. At his still-young age, he already has an almost encyclopedic knowledge about both teams and their players. Asked a question about either team's stats, he will answer accurately and color it with his take on the significance of the numbers. He wants to think about his upcoming test, but his mind keeps wandering to the game.

He'll go to tonight's game, as he usually does, with his father, Michael, who runs Vanderbilt's Rehabilitation Hospital and is a former team doctor with the New York Rangers. He's delaying leaving for school because he's upset that the local paper, the *Tennessean,* has not yet arrived, and he hates to miss sportswriter John Glennon's Predators' Notebook. It contains essential fodder for the intermittent discussions he'll have at school today with classmates who are equally fanatic about sports. Having two teams in Nashville has intensified the preclass, recess, lunch, and after-school discussions for Mike and his friends and made them more personal. They feel deeply about their hometown teams, and although they don't know who Mayor Phil Bredesen is or what he's done to bring the teams to Nashville, they're excited and proud that they have teams in Nashville that they can identify with.

7:45 A.M.
Brentwood, Tennessee

About twenty miles south, in the sprawling suburb of Brentwood, Scott Walker stirs awake after a restless night. It's earlier than he wants to get up because he awoke several times thinking about tonight's game. He needs to be at the Predators' practice facility in a couple of hours, but for now he'll just lie in bed and think about the Stars. He tries to visualize the last time they played them. *How long ago was it?* he thinks. *Oh, yeah, just a month ago. Seems like forever. Now twice in two nights. I'd like to meet the guy who schedules these things!* Floating through his mind go Modano, Nieuwendyk, and Hull. Getting a mental picture of these guys is not tough. They are distinctive. And because they're a Western Division team like the Predators, he'll face the Stars four times this season. Some of the teams in the East will play the Predators only once.

While he played in major junior and even in the AHL, Walker could get a good visual image of his team's next opponents. Typically starting the Monday following a weekend game, images of opposing players started to intrude into Walker's thoughts. These thoughts built during the week, reaching a peak on game day. But it was easier then, with fewer teams and games, and those played mostly on weekends. Now playing or traveling every second day, the season becomes almost a blur. And it gets harder to remember the cities, let alone the players. In the NHL it's tough keeping all the players straight. With more than 550 regulars and another fifty to sixty players in and out of the league, mostly due to injuries, sometimes he doesn't recognize some of the faces, let alone the names.

Unlike baseball, where teams play each other frequently and over several consecutive games, or football, with its far fewer games and a more predetermined set of plays, hockey players generally can't focus on particular players or key in on specific plays. As much as anything, players learn to instinctively react to patterns formed by the movement and positioning of their opponents, all the while keeping their heads up to avoid bruising checks, but with their eyes riveted on the puck. Much of their play requires instant reaction to rapidly occurring events with players changing shifts every forty seconds or so. Every player plays defense and offense, often switching from one to the other every few seconds. Even goalies, who now frequently leave the net to direct the puck in such a way as to start a breakout from their own end, participate in the offense.

The Stars' crafty center, Mike Modano, occupies center stage in Walker's mind. As a defenseman turned forward, Walker is sure he will get the job of checking the Modano-Hull line tonight. With his "in your face" defensive style, Walker often gets the nod to check the other team's top scoring line. Ironically Walker scored more when he played defense, but Vancouver, which drafted him and brought him into the league in the '94–'95 season, converted him into a checking, defensive forward.

Trotz, who first saw Walker play in the minors with Syracuse (Walker skated by Trotz's Portland Pirates' bench and taunted the team's tough guy), wanted his aggressive style for Nashville, and has added penalty killing and even some power-play responsibilities to his job. It's almost a tradition in hockey to get a nickname, and Vancouver Canucks Head Coach Jack McIlhargey dubbed Walker "Wild Thing" in recognition of his feisty, gritty style. The tag has stuck, but around the Predators, he's mostly known as "Walks."

After fifteen more minutes of thinking about the Stars, Walker finally gives up the idea of getting any more sleep and puts in a call to his parents' home in Cambridge, Ontario. Walker credits his father as being the biggest influence in his hockey career, and he talks to him almost daily. His mother, he says, deserves a lot of the credit for his success; she was often the driver to early morning games. His father has already left for work, so with his mother he discusses some details about his wedding this summer to Julie, a schoolteacher from Cambridge.

He finishes talking with his mother, hangs up, and again thinks about the game tonight and what he must do. Because he gets more ice time with the Predators than ever before in his six-year professional career, Walker is collecting the most points he's ever had (he'll get 40 before the end of the season, 15 goals and 25 assists). He collected 2 of those goals, big ones, as it turned out, in the Predators' 5-3 victory over the Red Wings in December. Like many hockey players, he often envisions himself scoring the winning goal in the Stanley Cup final.

We're a ways from that, he thinks, *but it would be great to get the winner against these guys from Dallas.* (He won't. But he will score 2 tonight and get an assist. One of them will be one of the most dramatic goals of the Predators' season, called a "spin-o-rama" by color commentator Terry Crisp. That helped the team take a 3-1 lead over Dallas in the second period. In what he will later confess was not a planned move, he tries faking a Dallas defenseman, but spins almost out of control, 360 degrees, before putting the puck past the Stars' Eddie Belfour.)

About thirty miles away, in yet another part of town, Pete Weber, play-by-play announcer for the Predators, is also getting his mind into tonight's game. Weber, a versatile broadcaster who has called the plays on TV and radio for baseball, football, basketball, and hockey for more than twenty-five years, is renowned for his ability to let the sometimes tongue-twisting names of many of hockey's Russian and European players flow fluidly across his lips. Many of the names, which give other broadcasters problems, seem easy for him. As a young college student, he studied foreign languages. Starting in college at his alma mater, Notre Dame, Weber's varied broadcasting career had brought him to Nashville many times in the past. Now here permanently, he viewed his position with the Predators as the crowning achievement of his professional life.

No stranger to hockey, Weber had been on the broadcast teams of both the Buffalo Sabres and the LA Kings, but like a few of the Predators management team, he had never been involved in an expansion franchise. As he always has, Weber is preparing diligently for the broadcast. He is using all his available time this morning to prepare for the game. This morning he is watching the last several Stars games that he's taped off his satellite TV service. He calls his counterpart in Dallas to get some insight on the latest happenings with the Stars.

Weber will leave home in time to meet his partner, Terry Crisp, for lunch and a discussion of their own "game plan" for tonight's game. But before he leaves, he consults some of his reference material for the latest stats on the Stars and the Predators. He is a stickler for preparation, with a passion for the stats, and by the time he settles into his seat in the broadcast booth this evening, he will be almost as well briefed as the Predators coaches.

8:10 A.M.
Gaylord Entertainment Center
Barry Trotz's Office

Assistant Coach Paul Gardner joins Trotz. Shortly afterward, David Poile comes in, and they talk in general about tonight's game. They will wait for the other assistant coach, Brent Peterson, before they cover the specifics. Peterson, like Gardner, is an NHL veteran, having played eleven seasons after breaking into the league in 1978 with Detroit. Known as one of the finest defensive players in the league, he turned to coaching at the end of his career. Prior to joining the Predators, he coached the WHL Portland Winter Hawks for seven years and led them to record performances, including winning the WHL championship (Memorial Cup).

Peterson, who is scheduled to be a bit late this morning, is stopping off at his church. A Mormon and an active member of the Church of Jesus Christ of Latter-day Saints, Peterson needed to see his bishop briefly about his oldest son, Ryan, who will be leaving for a two-year mission in Sweden later in the year. Peterson arrives about ten minutes later and the meeting begins.

Throughout the morning and early afternoon, the various combinations of the thirty-one members of the Predators hockey opera-

146

tions staff will meet in person or by phone to discuss players, watch game films, and review recent scouting reports about the Stars. Executive Assistant Kalli Quinn will help coordinate the steady succession of planned and impromptu get-togethers. In particular, she's arranged for Trotz to meet with the goaltending coach, Mitch Korn, who is in town for the game. Before joining the Predators organization, Korn spent several years with Buffalo coaching Dominik Hasek, the Sabres' four-time Vezina Trophy winner (voted by the league's GMs for best goaltender) and two-time Hart Trophy winner (the hockey writers' award for most valuable player). An excellent addition to the staff, Korn, who lives in Ohio, is in Nashville frequently to work with the team's goalies, who have kept him unusually busy this year with their multiple injuries.

8:15 A.M.
Gaylord Entertainment Center
On the Ice

Out on the ice, Tim Hild,* Ice Tech supervisor, is making his first of dozens of inspections of the ice prior to game time. Robert Courtney, a member of the Gaylord Entertainment Center staff, is anxious to ensure the ice is just right for the Stars' morning skate. He will be on and off the ice all day while regularly monitoring the computers that direct the machines that make the ice and keep it hard for the game. It was once a job that used hoses and shovels to keep the ice in reasonable condition, but today's teams expect the ice to be perfect, and Courtney uses the latest technologies to ensure it is.

Courtney's boss, Russ Simons, is senior vice president/general manager of Leisure Management International, a management company that is contracted by the Predators to run the facility on a daily basis. His full-time staff of thirty, several devoted solely to

---

*Some of the people named in this chapter joined their respective organizations later than the Predators' first season. For simplicity, names of current employees were used in this text.

147

the Predators, will supervise literally hundreds of part-time vendor employees before the day is out. The majority of the outside vendor support will be for the food concessions. Under the supervision of Sue Fullington, hundreds of people will wait on fans at the Sportservice restaurants and concessions stands this evening. Most will arrive several hours before the game and won't leave until after cleanup, usually another hour or so after the game is over.

9:30 A.M.
Gaylord Entertainment Center
Predators Administrative Office

In the cavernous space cluttered with the cubicles that house the Predators business team, Elaine Lewis (no relation to Mike), administrative assistant to both Craig Leipold and Jack Diller, is busy with the phones. Several business contacts and media people are calling to make arrangements to meet Craig or Jack. Since it's game day, both will be tied up with a variety of activities and meetings right through the day until the game and often several hours after that. Both Craig and Jack will be making the late-night trip to Dallas with the team. It's Elaine's job to balance all the requests and help the two manage their busy schedules, and despite the many demands, she does it with style, diplomacy, and a sense of good humor. For many of the callers, she represents the first-ever contact with the Predators senior management team, and she creates a positive first impression, portraying the open, friendly style the team wishes to project.

It's noisy all around her in the workplace, however, because the space that the administrative staff occupies has not yet been built into individual offices. Regular offices will have to wait until almost midway through next season. For now, everyone, including Craig and Jack, has an open cubicle. The open-door policy Craig brought with him from his earlier venture is superfluous here; he doesn't even have a door.

Not far from Elaine, Linda Adams, executive assistant to Tom Ward, and Kelly Preuett, administrative assistant, try to direct traffic for the beehive of activity that is the marketing department on game day. Despite the close quarters, the noise, and the sometimes frantic activity level, Elaine, Linda, Kelly, and over in the hockey office, Kalli, handle the calls and the internal commotion with quiet efficiency. To the outside world, their calm voices betray the intensity of activity inside.

In a conference room nearby, CFO Ed Lang has hastily called a staff meeting. Unlike a big company, the Predators have no set of policies and procedures developed over years of operation. As a classic start-up, they have some general business guidelines borrowed from other organizations, but the Predators must fill in the details as they go along. With Ed are his financial staff, Julie Gillen, director of finance, and accounting personnel Virginia Blount, Tracy Hardes, Betsy Shea, Denton McLane, and Susan Charnley. Ed also has responsibility for human resources, so the director of that department, Kim Marrone, is present, as are Project and Office Coordinators Scott Pilkinton and Robin Krokker. Jim Jones, who manages the information systems for Ed, is not present for the meeting. He is working with Scouting Coordinator Stu Judge and Hockey Operations Assistant Mike Corbett on a computer issue in the scouting database.

In another area nearby, the phones are ringing constantly, and the people assembled there are trying to answer each call on the first ring, all the while rapidly compiling the statistical results of last night's action in the NHL. With the constant demand from the media for fast, accurate, and up-to-date information, the communications group is kept busy all the time fulfilling special media requests and preparing publications, such as game program information, media guides, and the Predators fan magazine, the *Saber Tooth Times*, designed in-house by Maggie Bizwell. But game day taxes all their resources. Nashville, Dallas, and national media will look to them for detailed data on virtually every aspect of the Predators organization.

Under the direction of Gerry Helper, Frank Buonomo (manager of team services), Judd Hancock (communications coordinator), Gregory Harvey (communications assistant), and Ken Anderson (publications and Internet coordinator) compile player statistics and previous game statistics to provide to all media attending the game. Additionally they certify media credentials, and before game time, they ensure that the press box, the players' wives' room, and the media room are set up. This includes arranging for food for the media and, once the game has begun, preparing the media room for the postgame press conference. On road trips, Buonomo and occasionally Hancock accompany the team to handle routine travel and media activity in other cities.

Across the office, Tom Ward's staff in sales, marketing, game presentation, and fan relations seem to be moving in a dozen different directions at once. At the center of the maelstrom, Ward has to understand, manage, and lead them all. Most important on game day are the game presentation staff members, managed by Bryan Shaffer. They have to take care of a million details if the entertainment for tonight's game is going to work. They know their jobs and are developing a smooth routine with some 30 home games already under their belts. Much of the actual work was done the day before, but game day always brings changes. Tomorrow, after the game, Ward and the staff will scrutinize every detail of what went on. After a quick discussion with Bryan, Ward moves on to talk to his sales and sponsor groups.

The Predators' sales effort is headed by the always smiling and outgoing Scott Loft, director of ticket sales. A veteran of the initial season ticket campaign, he feels he knows almost every season ticket holder by name. Under his direction, the Predators are also setting expansion franchise records for attendance (they'll end the season with over 94 percent attendance and seventeen sellouts). Today, though, the reason for the meeting is the team's "Give & Go" program that allows season ticket holders unable to attend a game to donate those seats to the Predators Foundation for distribution to local youth charities. Scott and his team of five account representatives (Sid Chambless, Geoff Dunnuck, Slayton Gorman, Jonathon Tuschl, and Bill Walker), joined by the ticket sales administrative assistant, Annie Snelgrove, are already meeting with Gerry Helper's community development group, headed by Predators Foundation Executive Director Jenny Hannon.

With the team almost since day one, Hannon, along with Community Relations Coordinator Alexis Herbster, directs the team's relationships with various community groups. Herbster joined the team with Jack Diller from San Antonio. Hannon is from Nashville and provides the team with a vital, experienced link to the community. They have primary responsibility for the logistics of the "Give & Go" program, but need to work closely with sales. Also at the meeting is the marketing department's in-house graphic artist, Mike Towsen, because there is some thought that a new piece of literature may be needed.

The Predators create and print thousands of pieces of literature each year in the forms of game programs, schedules, and fan-oriented promotional magazines, posters, mailers, and other material. Printed material is one of Ward's largest budget items, and for many fans it is an important connection to the team. Ward insists that it is done right: consistent theme and graphics, well written, colorful, and quality printing.

The meeting seems to be on the right track, so after a few words of encouragement and direction, Ward excuses himself and goes to talk to the staff that run the various other aspects of the marketing group, club and suite sales, sponsor service, promotions, and fan relations. Each group will be busy tonight, and Ward wants to catch up with all of them so that he'll be well briefed by game time. It will take most of his day, and ultimately he'll be forced to reschedule a personal lunch meeting as the issues that need his attention mount and the time until the first face-off runs down.

9:30 A.M.
Centennial Sportsplex
Predators' Dressing Room

Less than five miles away from the frantic activity at the Gaylord Entertainment Center, at the Predators' new practice facility,

Centennial Sportsplex, several of the players have already arrived to prepare for their game and this morning's skate. Among them is Scott Walker. Walker, one of the few Predators already listed in the NHL Hockey Hall of Fame, holds the distinction of scoring the first ever NHL goal outside North America (against the Mighty Ducks in a historic game played in Tokyo). Just as some people viewed Cliff Ronning early in his career, observers thought Walker was too small for the NHL through much of his career. Over the past fifteen years, the average player height has increased several inches and the weight nearly 20 pounds. At 205 pounds, the NHL's average hockey player today would not look too much out of place in the NFL, and some, like Dallas Stars defenseman Derian Hatcher, at six feet five inches and 225 pounds, in the NBA. In every league he's played in, however, Walker has proved the skeptics wrong. On a Predators team that is generally much smaller than its opponents, Walker has made a significant contribution on and off the ice, particularly helping the team stay loose in the dressing room.

Hockey has a tradition that is true of virtually every team, and the Predators are no exception. Teams insist that they don't draft or trade for this particular characteristic, but every team seems to end up with a couple of players who enjoy playing jokes, particularly on rookies and those recently joining the team via a trade. Although harmless, the jokes have a real function in building morale and cohesion among the team members, and often keeping the players loose and relaxed during periods of tension and frustration in the long, often tiring, up-and-down season that most teams go through. Despite his aggressive, hard-driving style on the ice, Walker is usually at the center of the jokes in the Predators' dressing room. According to Coach Trotz, he is either the ringleader or the one closest at hand when the jokes occur.

Walker is planning a practical joke on Kimmo Timonen (he'll fill Timonen's skates with shaving cream), who was called up from Milwaukee in December and has already established his presence on defense. The joke will be the "official" welcome; his excellent play will keep him in Nashville for the balance of the season. A great skater and stick handler, Timonen already looks as if he might stick with the Predators on the basis of his heads-up play and ability to create offense.

From Kuopio, Finland, Timonen was acquired from the LA Kings. Over the course of the year, he will end up playing in 50 contests for the Predators, 29 for Milwaukee, and another 12 for Finland's national team in the World Championships. Walker has several accomplices who will distract Timonen while Walker gets ready. Several other players are in on the joke, but they are just spectators on this one. They are busy getting ready for the team practice.

Patrick Cote is keeping an eye on the action from the next room, where he is lifting weights in a facility that would be the pride of any professional gym. Cote, who broke into the league in '95 with the Stars, is particularly intent on a good showing tonight against his former team. Drafted by the Predators in the expansion draft, he is the team's tough guy who will ensure no one on any other team takes physical advantage of the smaller players for the Predators. He will lead the team in penalties this season, with 242 minutes. Generally a "plus" player (he's on the ice for more goals for than against), Cote is working hard to improve his overall skill level. He'll attend a special skills camp in Sweden this summer and will record his first NHL goal later in the season against Tampa Bay. He improves his on-ice toughness, too, training as a boxer in his hometown of Montreal.

Next door in the equipment room, Ville Peltonen (also from Finland) is preparing his sticks along with Sergei Krivokrasov. They'll shave and bend the blades and often slightly alter the shaft as well as apply a variety of colored tape to both the blade and the top of the shaft. Players like to take care of their own sticks but rely on Equipment Manager Pete Rogers and his assistants, Chris Scoppetto and Chris Moody, to handle the cleaning of pads and uniforms. The equipment staff often pitch in to assist players with medical braces and the like. Rogers also performs the critical function of skate sharpening.

Although players in other sports commonly call it a locker room, Canadian hockey players have historically called it a dressing room;

however, the custom is changing with the influence of U.S. and European players. The rich traditions associated with the room haven't changed, though. A hockey dressing room is the key place for all team business, positive and negative. The coaches use the room for pregame and between-period strategy reviews and the occasional pep talk, but it is above all the players' sanctuary. The constant and intrusive glare of the media is held at bay for a critical few minutes following a game for the players to collectively and individually unwind.

Over the years, much of the lore and many of the traditions of hockey have been born in the dressing room. For players it is a special place, and some will come here hours before game time to prepare, contemplate opponents, and build the special bond that defines a hockey team. It is a place for laughter and hope, and it serves as a refuge from the agony of a loss. Since early childhood, these players have spent almost as much time in the dressing room as on the ice. Often with little more than cold, bare cement walls and benches, few of those rooms held any of the creature comforts of today's professional dressing rooms, havens that include individual wooden lockers and large, immaculate showers. The players manage to pass the traditions down to each new generation. Among the key nonplayers in the Predators' dressing room is Locker Room Attendant Craig "Partner" Baugh, who ensures that the room is kept orderly and that all equipment is packed for transport.

Before leaving the dressing room, players and coaches listen to a visiting official from the NHL. His talk lasts about twenty-five minutes, and then he addresses a few scattered questions, primarily from the younger players. The official departs for the Gaylord Entertainment Center to repeat the talk for the Dallas Stars.

10:30 A.M.
Centennial Sportsplex
On the Ice

By 10:30, with Walker's joke and a presentation by a league official over, a relaxed Predators squad, joined by Assistant Coaches

Gardner and Peterson, file onto the ice. The coaches skate around to loosen up while the players, led by Captain Tom Fitzgerald, go through several minutes of stretches to warm up. Following their warm-up, they practice a series of action drills that keep the players in constant motion carrying the puck and shooting on the goalies.

After several such rapid-fire drills, the coaches divide the players and work on a focus area for tonight's game. Trotz wants more effectiveness out of the special teams, so Gardner takes the power-play units to one end of the ice for instruction, while Peterson works with those who get the call to kill penalties. Near the end of practice, Peterson works with a couple of the centers on face-offs (still sharp, he wins several of them).

When the players leave the ice, they'll walk down a corridor to the dressing room and pass under a sign over the door: "WINNING ISN'T A SOMETIMES THING." Tomas Vokoun stays behind to work a bit longer with Coach Korn. Joel Bouchard and Drake Berehowsky stay behind to help out with booming slap shots from the point.

10:30 A.M.
Gaylord Entertainment Center
On the Ice

The Dallas Stars, led by their assistant coaches, take the ice for a forty-five-minute skate. Because they have been playing well and traveling hard, Hitchcock has told the coaches to have fun today. They will skip tough drills and use the time to get loose and, as the players say, "get the legs going" for the game tonight.

After their light skate, they meet in the dressing room for an information session with Dennis Cunningham, the NHL vice president of security. An hour earlier, he was with the Predators for the same briefing. He'll visit each team this year to provide them with an update on league security issues. The NHL will provide teams with briefings on a variety of matters such as media relations, abuse, and player assistance programs throughout the year. These programs will be developed by some of the more than two hundred professionals in one of the three major NHL offices in New York, Toronto, and Montreal (the NHL also has a small office in Switzerland).

Sitting in on the briefing are the four officials and the alternates (referees and linesmen) for tonight's game. In total the NHL has some forty referees and thirty-six linesmen who travel North America to officiate at games. Another large group of off-ice officials (timekeepers, penalty box, and goal judges) from Nashville will work the game. Some, such as Nashville's Kirk Butler, have been around hockey most of their lives, having played goalie as a kid and continuing to play through adulthood in Nashville's old-timers' league. Kirk was among the first that the Predators recruited for the NHL to officiate at games.

10:30 A.M.
West Nashville

Mike Lewis has finished his exam, and as his teacher begins a new lesson, he begins to daydream about tonight's game and what food he'll buy at the arena.

Not too far from Mike's school, several players' wives meet to discuss their participation in next year's Toys for Tots and Second Harvest Food Bank programs. Both activities went well this year, and they want to get an early start on the planning for next year to do even better.

11:30 A.M.
Centennial Sportsplex
Predators' Dressing Room

The players and assistant coaches leave in small groups to eat (substantial) meals in nearby restaurants like Rotier's and McCabe Pub. They bulk up at lunch, not so much because of their workout, but because they won't eat again until after tonight's game. After lunch, most of the players return home for a nap or at least try to take one.

Some players seem to be able to sleep anytime or anywhere, while others find that the stress of the upcoming game keeps them wide awake. Although he usually doesn't do outside activities on game day, before he heads home today, Scott Walker goes for a very brief meeting with some people in the Nashville Public Schools, where he serves as the Predators' spokesman. An animal lover, Walker is also doing promotional work for the Nashville Humane Society.

One group of players arranged to have lunch together to discuss their band, Offside. Defenseman Joel Bouchard (drums), center Darren Turcotte (guitar), winger Denny Lambert, and center Sebastien Bordeleau (lead singer) discovered their mutual interest in music during the Predators' inaugural training camp. They now get together to jam and to practice for Predators' team parties. Today they're reviewing their performance at the Predators' Unmasked Ball, where they'd performed along with Amy Grant and Sons of the Desert. (The group is featured on a CD called *Check, Please,* released by the Predators in December 1999.)

Barry Trotz doesn't join any of the groups for lunch today as he usually does, nor does he go home for a nap. He's still in the coaches' room at the practice rink, doing a half-hour interview with a visiting newspaper reporter. That finished, he hangs around a while longer to meet with Robin Walsh, a local businessman and coach of Robin's son Ray's youth hockey team. Trotz has promised to help with some activities for youth hockey, and Walsh needs some of Barry's time and attention. When he's finished, Trotz will return to the arena for more meetings, paperwork, and game preparations.

Also staying behind is Mark Nemish, Predators strength and conditioning coach, who is meeting with Head Athletic Trainer Dan Redmond. Both are experienced professionals who have worked with a number of athletes from a variety of sports, from amateurs to the professional leagues. Their dedicated efforts are directed at keeping the Predators' players strong and healthy. Today, however, they'll confer for nearly an hour to review some persistent, nagging minor injuries to players that have thus far not cleared up.

After their meeting they call the head of the Predators' medical staff, Dr. Michael Pagnani (orthopedist), at Baptist Hospital. The Predators have an ongoing relationship with Baptist Hospital Sports Medicine, and its six-man team works closely with the players and training staff to assist in routine and emergency medical activities. In addition to Pagnani, the Predators' medical staff includes Drs. Richard Garman (internist), James McPherson (dentist), Daniel Weikert (ophthalmologist), Donald Griffin (plastic surgeon), and Bryan Oslin (plastic surgeon). Dr. Weikert won't make it to tonight's game, so another Baptist eye doctor, Ken Moffat, will attend the team in his absence.

12:30 P.M.
Downtown Nashville

Having lunch in a casual restaurant near the arena, broadcasters Pete Weber and Terry Crisp compare notes on what they have just seen and heard. They'd met at eleven o'clock to watch the Dallas Stars take their morning skate. Afterward, they'd stopped by the visitors' dressing room to chat informally with some of the Stars. The Stars, they'd noted, seemed on a high. Usually reserved Brett Hull was smiling and talkative. Modano and Nieuwendyk, always available to the press and very articulate, seemed even more so today.

"They are on a roll," says Crisp. "They can smell the Cup already."

"The road to the Cup runs through Denver and Detroit," counters Weber. At nearby tables, patrons of the restaurant recognize the two men and strain to catch pieces of their conversation.

After chatting with the two broadcasters, the Stars players go back to their hotel for a big meal, then a long, and for most, boring afternoon of hanging around. Some players walk over to Gruhn Guitars on Broadway to look at the largest collection of used guitars in the world. Others head to the exercise facility at the Renaissance Hotel to get in an hour of riding the stationary bikes. Still others watch TV, including the soaps or any current movies.

158

Some sleep for an hour or two, then reread the local newspapers for the second or third time today.

1:30 P.M.
Across Nashville

At more than three dozen locations around town, food concession and arena restaurant staffs are busy preparing for the thousands of meals they'll serve to tonight's crowd.

At a break between classes, Mike Lewis and his friends are debating who is the best playmaker among the Dallas Stars' "big three."

On the ice at the arena, Robert Courtney is making his tenth inspection of the day.

Over at the Renaissance Hotel, more than half the Dallas Stars are sleeping.

At her desk in the Predators' office, Elaine Lewis grabs a quick sandwich between phone calls. Just down the hall, Gerry Helper is arranging yet another media interview. Over at the ticket office, game day tickets are selling briskly, and already Scott Loft is predicting a sellout for tonight.

Craig Leipold and Jack Diller are in a conference room at the arena listening to a proposal for a new service provider for team travel.

David Poile is in his office talking on the phone with Stars GM Bob Gainey.

On the other side of the arena, Pete Weber and Terry Crisp are meeting with the director of broadcasting, John Guagliano, and his staff, Jim Corn (manager of technical services), Erik Barnhart (feature producer), Susan Morgan (traffic manager), and Peggy Bartishell (production assistant). They are working on the schedule for tonight's broadcast and lining up interviews and features for between periods. Joining them for the discussions is Robert Bouchard, the video coordinator from the hockey operations staff.

In Brentwood, Scott Walker returns home after his visit with the Nashville Public School administrator. He makes himself some lunch and then takes a nap.

3:30 P.M.

Walker wakes up from his nap and gets ready to leave for the arena. He needs to arrive earlier than usual because he's scheduled to meet Donna Gurchiek, team nutritionist. Most of Scott's teammates will be at the arena within the hour.

4:30 P.M.
Gaylord Entertainment Center

Vendor, service, concession, security, and a host of other people needed to work tonight's game begin arriving at the arena. The flood of people will continue until just before game time and then will disperse over a period of several hours after the game.

Down in the bowels of the arena, the coaches are informally chatting about last-minute issues, and the Predators players are going through their individual pregame rituals. Each will "put on his game face" in a unique way: quiet and reclusive or noisy and outgoing.

5:30 P.M.
Gaylord Entertainment Center

Security personnel, ticket takers, and door greeters assemble as the many doors to the arena are officially opened for the game. Outside, dozens of police and parking staff are directing the first of the flood of cars that will fill virtually every parking spot within a two-mile radius of the arena.

In restaurants around the downtown area, waiters are hurrying to serve anxious customers who want to eat and get to their seats with plenty of time for the pregame festivities.

6:15 P.M.
The Cumberland

Craig and Helen Leipold leave their townhouse at the Cumberland with their three youngest children for the two-block walk to the arena. As is usually the case, their attention is focused on keeping Connor, Curtis, and Bradford from ducking into the street. Fortunately Craig's oldest two boys, Chris and Kyle, are visiting from college and help with the younger ones.

A number of the Predators' fans stop Craig to wish him luck in tonight's game against Dallas. He knows he will need it.

6:30 P.M.
Gaylord Entertainment Center

In the Predators' dressing room, Trotz reviews last-minute instructions for his players and then calls on a number of them to review their assignments for tonight.

Just around the corner, the color guard and the person who'll sing the national anthem meet to review their approach for the opening of the game.

6:45 P.M.
Gaylord Entertainment Center

On the ice, both the Predators and the Stars are finishing their pregame skate.

Up on the main floor, Mike Lewis is beginning to eat pizza on the way to his seat.

In the broadcast booth, Pete and Terry are going through their pregame checklists.

The Predators game presentation staff members are frantically finishing their last-minute preparations.

High above the center ice, in the rafters, the Predators mascot,

Gnash, is fixing his harness for his dramatic entry down a heavy wire to center ice.

7:05 P.M.
Gaylord Entertainment Center

Fireworks explode over the top of the Jumbotron just seconds before the Nashville Predators file onto the ice through the gaping mouth of the huge saber-toothed tiger head that guards the way to the ice from the Predators' dressing room.

In the GM's box at the south end of the arena, David Poile, Ray Shero, and Assistant Coach Brent Peterson sit down to review their game notes for this evening.

The Predators and Stars line up on their respective blue lines for the singing of the national anthem.

Minutes later, one of tonight's two referees lines up for the face-off between Mike Modano and Greg Johnson.

7:49 P.M.
Gaylord Entertainment Center
Predators 2, Dallas 1

The first period ends, and the Predators and the Stars file off the ice to their respective dressing rooms. Once inside the quiet of the rooms, the coaches review what seemed to be working and what didn't during the first period. Many players remove much of their uniforms and pads to cool off during the brief time between periods. Others take off their skates and ask for the equipment managers to sharpen them.

Out on the ice, the Predators Puck Patrol sets up one of its between-period activities. At the south end of the ice, John Holmes waits on one of the two Zambonis that will shortly clear the ice.

In the stands, Mike Lewis leaves his seat and goes to the concession stand for some Dippin' Dots®, the modern ice cream served at the game.

162

Cliff Ronning skips the early part of the briefing in the dressing room and does an interview with Pete and Terry.

In the GM's box, Poile, Shero, and Peterson compare notes on the first period. Peterson will stay in the box and communicate by phone to the Predators bench through the second period. He will then join Trotz and Gardner behind the bench for the third period.

10:08 P.M.
Gaylord Entertainment Center
Game Over: Dallas 4, Nashville 3

Phil Sweetland, a Nashville-based sportswriter and the local stringer for the Associated Press, enters the Predators' dressing room to interview Scott Walker about his unusual "spin-o-rama" goal in the third period. Some players are riding stationary bikes, others are in the showers, still others are in the trainers' room getting patched up, and the rest are hurrying to finish dressing. They'll go out to the guest room for a brief chat with wives, family, and friends here for the game.

Frank Buonomo walks through the dressing room announcing that the team plane for Dallas will leave from the Nashville airport at 12:00 A.M. sharp.

The Predators equipment staff will pack the team's gear on a truck, drive it to the airport, and load it on the plane for the trip to Dallas. After arriving in Dallas, the equipment staff will unload all the equipment and take it to the Dallas arena in preparation for tomorrow's practice and game.

11:35 P.M.
Nashville Airport

Most of the Predators have already arrived and are seated in the rear of the charter flight that will take them, plus coaches, the broadcast support staff, several of the hockey operations staff, and Craig, Jack, David, Pete, and Terry to Dallas. As usual, they find

163

a heavy snack at their places, which is intended to take the edge off their appetites until they are airborne and can get a full meal. Some of the players dispense quickly with the snack and get immediately into card games that seem to pick up spontaneously from where they left off on the last plane trip. Although the stakes are notoriously low, the competition is intense. It seems that the lower the stakes, the higher the intensity of rivalry.

Back at the Gaylord Entertainment Center, some of the support and concession staff have left, but nearly one hundred remain doing the final cleanup and getting a head start on the preparations for the next home game.

In West Nashville, Mike Lewis is already asleep.

11:59 P.M.
Nashville Airport

The Predators' charter flight begins taxiing to the runway for its hour-and-a-half flight to Dallas. The word spreads quickly throughout the plane that despite their loss tonight, Coach Trotz has canceled tomorrow's practice to allow the players some much-needed rest.

While most of the players and others on the plane talk quietly in small groups, near the rear of the plane, Scott Walker closes his eyes and tries for the third time today to get a few extra minutes of sleep.

Across the aisle from him, Sergei Krivokrasov closes his eyes and imagines scoring the winning goal against the Stars in their next game (he will, with less than thirty seconds to go in the game, to give the Predators a 2-1 victory).

I Want Some More of It

I wasn't sure how it would go [on being acquired by the Predators]. At first, Nashville didn't strike me as a real sports town. Its reputation is for music. But the fans have definitely proved me wrong. They have really taken an interest in hockey and accepted us with open arms. Now they're the best fans in the league. I believe they're the loudest and most loyal. They show up and stay until the end of the game. In most cities these days there are empty seats by the end of the game. Not in Nashville, though, no matter what the score. When I read the papers in other cities, I find that the media and the fans are often so critical of their teams. We feel like our fans are behind us 100 percent. They're getting more knowledgeable all the time so I think they'll expect us to do a little better. I think that's good.

—#22, GREG JOHNSON,
NASHVILLE PREDATORS

You'd think hockey in a market like Nashville would take time to develop. It seemed like it exploded right from day one.
—#6, BOB BOUGHNER,

NASHVILLE PREDATORS

Sometimes the noise in our building is contagious, for both teams.

—DAVID POILE,
EXECUTIVE VICE PRESIDENT OF HOCKEY OPERATIONS/
GENERAL MANAGER,
NASHVILLE PREDATORS

Our fans are really loud. Right after we've scored, I can't hear a thing. It's that crazy and that loud. From a player's standpoint, it's unbelievable to hear that noise. Around the league there are some traditional arenas that aren't anywhere near as loud, and probably never will be. I love the noise because it's the excitement of the fans. Hopefully that will never change.

—#12, ROB VALICEVIC,
NASHVILLE PREDATORS

Nashville, Tennessee
February 23, 1999
4:30 P.M.
Gaylord Entertainment Center

Manned by smiling ticket takers, guards, and people handing out promotional items (tonight it's pucks for all the children under age 12) and free Predators Press programs for the adults, the doors typically open at 5:30 P.M. sharp. Tonight they are open an hour early for fans wanting to attend Predators University's pregame discussion, Hockey 101. The banter between those at the doors and those entering for tonight's contest is light and fun. Everyone coming into the arena gets a smile and a genuine "Hello." It's Nashville at its best: smiling, friendly, and easygoing. By 5:30, a large number of fans are already arriving at the arena. Although the game itself won't start for another ninety minutes, most of the early crowd is here for the pregame activities.

PREDATORS UNIVERSITY

A periodic educational program, Predators University brings many of the fans to the Gaylord Entertainment Center early. Predators University offers an opportunity for the fans to hear people such as broadcasters Terry Crisp and Pete Weber (Weber is referred to as the "Professor") explain the rules, strategies, and finer points of hockey.

Among the courses offered by Predators University is Hockey 101. Hockey 101 is a regular feature on Fox broadcasts of games for TV audiences and on the Jumbotron during games for fans in the arena. For TV, Crisp tapes a segment on a specific hockey tactic or skill and, often using one of the Predators players, demonstrates

167

it for the home audience. Such educational activities are a key part of the Predators' strategy to create knowledgeable fans. The Predators also provide in-arena headsets for newer fans to hear the radio broadcast and get explanations of important on-the-ice action. Predators University, Hockey 101, and a number of other programs are part of the Predators' effort to educate fans.

"We believe strongly in the education process," says President Jack Diller, "so we invest heavily in Predators University, Hockey 101, and similar kinds of programs. We reach out to our audience to explain the finer points of the game. And we go to great lengths to showcase the game on television. But I believe that we won't be successful unless we get people in this arena to see the game firsthand. Once they've seen the game live and we've explained it, they're sold."

Educating—and developing—the fan base is so important that it is understood as a shared responsibility for everyone in the Predators organization, but the formal job belongs to the marketing and the communications and development departments. Heading the latter is Gerry Helper, a longtime hockey executive who, like Terry Crisp, joined the team from Tampa Bay.

Helper couldn't have a better name. His entire personality, demeanor, and passion are geared to help people get to know and love hockey. The job seems to come easily for him. He lives and breathes it.

Born and raised in "hockey country," in northwestern New York State, just outside Buffalo, Helper grew up a devoted Buffalo Sabres fan. Although he now has an unwavering allegiance to the Predators, he admits that when the Sabres played the Dallas Stars for the Stanley Cup, his loyalties were torn, if only for a while. "The Stars are in the Western Division, like us, so I guess I had to pull for them a little," he says. "But in the end, old loyalties die hard. In my heart I suffered with the Sabres." Predators' fans can forgive Helper's discomfort about the Sabres' series. The Sabres hired him for his first job in professional sports after graduating from St. Bonaventure.

In the mid-1980s, Helper went on to work for four years for the NHL in New York, first as director of information and later as director of public relations. He went to the Tampa Bay Lightning in 1991 as their first vice president of communications. A consummate communications professional, he added the role of community development when he joined the Predators, and he now serves as vice president of the Predators Foundation.

The role of communications and development chief requires long, hard hours, but hours that Helper gladly puts in. His work with the foundation brings a great sense of accomplishment and pride. He points out, "While I truly love hockey, and my job has me talking hockey virtually every day and most nights, I have really enjoyed seeing all the good that the Predators can do in the community, especially for kids. We try to help a lot of organizations, but for the Predators, kids come first."

While the Predators Foundation quietly supports a large number of children's organizations away from the arena, efforts on game night focus unabashedly on kids. Hockey is big business and the sophisticated marketing campaigns are aimed at primarily businesses, but by 5:30 P.M. on game day, the arena has become a kid's paradise. The ground floor is filled with booths and activities designed to engage, educate, and entertain young fans.

By late afternoon on game day, the Predators' Kroger/Nabisco Puck Patrol, a group of four young people in bright yellow T-shirts, are getting their "game faces" on. They organize a number of kid-friendly activities and crowd-pleasing routines.

Most of the rest of the fans will be in the arena and in their seats well before game time because there is a lot of action on the ice and elsewhere in the arena. When the fans entered the arena, they received a free program (many sporting events charge for such a program) and often a promotional item provided by a sponsor. During the course of the first season, the Predators and their sponsors gave away a variety of premium gifts, such as a team poster sponsored by the *Tennessean,* a magnetic schedule from Baptist Sports Medicine, T-shirts from Fox Television, and goalie Mike Dunham growth charts from Purity Dairies.

The Predators' promotional programs, which are under the

direction of Director of Marketing Randy Campbell, are ongoing and occur outside the arena as well. This year, for example, Pepsi used special Predators material on cans, and Purity Dairies produced a hugely popular ice cream, Predators' Crunch. These promotional programs don't happen without a lot of work. Managing this effort for the Predators is Promotions Manager Polly Pearce.

6:25 P.M.
Pregame Warm-Up

Both teams enter the ice for a brief warm-up before the game. Throughout the arena, fans are buying food and souvenirs. On the Jumbotron, the short videos give fans various information about the game, such as the Chevrolet Keys to the Game. The keys explain a couple of significant areas (controlling face-offs, power play execution, etc.) that the teams must do well in order to win. A humorous video warns fans to be careful of getting hit by pucks flying into the stands.

All these presentations—fun, educational, inspirational—are carefully organized, rehearsed, and choreographed into a production worthy of the Broadway stage. With nearly a thousand video and animation clips prepared for use on the Jumbotron, the production room resembles a TV control center. All these activities are coordinated by Game Presentation Manager Bryan Shaffer with an assist from Promotions and Entertainment Coordinator Christel Foley. About twenty minutes before game time, the clock begins a countdown, and the promotional events begin in earnest.

6:45 P.M.
Gaylord Entertainment Center

About 6:45, the lights are dimmed, and the First American Flying Tiger (a large self-propelled, remote-controlled balloon in the shape of a saber-toothed tiger) is lowered from its perch and circles the arena, dropping tickets for T-shirts and other prizes. As it completes its turn around the arena, the lights dim and a video begins that features a saber-toothed tiger breaking through the sidewalk in front of First American Bank and then prowling through the familiar landmarks of downtown Nashville. He climbs atop the BellSouth Building and jumps through the roof of the arena onto the ice. Another video highlights the Predators breaking through the logos of their main division rivals.

Then the Predators mascot, Gnash, a saber-toothed tiger, under the direction of Brett Rhinehardt, makes his entrance— often rappelling from the top of the arena. Gnash is joined by the Kroger/Nabisco Puck Patrol, and they rev up the crowd by launching T-shirts and other souvenirs high into the seats.

GNASH

The story of how the Predators came to have Gnash, their logo, and even their name is every bit as intriguing as getting the franchise itself. Craig Leipold explains, "People had their favorite names and the ones they disliked. We looked at a lot of names: the Fury, the Wild, the Ice Tigers, and many more. Everyone lobbied for favorites. And we had a couple of false starts. Tom Ward was involved in the attempt to get an NHL franchise in Virginia, and they were going to call that team the Rhinos. So he was pushing for the team to be called the Rhinos. Other than Tom, no one much cared for that one!

"My first choice was the Nashville Edge. I took Edge from the Edge shaving gel, one of my wife's most successful products at SC Johnson. We did some initial focus group testing, and Edge came back as a really strong name for a hockey team. That was my idea, not Helen's. Helen totally separated herself from that. She said she didn't understand why I would want to use the name. But it didn't matter because the name died when Commissioner Bettman heard about it. When he picked up that Helen's family owned Edge shaving gel, he called me and said in no uncertain terms: 'No, get rid of that idea,'" remembers Craig.

"My second choice was the Predators. I don't recall the moment that the name popped up. I don't recall who said it or where it came up in the process, but it struck a chord immediately."

The Predators were in search of a name that would go with their logo, which was decided on before the name. The logo, announced at a press conference at the headquarters of First American Bank, was a saber-toothed tiger. The remains of the tiger, a fierce predator that lived during the Ice Age, had been discovered in Nashville when building crews were excavating the foundation for the First American Center in 1971. The several-thousand-year-old remains, one of five such discoveries in the U.S., had become a local symbol of the city's early history. JDK Design in Burlington, Vermont, along with Nashville's Dye Van Mol & Lawrence created the logo.

The Predators knew they had a winner for a logo when they saw it. It gave them not just a logo, but a first-year promotional theme, "The Ice Age Returns," and significant visual images for a franchise that still didn't have anything tangible to show its fans. In choosing a name, they wanted a tie-in to the logo, something that would capture the determination and grit of the organization, but that also would evoke the spirit of Nashville.

"We wanted a name that would complement our logo, the saber-toothed tiger, which was indigenous to Nashville," says Leipold. "The dictionary describes this tiger as a predator. It was king of the Ice Age. That's how we ended up with the term.

"However, Helen was concerned about the name originally because she thought it might be a negative for some people. She suggested we test it carefully. So we did. Extensively. With focus groups of men, women, and children. We tested it and tested it and tested it and tested it again. No negatives ever came up. In all the focus group testing, Predators came out as a great name. To virtually everyone, it was a ferocious animal that suited a hockey team. People in Nashville loved it because it tied to the city's history."

To make the final decision, though, the Predators did what they so often do—they asked their fans. The response in favor of the name Predators (2 to 1) was overwhelming. The name was announced at a special press conference at the Wildhorse Saloon on November 13, 1997. Subsequently team colors (blue, silver, orange, steel, and gold) and their home and away uniforms were announced at a ceremony at Cool Springs Galleria on February 12, 1998.

Although the idea for Gnash came sometime later, he has become a crowd favorite at games and the many promotional events he attends for the Predators. Despite his ferocious name and appearance, Gnash is loved by young Predators fans, who often line up to hug him.

"Gnash works on several levels," explains Leipold. "He represents a very ferocious animal, he has many features that could be scary, but the kids love him. We spent a fair amount of time strategizing on the kind of mascot we wanted—the soft, warm, huggable type or the tough, athletic one that seems to say, 'Give me a high five.' We're fortunate. We got both with Gnash. I think that's a real tribute to the personality of the person [the identity is a secret] who plays Gnash."

Game time has almost arrived, and the Jumbotron is alive with player information and starting lineups. With just a few minutes to go, the lights are dimmed, and a multicolored laser show begins: it features the Predators logo, a running tiger, and finally the words *Nashville Predators* on the ice. It concludes with fireworks out of the top and bottom of the Jumbotron. Next, a huge saber-toothed tiger head is lowered to the ice, and the Predators skate out through its mouth onto the ice.

Both teams circle in their own ends of the rink until the announcer asks everyone to stand for the national anthem. It is sung by a visiting country music star or someone from the community who has auditioned for the opportunity. Mindy McCready sang the anthem on opening day, and other stars who have sung the anthem include Terri Clark, Bryan White, Pam Tillis, and Trisha Yearwood.

7:05 P.M.
First Period

Once the game starts, the other show gets under way. Throughout the game, various activities excite the crowd and fill in the breaks in the action on the ice. Early in the game, for example, two fans sitting in the very top section of the arena are selected for Windex on the Glass seats at ice level. The two are escorted by the Puck Patrol to their game seats while the theme song from the television series *The Jeffersons*—"Moving on Up"—plays. In front of the seats, members of the Puck Patrol are eagerly cleaning the glass. A little later in the game the Puck Patrol is back in the stands with a contestant for Applebee's Trivia, where the contestant's knowledge about the Predators is tested. And then Jim Knott, the in-arena host, is up in the 300-level seats selecting someone to ride the Bud Light Zamboni during the first intermission.

7:49–8:04 P.M.
First Intermission

The intermissions between periods give the Predators' game presentation staff a chance to be their most creative. Every night there is a different set of crowd-pleasing activities. Tonight, for example, it's the Mini Zamboni Races; four contestants (randomly selected by the game staff before face-off) ride pedal-powered mini Zambonis around the ice. The first contestant to complete two laps wins a Predators prize package. Over the course of the year, nearly a hundred such events will take place, some around holiday or hockey themes, but always involving the fans. The event finishes, then two Bud Light Zambonis take the ice with a lucky fan atop one of them.

"Florida was one of the original teams that did things in between periods for the fans," says Tom Fitzgerald. "You didn't see that too often around the league before. You wouldn't see entertainment in between periods at Chicago Stadium or the Boston Garden. I never saw that when I first broke into the NHL. Even to this day, many of the older teams don't do stuff like that. I guess it's just not in their tradition.

"I'm glad we do that in Nashville for our fans. The team is committed to the concept of an entire entertainment experience. The players try their best to provide exciting hockey, and I like the fact that the organization ensures that the rest of the experience of coming to the arena is an enjoyable one."

One of the enjoyable experiences of coming to the arena is eating. And everyone seems to partake. The arena offers something for every taste, from traditional hot dogs and pizza to gourmet meals. Some fifty vending locations on the main and top floors serve the vast majority of the fans who go to their seats to eat.

On the second and third floors, a variety of options are offered, including the elegant Arena Club, operated by Levy's Restaurants and managed by Craig Grimes, director of operations, and Supervisor Greg Coston. Even though there are only 41 home games, Executive Chef Laurie Potts works full-time getting ready for game days. Laurie spends several days specifically getting ready for diners at each home game. The meals she supervises are buffet, to ensure fast service, but the fare is gourmet. Some fans already consider it one of the finest eating places in Nashville and lament that it's available only on game days. The restaurant ambience, with dark oak paneling and Predators memorabilia as décor, reflects the quality of the food.

Around the rest of the second floor and much of the third-floor Club Level are 74 corporate suites and 1,800 club seats. These areas are served by Club/Suite Executive Susie Masotti and her premium seating team, which includes Britt Kincheloe, Evelyn Finch, Myron Murray, and Sponsor Services account managers Holly Conner and Jennie Wise and Corporate Sponsorship sales executives David Nivison, Bill McKay, Tommy Lynch, and Allison Gay are often found throughout the arena during games, hosting sponsors and ensuring smooth operation of this important part of the fan base.

However much the Predators devote their efforts to kids, a big educational job was aimed at the corporate community. "The real education process we went through," says Jack Diller, "in my mind, was with the business community, demonstrating what it was we were selling. We had to convince them we were selling an opportunity to do business rather than them focusing on the number of games. Scott Loft, now our VP of sales, worked up a scenario to demonstrate the value of taking different clients to games throughout the season. At the end of the year they could see how they'd supported millions of dollars' worth of business. That was really a revelation to the business community."

Is it working? According to Jack Diller, it is. He says, "I think it's worked on most accounts. I think our gut tells us it is working, and our formal research proves it. On the fan side, we're expanding a base of people who just love the game. And businesses are finding that this is a great way for them to build relationships with customers and employees.

"Part of our dedication to outrageous service is recognizing that sometimes we mess up. We try to make sure we do our best. But in the old Disney tradition, when we make a mistake, we make sure that the problem becomes an opportunity."

Diller notes that even the people in the hockey operations area make suggestions about the entertainment aspects of the game: "The hockey side buys into the outrageous service idea and makes suggestions. We would be missing the boat if we didn't try to get as many contributions as we can. Our staff has grown from five to more than sixty, and we seek input from everybody. Occasionally we just step back and spend a day looking at some bigger issues that we don't really have the time to address on a day-to-day basis. In those sessions, everybody is expected to contribute, and not just about his own function."

Up until now he was not a believer in mission statements, particularly ones that got tacked up on the wall and ignored. Diller admits, however, that in the Predators' case, it has become a guiding principle of everything they do, even on the ice. He points out, "We incorporate the mission statement into what we do with the players. And the good news is that they are such a great bunch of guys. They are so much a part of the community. They live here. They have their families here. We talk to the players about how important they are in the community, about how visible they are. How important it is starting out that they not only represent themselves, but that they also represent the franchise. When they go to Kroger, they are representing the franchise.

"Our guys are always thinking about going out of their way to do the extra thing. These players are careful in what they do, the way they conduct themselves. That's important with any franchise, but it's particularly important in a small market—and in one just starting out. Craig has told them that he believes that his personal reputation is on the line. That every one of them represents him and his family.

"We recognize that we are talking about human beings. There will be times when it doesn't work. The key, though, is what you do about it. If your game plan is never to make a mistake, you're doomed. Our game plan is to be very well prepared, make as few mistakes as possible, and if we do mess up, then do something about it. Our people have come to understand that serving the customer, and doing all those other things, is the most important part of their jobs."

8:04 P.M.
Second Period

At 8:04 P.M. the second period begins.

Shortly after the hockey game resumes, the Puck Patrol is back in the crowd throwing out T-shirts, cookies, and other food items provided by Kroger. Among the other items the Puck Patrol regularly distributes are Regal Cinema movie balls (T-shirts rolled up with movie passes inside), T-shirts from different sponsors, Wendy's plush Gnash doll, Shoney's Christmas bears, Dodge Silverado can holders for vehicles, and a host of other items.

Early in the second period there's a break in the action on the ice, so the game day staff runs a regular Predators feature, Sing for Your Supper, courtesy of Outback Steakhouse. In this promotion, a selected fan sings part of a song with musical support, then the latter part without. Fans react positively to tonight's performance, and the fan is awarded a certificate for a free meal. Play resumes, and the staff waits for another break in the action. At the next break, a promotional event pits two fans against each other in a dance contest, with the audience selecting the winner with applause. This promotion is Dance for Your Dinner, and the winner receives a meal certificate courtesy of the Wildhorse Saloon.

"When we were starting this franchise," says Jack Diller, "there was no question in my mind we would develop each night as though we were in the entertainment business. We scouted other teams for the game presentation. For example, if I go with the team to Florida or Phoenix, I look at everything they're doing there—the service, the entertainment, the music, videos, etcetera—not just the hockey.

"In many ways, we have a tougher job than, say, a rock concert. They put on the same show in maybe forty-one different cities. We put on a different show forty-one times to much the same audience. We have to be constantly innovating. We develop new ideas. We choreograph, rehearse it, critique it, then try it during a game. And the next day we review and evaluate what we've done. We examine whether it worked and why or why not. We talk to fans about what they thought. Then we decide whether to keep it, change it, or try something new. For us, it is a constant routine of invent, test, try, and evaluate. Then we start all over again."

Does all the noise and activity distract the players or detract from the game? Captain Fitzgerald expresses the general sentiment of the players when he says they all like to see the fans enjoy the entire package of entertainment that the Predators present at the games: "I love to see people coming to the game and be excited about it. Not just for the hockey but about everything that goes on. One of my favorites is the Windex bit, where fans get to move down to those seats down on the front row. It's great."

While not every player takes in all the extra action surrounding the game, Fitzgerald often does and actually uses it to his advantage as a player. He says, "I'm aware of everything that goes on. I find that is the way I stay in the game, not too tense, more relaxed by noticing what's going on around me.

"And I think it's great for the fans, too, especially the kids. I think it's a win-win situation by having all that extra stuff going on. The fans love it, and the players do, too, even the visiting teams."

Fitzgerald adds, "The guys I've spoken with on the other teams like coming to Nashville. They really do. And it's not just for the country music. That's a big part of it, of course. A lot of hockey players are country music fans. A few years ago, the word around the league was that San Jose had the best fans in the league because they were the loudest. But not anymore. Nashville is. Because of the way the arena was built, with the acoustics in the building, the place just rocks. It's so wild."

Rob Valicevic agrees wholeheartedly: "I don't think the noise and the entertaining activities that go on detract from hockey at all. People come to a hockey game to have fun. Not only to watch the quick action on the ice, but also to enjoy the surroundings. Hockey's supposed to be entertaining, and in Nashville, it is."

"We like the idea of making this place as easy as possible for kids," says Diller. "We've been lucky in having so many weekend games. From my own experience as a parent, we prefer weekend games. My youngest daughter, Mary Clare, is twelve, and during the week my wife, Holly, and I would rather she were focused on school. On the other hand, it's easier for kids to be here during the week than someplace like New York. We start at seven o'clock. It's a good illustration of our mission statement. When we started out, I wondered, 'What time should we start the games?' Well, the answer was to ask our fans. In every instance we try to find out what people want and figure out how to accommodate it."

PIONEERING PARTNER

Craig couldn't have chosen a better partner than Gaylord Entertainment. With a century of experience in media, family entertainment, and sports, Gaylord is the perfect complement to the business experience of Craig, Jack, and the senior Predators staff. The original E. K. Gaylord, who founded the company, went into the newspaper business in Oklahoma before it was a state. A journalist from Colorado, Gaylord first ventured into the "Indian

179

country" of Oklahoma as a pioneer and then formed his newspaper. Mr. Gaylord addressed the Oklahoma legislature at the age of one hundred and worked until the day he died, the following year. His pioneering spirit and basic values of good citizenship and hard work pervade the company to this day.

The country's first computerized typesetting was used at the Gaylord newspaper in Oklahoma. As new media were introduced, Gaylord became one of the first companies west of the Mississippi to own radio and then TV stations. Gaylord operated the first successful independent TV station in the country in Dallas. Always a leader and innovator, Gaylord recognized early on the value of program content and became involved in several sports ventures, including minority investments in the Texas Rangers in baseball and the San Antonio Spurs in the NBA.

Gaylord Entertainment was an early and enthusiastic supporter of the arena because a quality venue for country music artists was needed. Media reports to the contrary, Terry London, CEO of Gaylord Entertainment, says the company was never interested in the full ownership of the Predators. "Owning the entire team would not be a good asset for a public company like ours," notes London. "Our partial ownership in the Predators is a community-oriented investment. Our corporate values, from the original Mr. Gaylord to the current generation of the family, are to give something back, to improve the communities in which we operate. When I was with Gaylord in Dallas, I saw what sports could do for a community. With Dick Evans, we had a knowledgeable sports executive who understood the business and the people. But when we decided to invest, we did it because it helps Nashville, and over the long term, what improves Nashville helps our business."

Under London's leadership, Gaylord has transformed itself into an entirely new company with a new focus and approach. "Basically," he says, "we've sold off those assets that weren't going to help us grow in the new economy, and we're leveraging our assets, great brands like the Grand Ole Opry and Opryland Hotel, into new markets. We are now the leading producer of Christian music [the music industry's fastest-growing genre], are building new hotels, and moving aggressively into the Internet. Some of these investments will take time to mature, but we are patient, long-term investors. We've created enormous dividends for our investors, and I believe we'll do even more for them in the future.

"At some point in the future, we may not be part of the Predators, but for now, we relish our participation. I didn't know Craig at first, but I knew Jack from our investment in the Spurs. As Craig and Jack are such great operators, we don't have to spend any appreciable time on it. So, like everyone else in Nashville, we can just enjoy it."

As CFO of the company when the idea first came up, London admits that he was a bit skeptical. But he talked to friends in Dallas about the Stars, who had relocated to Dallas two years after he'd moved to Nashville. "They convinced me," he says, and he now thinks that hockey is the best sport for Nashville. "My father was a football coach, my best friend is in the PGA, I played basketball in college, and I was involved for Gaylord in the Texas Rangers baseball team. But I didn't know what to think of hockey. After watching what's gone on, I know the Predators will be a good investment for us, but in the meantime, my family and I have fallen in love with the game."

An important part of Gaylord Entertainment's involvement in the arena is the purchase of the naming rights. It's part of the long-term strategy of leveraging the company's entertainment brands. "We are trying to take our brands, including the corporate brand, to the next level," he says. "Look at our world-renowned Grand Ole Opry brand. Country music is the only music genre in the world to have a home, the Opry. And if you look carefully at our businesses, like the Opryland Hotel, you'll see we are in the 'experience' business. We are extremely well known in this market, and are perceived in the corporate meeting and hospitality business as better than anyone else in presenting the entire package—lodging, food, and entertainment. The only thing that was missing was awareness outside the industry of our corporate brand. Those that know us know that the Gaylord name represents honesty, integrity, and quality. We need more people to know that. That's why we think the arena name is a good investment.

"Building corporate brands is expensive and takes time. The opportunity to build our name around the arena venue in Nashville, our home now and forever, was just too good to pass up. Wall Street beats us up, looking for short-term results, but we are patient, long-term investors, and we are going to invest in our brands for the future. We are absolutely building value for our investors over the long term."

London adds, "Our goal is to create entertainment that makes a positive difference in people's lives. We believe strongly that our investment in the Predators and the arena is an important part of that."

The majority of away games are televised on Fox and WNAB. All Nashville Predators games are broadcast on Gaylord's WTN 99.7 FM on radio. Manning the radio booth are play-by-play man Pete Weber and color commentator Terry Crisp. While many teams leave the broadcasting to local or national TV and radio affiliates, the Predators produce and manage everything themselves. "It allows us to provide sponsors with a complete package," says the Predators' Tom Ward. "We have a complete team in place with Pete and Terry, VP of Broadcasting John Guagliano, who also produces the show, and Erik Barnhart and Robert Hill, who do features. Susan Morgan handles the traffic and ads. They represent the Predators so well, it's a win-win situation for everyone."

8:58–9:13 P.M.
Second Intermission

At 8:58 P.M. the buzzer sounds, ending the second period. As the teams skate off the ice, the Kroger/Nabisco Puck Patrol is on the ice again with another promotional event. This time it's the Pepsi Predator Ball races. Two contestants (randomly selected earlier) are put inside giant blow-up hamster balls. They run inside the balls from one end of the ice to the other while moving around obstacles. The first to cross the goal line after completing the obstacle course wins. Other popular features have included the Dodge Truck Shootout (fans have an opportunity to win a Dodge truck), Concentration (fans test their memory skills), and Musical Chairs (the traditional game played with five fans and Gnash).

9:13 P.M.
Third Period

As the players return to the ice, the in-arena events start again. Back in the stands, the Puck Patrol is hard at work. It's soon time for the T-shirt Target. From the 100-level seating, a fan using a slingshot tries to hit one of three targets set up in the 300-level seating with a T-shirt. Then the Patrol hands out balloons to people sitting in and around section 110/111 behind the Nashville goal (to distract opponent shooters), and during the last five minutes of the period, the patrol will be at the band stage area with Gnash for more fan exhortations: the noise meter, the song "YMCA," and the wave. Also during the period, the Fan of the Game is determined (by a fan "noise" vote), and the season ticket holder of the game is announced.

Up in the radio broadcast booth, the radio crew readies the return from a commercial break. It's near the end of the game, and Terry Crisp is preparing his Mercedes' 3 Stars of the Game selections. First, though, he'll describe what he thinks the Predators must do in the final few minutes of the third period.

"CRISPY"

In the broadcast booth, as he was on the ice, Terry Crisp is an original. As a player, he had sheer enthusiasm and joy for playing the game that always shone through. He was a tenacious checker and skater, and his energy and feel for the tempo and structure of the game made him an essential part of two Stanley Cups with the Flyers. A constant and dedicated student of the game, Crisp would probably have become a high school teacher and hockey coach

183

had his skills and dedication to hockey not carried him to places he couldn't have imagined growing up in Parry Sound, Ontario.

Perhaps he comes by his originality naturally. He was one of the original players in St. Louis when they were added to the league in 1967, and a member of the original New York Islanders when they expanded in 1972. When his playing career was ending, Crisp loved the game so much that he wanted to stay involved. He moved on to coaching and guided the Calgary Flames to a Stanley Cup in 1989.

But he once again succumbed to the lure of expansion, joining the Tampa Bay Lightning as head coach in 1992. He became the longest-serving head coach of an expansion team in NHL history, leading the Lightning during 391 games.

In the nickname-crazy tradition of hockey, he is known affectionately as "Crispy." He has brought boundless enthusiasm and a ready smile to every team he has been around. Despite being a player on two NHL expansion teams, Crisp says that Tampa Bay and Nashville are the two expansions he relates to most: "As a player, you get totally preoccupied with playing, getting ready for the next team coming to town. So you miss a lot of the excitement surrounding expansion. As a coach and now a broadcaster, I've had a better chance to see the big picture. To me, both Tampa Bay and Nashville almost seemed to be an 'awakening,' waiting to happen. I don't know, maybe it's the era, maybe it's our time or our young stars. But it seems that every time somebody says something can't be done or won't be done, well, it happens!

"I mean Bill Gates has taken us into a whole new era in business. Now hockey has done the same thing. It's going into markets where hockey has no history and succeeding beyond anyone's imagination. Growing up, I never thought I'd spend a good part of my career in Florida. Florida! In those days Florida to me was palm trees and orange juice! Now there are two NHL teams in Florida and some minor-league teams as well. Then suddenly I get this great opportunity to come to Nashville and I think, *Nashville? Okay, Nashville!*

"It seems that the people here were just waiting for hockey. When the car companies [Nissan and Saturn] moved here, I think that Nashville decided it wanted to be a big-league city. So they went out and got the big leagues. The Titans in the NFL and the Predators in hockey. That, along with the marketing this team has done, are the two biggest factors in the Predators' success."

Crisp also believes that being an expansion team helped immensely in getting the Predators established on a solid footing. "People like the idea that the team was born here," he says. "People have more of a long-term commitment when it's your own. The Nashville Predators were born in Nashville; they will be raised in Nashville; they are Nashville."

His broadcast partner, Pete Weber, agrees: "There is no question in my mind as well that the expansion aspect of it helped. Not just the automakers and medical industry, but many other people and companies who are flocking to the Mid-South helped quite a bit. They were all looking for something in common, something that was uniquely theirs. I think the Predators are that common bond for the long-term residents and the new folks alike.

"But," says Weber, "it was no small marketing effort from the people in the early days behind the scenes. I remember them in what then passed for offices, using three card tables, two telephones, and a fax machine. They made it happen. They helped this dream get going. I don't care that Nashville was ready for it, it took these guys to make the magic. They created the buzz."

THE BUZZ

Tom Ward credits his staff with getting it right. He believes that one of the keys to marketing success is to get the right buzz. And the Predators marketing and communications staff seemed to get the right buzz almost from the start. Soon after the franchise was awarded, it seemed that everybody in Nashville was alive with excitement about the Predators. Everybody was talking about the team.

The momentum, the buzz, grew throughout the summer of 1998 and reached a pitch after the season started. Everybody seemed to be saying, "Been to see the Predators? You just gotta go to a game." By midseason it was hard to find anyone who hadn't been to a game or wasn't planning to go. Everyone who had been had the same thing to say: "Had a great time. Fun, entertaining, really enjoyed it."

Tom Fitzgerald says the buzz wasn't lost on the team: "People told me before I came here that Tennessee was football country. And I'm really pleased to see how well the Titans have been received. But I was concerned. I wondered, 'Will hockey go over in Nashville?' It's supposed to be a nontraditional hockey market. But the people in the front office got it right. We all heard the buzz. From the beginning, it just felt right. We heard it loud and clear from fans. Often, if things are not going well, the first you hear about it is from the fans. But in Nashville, right away, before we even started to play, the fans were telling us, 'Hey, you guys are doing it right. Management is doing it right.' Sometimes you're not even aware of the impact you're having, but fans let you know pretty quickly what they like and don't like. Somehow everything we did just seemed to connect with the fans."

For Predators defenseman Bob Boughner, no fans are more important than the kids. He and his wife, Jennifer, have two, a son, Brady, and a daughter, Molly. Boughner grew up in Canada and broke into the league with the Buffalo Sabres in 1995. Acquired by Nashville in the expansion draft, Boughner quickly established himself as a stalwart on defense. In a city known for its music blockbusters, "Boughner's Greatest Hits" have become a fan favorite. While his leadership and tough, physical play have made a big impression on the ice, his leadership in off-ice activities is equally meaningful, but in a quieter way. He frequently purchases tickets for youth groups and has been very active in the Kids Escaping Drugs, a program that helps rehabilitate children with drug and alcohol addictions.

10:08 P.M.
Game Over

Fans are encouraged to stay after the game for various events. At Thanksgiving, it was the Turkey Shoot; any fan could win a turkey, courtesy of Kroger and Honey Suckle White. During the inaugural season, more than three hundred turkey certificates were awarded.

Even though the Predators lost, it has been almost a magical evening for the young fans. You can see it by the look in their eyes. For them, game night is everything. The hockey, the videos, the music, the souvenirs, and the food—all add to a great night's entertainment. For the adults, it's more about the game, but they, too, appreciate the hard work and the outrageous customer service.

"Our service model and philosophy are similar to those of Southwest Airlines," says Diller. "We haven't patterned ourselves after them, but we are both in businesses that maintain long hours, and we have the same degree of expectation about what's supposed to happen on a given day. They offer a superior product and wonderful service at value prices, and we believe we do as well. We both also employ a lot of enthusiastic young people. I fly a lot with Southwest, and I always ask their employees if it's a good place to work. They tell me, 'Yes, it is!' That's the kind of response I hope we get from our people because that translates into good service for our customers."

The Predators marketing and game presentation staff want the fan experience to be a complete one. They try to manage every part of the experience to ensure a total experience for their fans. They even worry about traffic patterns coming and going from the arena. A number of regular fans come from as far away as Chattanooga (a two-hour drive), and some occasionally from Knoxville (nearly three hours away). The Predators want the out-of-town and local fans to find traffic that flows and parking that is clean, convenient, and well supervised. Fortunately the Nashville Police Department and the parking facilities' managers, such as locally based Central Parking System (the world's largest parking and transportation management company), are both cooperative and professional. The team meets with all those involved on a regular basis to ensure that the fans continue to have a positive experience.

Despite the hundreds of hectic hours of behind-the-scenes efforts over several days, the Predators game presentation staff will start first thing the next day following the game to dissect every instant of the game presentation. They'll analyze in minute detail what worked and what needs to change.

For fans, though, the game this night, February 23, ends for them as the season began, full of excitement, noise, fun, and surprise at the videos, the contests, and the hockey. As the season progressed, they came to expect more with each passing game. Their very high expectations for something special from the Predators started with the opening night. The surprises continued right through the last game of the season when players literally gave them the shirts off their backs in an emotional, season-ending finale. But if Nashville's love affair with its hockey team began nearly a year before with the visit of the NHL Governors, it reached a crescendo with the opening game, October 10, 1998.

OPENING GAME

The owner's box was full of family: Helen; all five sons; Craig's brother Lance and his family from Dallas; Helen's brothers Curt and Fisk and their families from Racine; Helen's sister Winnie from Norfolk, Virginia; and both Craig's and Helen's parents. For Craig, though, all the pomp and rituals of the occasion required him to be available for myriad meetings and special events over the preceding weeks and continued through tonight's ceremonial opening face-off.

Craig wanted this night, more than anything, to be a family time. Making the event even more poignant, it was his mother's birthday. Always supportive of Craig's endeavors, Betty Jo had typically been the one to keep such achievements in perspective. Surveying the more than seventeen thousand fans, the noise, the color, and the drama surrounding the opening night, she turned to Craig and jokingly said, "Craig, it was very sweet of you to arrange all this for my birthday."

Her comment to him broke the tension of the previous weeks and months preparing for this special night. For nearly three years

Craig had been focused on little else than getting a sports franchise. Now it was finally happening, and for the first time in many months, surrounded by family, he could relax and just be a fan.

If it was a historic high point in Nashville sports history, it was also the beginning of Craig's conversion from just an owner to an owner-fan. Some sports owners seldom attend games; their interest is strictly financial. But for Craig, from that first face-off, the attraction became emotional. He later told the media, "It's hard not to love this team. I don't just go to all the games because I'm the owner. I go because I'm a fan." And from the very start, the Predators created an emotional bond with their fans that will surely stand the test of time.

Like an opening night on Broadway or perhaps the Academy Awards, the Predators choreographed their historic first game in Nashville to create a level of excitement and anticipation that would last all season. Despite local and state dignitaries and NHL officials in attendance, on opening night, players and fans were the center of attention. Players arrived in limousines and Humvees and entered the arena on a red carpet to the cheers of fans.

Every fan received a commemorative ticket holder and a logo lapel pin from First American and BellSouth. Craig greeted fans as they entered the arena and signed autographs for hundreds of people. It was, in many ways, his finest hour, and the fans showered him with their appreciation that night.

Attorney Tom Sherrard, who had worked as closely with Craig as anyone in Nashville in putting the franchise together, perhaps sums it up best when he says, "Craig, unique among sports owners, has an ability to relate to everyone. He sees himself as an ordinary guy in an extraordinary situation. He listens to people with a true, genuine desire to hear and learn. He thinks everyone's opinion is important to him. He genuinely loves his job and takes seriously his responsibility to the fans. While he is technically the owner, he truly believes the Predators are Nashville's team, and he is just the caretaker. The fans sense his genuine character and straightforward honesty. It works well in Nashville because that's the kind of people we are. On opening night, I wasn't surprised to see that his autograph was more sought after than any of the players'.'"

On opening night, Craig saw that three years of work and planning had finally paid off. On the street outside the arena, the noise of the crowd was exhilarating; inside, the air was alive with music. The pageantry of the color guard, the national anthem, and the ceremonial face-off seemed to dramatically raise the level of anticipation. The mood was electric. The crowd literally vibrated. During the entire game, they cheered nearly every time the Predators got the puck or goalie Mike Dunham made a routine stop. Despite a 1-0 loss, the fans enjoyed every minute.

For the players, such emotional fan support is critical. Bob Boughner recalls the players' astonishment at the fan reaction to the Predators' first game: "The players really key off the fans' reaction to a game. I've been involved in some emotional games, but nothing like that first game we played in Nashville. Even though we lost, afterward the people were standing on their feet giving us a standing ovation like we'd just won the Cup. Not one person left his seat. Then we won the second game, and the response was even better. It's been that way all season. It's an amazing feeling playing here. I even get the same response outside the arena when people find out I'm one of the Predators."

The dramatic success of the Predators' inaugural season has become a benchmark not just in hockey, but in all sports. Jack Diller maintains that the team's success, on and off the ice, is all about people: "Our people created a highly successful new franchise from the ground up. Our success, I believe, is based on two things. We hired experienced people, but more important, people with an intense desire to succeed."

As Nashville and Middle Tennessee were to find out, the arrival of the Predators brought more than just success for the team, more to cheer about than just goals. The Predators significantly stimulated the economic and social vitality of a city and region already on the move.

Power Play

The Predators' home games have become "the place to be" to provide a premier entertainment experience for business clients and potential customers. In fact, the Chamber has found Predators' games to be a great way to show off our community's spirit and energy to economic development prospects.

—MIKE ROLLINS, PRESIDENT,
NASHVILLE AREA CHAMBER OF COMMERCE

As an economic catalyst, what more could you want . . . civic pride, a packed downtown, worldwide press, and plenty of Red Wings tourists. The Predators were a great shot in the arm during a typically slow period in the hospitality industry.

—BUTCH SPYRIDON, EXECUTIVE VICE PRESIDENT,
NASHVILLE CONVENTION AND VISITORS BUREAU

One of the reasons I moved to Tennessee was the Nashville Predators!

—DR. CHRISTINE HOFFMAN,
FAMILY PRACTICE, MURFREESBORO, TENNESSEE,
FORMERLY PROFESSOR OF MEDICINE,
EAST CAROLINA UNIVERSITY

C hristine Hoffman, M.D., is a vital part of a busy family medicine practice in Murfreesboro, Tennessee, just thirty miles from
Nashville. Earlier, as a clinical instructor of medicine at East
Carolina University, a relatively isolated school in the eastern
Carolina mountains, she had dreamed about putting her academic
work into practice. She is passionate about helping families, especially kids, and she dreamed about a new life with her own family
in a place that offered a rich variety of family-oriented activities. As
an accomplished doctor, with an exceptional academic record, she
could have gone anywhere in the country. In fact, she had been
enticed by offers to go to a number of exciting places.

But Dr. Hoffman had another passion—sports. To her, it's an
essential part of life. With a multitude of opportunities to choose
from, wherever her work took her, professional sports events were
sure to be available. About the time she and her family were making the final decision on a move, she got the word that the Predators
were coming to Nashville. She decided she'd join them. When she
carefully weighed all her options, she says her decision was easy.

Not every doctor, family, or company that moves to Nashville
does so because of the Predators. But professional sports teams, such
as the NFL Tennessee Titans and the NHL Nashville Predators, add
many tangible and intangible benefits to the community.

In their short history, the Predators have had a major impact on
the city of Nashville and the Middle Tennessee area. They've
brought in millions of dollars in direct revenue, created hundreds
of direct and indirect jobs, made vital contributions to the dramatic
resurgence of downtown Nashville, and created national publicity
for the city's tourism industry.

These indisputable benefits are only the beginning, however.

The team has electrified the city and built up the region's "brand image" around the U.S. and the world. Along with the NFL Titans, the Predators have launched Nashville into the big leagues and increased civic pride. This boost to the city's image has an impact on everything from property values to company relocation and executive recruitment.

The team has generated millions in free press for the city, attracting tourists and new commercial activity. Virtually every major newspaper and TV outlet in the country has run a story on the amazing success of the Predators. "What They're Saying About the Predators" provides a good indication of what the media had to say during the team's first year.

WHAT THEY'RE SAYING ABOUT THE PREDATORS

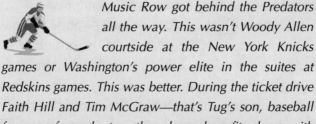

Music Row got behind the Predators all the way. This wasn't Woody Allen courtside at the New York Knicks games or Washington's power elite in the suites at Redskins games. This was better. During the ticket drive Faith Hill and Tim McGraw—that's Tug's son, baseball fans—performed at a three-hour benefit along with Delbert McClinton. McClinton introduced the Predators' fight song ("Welcome to Dixie when you walk in the door, but you better be ready for the Third World War"). He reprised the song at the regular season opener. Trisha Yearwood has agreed to sing the national anthem twice. Barbara Mandrell, whose son, Nathan, plays in the Nashville Youth Hockey League, invited everyone in the Predators organization to a reception at her 30,000 square-foot log home last month.

—MICHAEL FARBER, SPORTS ILLUSTRATED

From an on-ice viewpoint, it's clear that GM David Poile has surpassed all expectations . . . The team is both fan-media friendly and forges that image on a daily basis.

—FISCHLER REPORT

But the group attracting the most attention is the one pounding out the hits at the Nashville Arena. And so far, on the street where dreams of becoming a big star are born and dashed every day, the newest act in Music City—the Predators—is hitting high notes on the ice and in the stands.

—BRUCE GARRIOCH, OTTAWA SUN

Across the street from the Ernest Tubb record shop and down the block from the Blue Grass Inn and the Gibson Café and Guitar Shop is the newest star factory in Music City. But it's not a honky-tonk. It's a hockey tonk . . . The unlikely pairing of a northern-rooted sport and a smallish southern city devoted to football, NASCAR and country music has sparked an instant infatuation, uniting worlds that turn out to be surprisingly alike.

—HELENE ELLIOTT, LOS ANGELES TIMES

Nashville has fallen in love with hockey . . . Local newspaper columnists have raved about the game they admittedly know little about . . . They cheer the hits, the goals and even the loss on Opening Night . . . The New Ice Age, as they call it here, is red hot . . . But as much as the city has fallen in love with the game, the players have fallen in love with Music City.

—MARK MILLER, CALGARY SUN

The Nashville Predators have made a good first impression in a state known more for country music and college football than hockey.

—JIM SMITH, NEWSDAY

When ice hit area roads last week on the same night the Predators faced the Detroit Red Wings, the Predators management reacted with a smart gesture that should help endear the team to its new home. The Predators announced that fans who didn't want to brave the icy roads to see the sold-out game would be able to exchange their tickets for one of three January games. Such a weather-related ticket swap is highly unusual in professional sports . . . Predators management has demonstrated repeatedly from the day the franchise was announced that it understands the need to build a market for the sport and for the team . . . In addition to winning the game, they won another measure of support from their hometown.

—EDITORIAL, TENNESSEAN

Truth is, the Predators are more than a team located in the nation's country music capital. They're also a decent hockey team . . . Nashville General Manager David Poile, Washington's former GM, built the Predators through the expansion draft and with a variety of shrewd deals associated with the draft. He stockpiled extra players and draft choices from teams in exchange for bypassing some of the players available on their unprotected list . . . The Predators don't need a trap. They take their name seriously. They seek and destroy.

—DAVE LUECKING,
CBS SPORTSLINE PRO HOCKEY WRITER

To all those people who said last summer that the idea of NHL hockey in Nashville sounded strange, the verdict is in. You were right. It was wonderfully strange . . . Those who attended the game Saturday could savor a proprietary sense of being present at the creation, of being Founding Fans—and the Predators could position themselves, with certain legitimacy that extended beyond the hype, as Nashville's team . . . Here's the really weird/wonderful thing: for whatever reasons fans seemed to embrace their new hockey team—civic pride, love of the sport or excitement over a new municipal toy—the players appeared to reciprocate the feelings . . . Whatever the conclusion you draw, though, it's fair to say this much after one game: These folks know how to put on a pretty fair coming-out party.

—R*ANDY* H*ORICK,* N*ASHVILLE* S*CENE*

Down on the ice, the game's up-close speed is dazzling. It's like Daytona without bumpers. The only difference is, when a hockey player crashes into the wall he doesn't burst into flames. Usually, the action was a puck-whacking, glass-slapping blur. Non-stop. The other night, I was channel-flipping between a Predators game and the World Series. I left the baseball game for a minute and saw 10 shots, three scuffles and two face-offs. When I returned to the game, the pitcher was still waiting for the signal. It's frantic, fast and fun. And there's plenty more where that came from.

—L*ARRY* W*OODY,* T*ENNESSEAN*

Just two games into the first hockey season of the rest of my life and I confess: I like it, I love it, I want some more of it . . . It is the hustle, determination, work ethic such as Fitzgerald and friends have displayed in the first two games that will endear them to Nashville sports fans . . . It has been what Barry Trotz promised as he and General Manager David Poile built the roster. A team which makes up for being short of talent and scoring punch with blue collar effort. They will bring their lunch pails to Nashville Arena every night.

—JOE BIDDLE, *TENNESSEAN*

It's [hockey in Nashville] going to work big time. It's only going to get better and better. The people are fantastic. The crowd is loud, they're alive. They're even getting to boo the referees now and they're even starting to boo the Predators if the power play's brutal. So, that's a real sign of learning the game. The stars have been great. You saw the excitement. Barbara Mandrell sat down and talked to us for over an hour about the Predators. It's going right through the community. You walk into a bar after the game and they're talking hockey. They're wearing Predators sweaters. This city is doing it right. Everybody else should go to Nashville and see how this city's doing it because it's going to be a blueprint. It's an excellent, excellent organization.

—BARRY MELROSE, ESPN COMMENTATOR

PLAYERS OFF THE ICE

An often-overlooked area is a team's contribution to the local quality of life. The Predators have repeatedly shown their commitment to the city through charity and fund-raising activities. The team has already lent its support to more than forty charities. The Predators Foundation allocates funds and facilities directly to the community, and team management routinely donates tickets to local charities. The team focuses much of its effort on kids. The players have donated time and money to such organizations as Youth, Inc., the Nashville Children's Theater, and the Ronald McDonald House. In these endeavors and more, the players, staff, and spouses have been generous with their time and have made a major effort to contribute to the community.

According to GM David Poile, being part of the community is an important part of what the Predators are all about: "That's part of the total package of what we've brought to Nashville. We are a Nashville team both on and off the ice. We try our best to ensure that fans have a good time when they come to a game, whether we win or lose. No team can guarantee a win every time, but we can guarantee we'll try our best every time. We will always be well prepared and will make our best effort.

"We can make that claim because I know that our coaches and players care. It's a little bit different in some more established markets or in bigger markets. In many of those places, all they have to worry about is the game. But we recognize that our players are fairly visible in the community. We believe the entire Predators family—players, coaches, support and management staff, and even spouses—has a bigger role in Nashville. We're part of the community on more than just game days."

It also comes as no surprise that many team members have been especially big supporters of youth hockey. The NHL established a Fan Development program in 1993 that continues to grow. Through this program the Predators have supported the Street Pride street hockey program (sponsored by Nike and the YMCA). The league also sponsors a variety of street hockey tournaments. The team has taken these efforts a step farther; players hop into a team caravan (the Predators Prowler RV) to teach children in nearby cities about hockey.

For many of the Predators, youth hockey is more than just part of the Predators' fan development business. Captain Tom Fitzgerald is among those with kids growing up in Nashville, and he's anxious to see his boys play if they are so inclined. He has three boys, but only one is old enough to play youth minor hockey.

"He plays every Friday night," says Fitzgerald. "I get to see him play often, but because of our travel schedule, I can't get to every game. I'd like to, though, because it's so much fun. He's five. He loves soccer, too, and plays on a soccer team. He likes hockey, but he could play soccer all day. Soccer is a great sport for kids, but I think he is going to like hockey. He skates pretty well for a five-year-old.

"To try to gauge his progress, I asked my dad, 'When I was five, what was I doing on the ice?' I think kids start things so much earlier these days. It's amazing. In some ways, I think, you can start kids too early; it's more for the parents than the kids. Just to have the kids busy. Fortunately I got a great start as a kid."

The Predators and the Fitzgerald family were pleased to find a strong youth hockey program already operating in Nashville. By comparison, in Florida, the Panthers team was the catalyst for the youth program. "It was nonexistent when we got down there. From day one, youth hockey had only one rink and not many teams. As the Panthers caught on, youth hockey kept growing," says Fitzgerald.

Having the Predators in town has added momentum to a youth hockey league that was already starting to make waves. In 1997, the Bantams, a group of fourteen- and fifteen-year-olds, won the Southeastern District championship. They defeated teams from Atlanta and West Palm Beach before upsetting a team that came into the final with a 62-0 record.

The youth hockey league now has almost five hundred players, including girls, ranging in age from five to seventeen. Early on, many of the players were transplant kids, hailing from traditional hockey cities. Since the Predators came to town, however, youth and adult hockey has exploded with Nashville natives and hockey novices.

"We started with a great base in Nashville, and I think you're going to see that keep growing," Fitzgerald points out. "Already, the growth of the enrollment for Nashville is just amazing. Our new practice facility is helping with ice time, but we still don't have enough facilities. I think we'll see a lot of new rinks in Nashville, in Brentwood, and in other places around Middle Tennessee."

Opening the Centennial Sportsplex training facility for the Predators was a big boost to amateur hockey players. The facility doubled the public ice availability in the city, and with the Predators using it a maximum of three hours per day, it is a big benefit to hockey players, figure skaters, and recreational skaters. John Holmes, the facility coordinator, says that they can now accommodate almost one thousand people, with skaters ranging from three-year-olds to people well into their seventies. "We often have grandparents come in to skate with their grandkids," Holmes notes.

The facility has been a boon to local leagues, increasing the number of games, practices, and clinics. The old-timers' leagues started nearly twenty years ago. With ice being such a rarity before, teams often didn't finish up until after midnight. Now they are able to play at a time more suited to those with middle-aged schedules (and bodies).

The Sportsplex has hosted some big events as well, including a regional figure skating championship. It hosted a Country Western Tournament for youth hockey in 1999, bringing in kids from such faraway cities as Toronto and Tampa Bay.

Playing hockey in a city with a new NHL franchise is naturally more exciting for youth hockey players, but it also brings a new level of intensity to the competition. For the boys in Tom Fitzgerald's family, is there a lot of pressure on youngsters whose father is captain of the Nashville Predators? There has to be, but Fitzgerald is aware of it and tries to minimize it.

"You know what," Fitzgerald says of his oldest son, "he loves hockey. But I don't put any pressure on him, nor will I on the other two boys. The oldest has just turned five, and he's playing with six-, seven-, and even some eight-year-olds. That's pressure enough for him. I don't want to push him. I don't want to turn him off.

"My mother was a real 'hockey mom' for my brothers and me, but she kept things in perspective. I learned a lot from that. When my oldest son first started hockey, he wasn't always sure he wanted to go. And I was okay with it. I said, 'Fine, you don't have to go.' I wasn't worried, and I wouldn't press him. If he wants to play, great. If not, that's okay too."

Fitzgerald continues, "My wife is not an experienced 'hockey mom.' She grew up with basketball, baseball, and football with her brothers. This hockey stuff is all new to her. But we are really pleased to see the availability and growth of youth hockey in Nashville. It says a lot about the future of the Predators in Nashville, but more important, it adds a great new opportunity to learn to play and love hockey. With the old-timers' leagues here, there is an opportunity in Nashville to play recreational hockey nearly your whole life. And hockey is a sport that you can play almost as long as you can walk.

"My middle guy, who is two and a half, loves Rollerblades. He and my older boy play hockey on Rollerblades in the garage, just like it's a hockey rink."

Fitzgerald vows to be vigilant in keeping future family rivalry in check: "A professional athlete in the family can be hard for others. My middle brother, who is only fifteen months younger than I am, went through that. Whether it was in baseball or hockey, he was always playing in my shadow. I know my parents were concerned about it. My parents were good role models for me. My brother never played professionally, but he's found his own role as a scout for the Columbus Blue Jackets."

Most of the kids who play youth hockey will never make it to professional hockey or play in college. But by learning the game firsthand, feeling the emotion of the sport, and enjoying the camaraderie of a hockey team, they'll be the fans for the Predators in years to come.

Fitzgerald says the players are aware of how many young fans they attract to a game: "Since most of us have young and growing families ourselves, that's pretty important to us. I think having games at 7:00 P.M. helps. And the family-oriented entertainment atmosphere of the arena is very positive too. From the bench, we can see how much fun the kids are having."

But the kids certainly aren't the only ones to benefit from the Predators' presence. Nashville as a whole is seeing major economic benefits.

BOOMTOWN

Nashville is the capital of Tennessee and a vital transportation, business, and tourism center for North America. Nearly 50 percent of the U.S. population lives within five hundred miles of Nashville.

The area benefits from low unemployment, consistent job growth, substantial outside investment and expansion, and a broadening of the labor force. Several highly ranked colleges and universities provide a steady flow of skilled management and technical talent.

The Middle Tennessee region tends to outperform the state and nation throughout all stages of the economic cycle. The city is a leader in publishing and printing, finance and insurance, health care services, music and entertainment, transportation, technology, higher education, and tourism. With the Grand Ole Opry, the Opryland Hotel, the country music recording industry, and a multitude of historic sites, Nashville is a major tourist and entertainment destination. It hosts some of the largest conventions in the country.

The biggest player in Nashville's entertainment and convention businesses is Predators minority owner Gaylord Entertainment. The company, whose name adorns the team's arena, owns the high-profile Grand Ole Opry, Ryman Auditorium, and Opryland Hotels, as well as a portfolio of entertainment and publishing enterprises. Gaylord employs approximately 6,400 people. For a closer look at the man at the helm of this empire, read "Terry London, Standing Tall."

TERRY LONDON, STANDING TALL

Terry London, President and CEO of Gaylord Entertainment, is quiet and unassuming, but he brings a commanding presence when he walks into a room. With his tall frame, he still looks like a basketball player. No stranger to competitive sports, he played basketball for legendary coach Hank Iba at Oklahoma State. And the Predators are not London's first foray into a professional league, as he was involved earlier with the Texas Rangers.

London worked as a CPA before joining Gaylord Broadcasting Company in Dallas, in 1978. He worked his way up through the financial ranks and came to Nashville in 1991 as Vice President and Chief Financial Officer. He was promoted to his current position in 1997 and has guided the company through a historic restructuring, dismantling parts of the organization and growing others. Gaylord sold off its TNN and CMT cable channels and a Dallas TV station to CBS and shut down its Opryland amusement park to build a giant shopping and entertainment complex. Meanwhile, London made investments in new Internet companies and initiated the investment in new Opryland Hotels in Orlando, Dallas, and Maryland.

Thankfully for Nashville hockey fans, with London at the helm, Gaylord stepped up at a crucial point to buy a key stake in the Predators organization. Gaylord Entertainment reaffirmed their commitment in the

Predators when they bought the naming rights to the arena. Terry and his wife, Nancy, can be found at virtually every Predators game cheering for their team. Many believe they compete with Craig and Helen Leipold and Phil Bredesen and wife Andrea Conte for the title of the Predators' biggest fans.

Gaylord Entertainment has continually demonstrated its commitment to Nashville and has played a major role in the growth of the local tourism industry. "We want to be a leader in this community because it's a special community and there are a lot of good things happening," London says.

Like Craig Leipold, London has his eyes fixed clearly on the future. "We believe that a company either grows or goes backward," he says. "Either it does the best that it knows how to do or it fails." Like the Predators' strategy of building for the future, London takes the long view. "We've been a long-term manager of business. We're not driven by earnings per share." With Terry London's vision, including building a company that could one day be as big as Disney and Time-Warner, the Nashville community will likely find that they've found a powerful partner.

NASHVILLE FANS:
SUPPORTIVE AND ENTHUSIASTIC

Although the area has had many active minor-league sports in the past (principally the Sounds baseball team and in hockey, the Knights), the 1990s saw the arrival of a variety of new sports franchises, including the NFL Tennessee Oilers, who moved into their new stadium in 1999 as the Tennessee Titans. Others include the Kats arena football, minor-league basketball, and soccer.

In addition, Nashville has always been highly thought of as a college sports town, with football (including Vanderbilt, Tennessee State, and Middle Tennessee State Universities in nationally ranked conferences) and basketball (with dozens of existing men's and women's teams, including the nationally ranked Vanderbilt men's and women's teams) being the most popular.

Nashville fans have enthusiastically supported the arts, with a world-class performing arts center, and performing arts companies in dance, opera, theater, and symphonic and chamber music.

The Predators are located in Nashville; however, the economic impacts have accrued to the entire Middle Tennessee region. Several studies of the economic impact of sports have found that the economic benefits seem to affect all cities in a region.

The impact of a sports franchise is greatest in smaller markets such as Nashville. While the largest cities view sports teams as important pieces of their overall cultural package, in many less-populous cities the teams have become inextricably linked with the city's image. "Sports means more to Oakland," says a former city manager. "It makes less of a difference to New York, San Francisco, or Chicago."

According to Bernard Manekin, a Baltimore developer who has been chairman of a commission studying the economic impact of sports in Maryland, sports franchises are "terribly important for the psyche of a city, particularly for cities not considered the 'glamorous' cities. Pro sports franchises stir the heart of the citizenry in Baltimore more than they would in Los Angeles or New York."

PREDATORS' ECONOMIC CONTRIBUTIONS

To assess the potential economic impact that the Predators would have on Nashville, an independent study was undertaken at Vanderbilt University's Owen Graduate School of Management. Assisting the study's author, Rick Oliver, economics professors

Luke Froeb and David Scheffman provided guidance about specific areas of interest. The economic impact model they used followed that developed by Dr. John Connaughton of the University of North Carolina, a widely recognized expert in the field of economic impact studies. The Nashville Predators, the National Hockey League, and the Nashville Area Chamber of Commerce provided factual information on the Nashville economy, arena seating, ticket information, schedules, and more.

The study revealed that the Predators created some $82 million in new economic activity in Middle Tennessee in the first year of operation. Overall, the Predators will create nearly $470 million in new economic activity within the first five years. These figures include arena revenues, such as ticket sales and concessions, as well as off-site expenditures for hotel rooms, food, and entertainment.

NEW OPPORTUNITIES

The Predators have created jobs—and not just for players, coaches, and administrators. Studies estimated that the Predators created the equivalent of 123 full-time jobs in the first year and will create 616 jobs over five years. The team also created opportunities for a variety of entrepreneurs.

Beverly Cole is one example. This native Nashvillian in her sixties closed down a declining antique store and opened the Hockey Stop Pro Shop in its place. Beverly's love of the game goes way back to when hockey games were still a novelty in the South. "We went to Municipal Auditorium when the Dixie Flyers were here in 1963 and there was no glass on the boards, nothing between you and the ice. It was pretty dangerous," she says.

Her grandchildren now play in youth hockey leagues, which led to the idea for her shop. Beverly told a reporter from the *Tennessean*, "One Christmas we found the only way to buy hockey equipment for our grandchildren was to order it [through the mail]. So we opened this [store] and haven't slowed down since." As for those who say that tax dollars shouldn't go toward sports teams, Beverly doesn't mince words: "I'd rather dodge a pothole and go straight to the hockey game than to sit on my hoo-hah and complain."

The Predators are creating literally millions of dollars' worth of free publicity for Nashville's tourism industry. While Nashville has scenic beauty and rich historical treasures, its main competitive advantage in recent times has come from the man-made aura of its music and entertainment industries. Nashville's main attraction needs to be constantly reinforced in the minds of tourists and those who influence the flow of tourists and conventions.

With the fast-growing interest in hockey, and the resulting increase in media coverage, the Nashville Predators will be constantly referenced—in newspapers and magazines, on TV and radio, and even across the Internet—primarily in the United States and Canada, but also around the world. Such exposure is difficult to measure, but if the city had to pay for it in the form of advertising, the cost would run into the millions.

NASHVILLE "BRAND EQUITY"

The Nashville Predators have quickly made a huge, even if unmeasurable, impact on the equity or value of Nashville's brand image.

An illustration comes from Columbia/HCA CEO Dr. Tommy Frist, who arrived in Europe with a trade mission from Nashville late in the Predators' first season. The immigration official examining his passport noted he was from Nashville and started to name the various Predators players. Curious, Frist asked the official how he knew so much about the team. "We watch Nashville play on TV here quite frequently," the official replied. "We know all about Nashville!"

The presence of the Predators in Nashville, along with the Tennessee Titans, assists the city in its ongoing efforts to recruit new companies and more jobs. The teams also add to the rich diversity of life in Nashville and can only create more enthusiasm and excitement about the community. As the Titans proved in their 1999–2000 season, a championship team can quickly electrify a city and can boost its national and international stature, seemingly overnight. Nashville's football and hockey players have supported each other from the start, and both sets of players are hoping the Predators can follow up on the Titans' success. When Titans tight end Frank Wycheck appeared at a press conference during the Super Bowl, he sported a Predators cap.

Few would deny that you can feel the buzz about a city and that this feeling has a major impact on everything from civic pride to company relocation. Recruiters can more easily lure top executive talent to the area. Today, company location decisions are increasingly a function of quality-of-life issues, such as education and entertainment. Nashville needs to compete, to constantly invest in things that enhance its quality of life. Obviously sports alone cannot do it. But the absence of sports—major-league sports—for a city of Nashville's size creates serious competitive disadvantages.

The Predators have had a major impact on the Nashville downtown area and will continue to stimulate additional new development. It is nearly impossible to directly attribute additional development to the presence of the Predators or the Gaylord Entertainment Center, yet everyone would agree that both had a role in the dramatic redevelopment of downtown Nashville. The face of the city has changed dramatically in the past ten years. The arena, the convention center, the renovated Ryman Auditorium, and other such landmarks have become the anchors for a downtown renaissance that should continue. Such projects create an enhanced environment for tourists and are positive market signals for those who invest capital in private developments. The Predators are a significant part of the balanced development— business, arts, sports—of downtown Nashville.

What's happening in Nashville has been repeated throughout much of the southeastern and southwestern U.S. Most of the NHL's expansion teams and team relocations have taken place in these areas. In the 1990s, new (or relocated) NHL teams appeared in such nontraditional hockey markets as San Jose, Anaheim, Tampa Bay, Miami, Denver, Raleigh, Atlanta, Dallas, and Phoenix. In the 2000–2001 season, franchises will begin play in Columbus, Ohio, and St. Paul, Minnesota. The Nashville Predators made their debut in October of 1998, and the Atlanta Thrashers began in 1999. For a brief overview of the colorful history of the National Hockey League, see "A Quick History of the NHL."

A QUICK HISTORY OF THE NHL

1917: The NHL is organized in Montreal, with Frank Calder elected president and treasurer.

1923: The NHL, formerly made up entirely of Canadian-based teams, grants its first U.S. franchise to Boston.

1923: Foster Hewitt broadcasts radio's first hockey game.

1927: Game is standardized at three twenty-minute periods of stop time.

1933–34: The first NHL All-Star game is played in Toronto as a benefit for injured Maple Leaf "Ace" Bailey.

1942–43: Frank Calder dies in Montreal. Mervyn "Red" Dutton becomes president.

1943: Hockey Hall of Fame is established.

1943–44: Center-ice red line is introduced, marking an unofficial start to the NHL's modern era.

1944–45: Maurice Richard of the Montreal Canadiens becomes the first player to score 50 goals in a season.

1946–47: Dutton retires and is succeeded by Clarence S. Campbell.

1956–57: Standardized signals for referees and linesmen are introduced.

1957–58: Maurice Richard becomes the first NHL player to reach 500 career goals.

1960–61: Gordie Howe becomes the first NHL player to reach 1,000 career goals.

1966–67: NHL doubles in size from six teams to twelve. Chicago, Boston, Detroit, Montreal, Toronto, and New York are joined by Philadelphia, Pittsburgh, St. Louis, Minneapolis–St. Paul, Los Angeles, and Oakland, California.

1968–69: Phil Esposito of the Boston Bruins becomes the first NHL player to score 100 points in one season.

1969–70: Bobby Orr of Boston becomes the first defenseman to collect 100 points in a season.

1970–71: NHL increases to fourteen teams by expanding to Buffalo and Vancouver.

1970–71: Esposito becomes the first NHL player to pass 60- and 70-goal plateaus in one season and finishes with 76.

1972: A team of NHL stars represents Canada in an 8-game series against Russia. A goal by Toronto's Paul Henderson with thirty-four seconds left in Game 8 gives Canada a dramatic series-winning 6-5 victory and a 4-3-1 triumph in the league's first international foray.

1972–73: Atlanta and the New York Islanders are added, boosting NHL membership to sixteen franchises.

1974: The Philadelphia Flyers become the first expansion team to win the Stanley Cup.

1974–75: Kansas City and Washington become the NHL's seventeenth and eighteenth teams.

1976: The first Canada Cup is played. Canada sweeps Czechoslovakia in 2 games in the final of the six-country tournament, in which professional players are used.

1977–78: Clarence Campbell retires as NHL president and is replaced by John A. Ziegler Jr.

1978–79: Cleveland and Minnesota franchises merge into one team that plays its home games in Minnesota.

1979: World Hockey Association closes operations, and four of its franchises are absorbed. Hartford, Edmonton, Quebec, and Winnipeg swell NHL membership to twenty-one teams.

1980–81: Atlanta franchise shifts to Calgary.

1981–82: Wayne Gretzky sets NHL record with 92 goals and 212 total points in one season.

1982–83: Denver franchise shifts to New Jersey.

1984: Canada regains Canada Cup with 2-game sweep of Sweden in tournament final.

1987: Wayne Gretzky passes to Mario Lemieux for the winning goal in a 6-5 triumph that gives Canada the rubber match in a 3-game tournament final against Russia.

1991: Canada sweeps Team USA in the final of the last Canada Cup.

1991–92: A franchise is added in San Jose as the NHL celebrates its seventy-fifth anniversary season.

1992: Gil Stein becomes NHL president.

1992–93: Teemu Selanne of Winnipeg sets a rookie-scoring record with 76 goals and 132 points. Ottawa and Tampa Bay are added, boosting league complement to twenty-four.

1993: Gary Bettman becomes the first commissioner in NHL history.

1993–94: Anaheim and Florida franchises join the league.

1993–94: Minnesota North Stars move to Dallas as the Dallas Stars.

1995–96: Quebec franchise shifts to Denver.

1996: Team USA wins the first World Cup of Hockey international tournament.

1996–97: Winnipeg franchise shifts to Phoenix.

1997: Hartford franchise shifts to temporary quarters in Greensboro, North Carolina, while awaiting permanent quarters in Raleigh.

1998: Nashville Predators franchise is added.

1999: Wayne Gretzky retires. Atlanta Thrashers franchise is added.

2000: Columbus, Ohio, and Minneapolis–St. Paul franchises give the NHL thirty teams at the start of the millennium.

THE NATIONAL HOCKEY LEAGUE

Hockey's origins can be traced back to the Middle Ages when northern Europeans played a ball-and-stick game using primitive ice skates. Meanwhile, Native North Americans were playing a game even more like modern hockey, using field tools with curved ends. The French explorers watched the Native Americans play the game called *hoquet*. The first formal game is believed to have been played in Ontario, and the first recorded game was played on the Montreal campus of McGill University in 1875.

The National Hockey League (NHL) was established in 1917, making it one of the oldest professional sports leagues in the world. Only major-league baseball is older. Many rules and teams have changed since the first NHL game, but the puck remains exactly the same. The teams in the NHL compete for the Stanley Cup, the oldest sought-after team sports award in North America.

The "coolest game on ice" is played at high speeds, by players averaging around two hundred pounds. Hockey is a grueling sport that demands stamina, strength, and strategy along with both individual and team skills.

For most of its history, the sport was largely a phenomenon of the northeastern United States and Canada. Until 1972, when a short-lived Atlanta franchise began play, there weren't any teams in the southern U.S. That is no longer the case. Today, hockey's popularity and appeal are global.

When Gary Bettman became NHL commissioner in February of 1993, he became head of an organization that had a public relations and marketing staff of one, a tiny TV cable contract, and according to one media analyst, "no vision." Now, the league has broadcast agreements with Fox, ABC, ESPN, and the Canadian Broadcasting Company. Every game is broadcast live on NHL.com. Sales of NHL-licensed products have risen to more than $1 billion annually, with double-digit increases each of the past few years.

International broadcast revenues were up 27 percent between fiscal 1997 and 1998, and eighteen international syndication partners telecast NHL games during the 1997–98 season. The 1998 Stanley Cup Finals were broadcast in 187 countries worldwide, from Albania to Zimbabwe.

Over the past several years, interest in hockey in the United States and around the world has skyrocketed. Surprising to many observers, but perhaps not to the NHL, the expansion of the league into the southern and western parts of the United States has been among the most successful strategies in sports history. The NHL rivals baseball for its international stature and players. Today, about 60 percent of NHL players are from Canada, about 20 percent are from the United States, and 20 percent are from around the world, principally Western and Eastern Europe. Over the past ten years, the percentage of European-born players in the league has increased 192 percent. The league now consists of twenty-eight teams across North America and will grow to thirty by the 2000–2001 season (with the addition of Columbus and Minneapolis–St. Paul).

In 1997, the NHL played its first regular-season games off the North American continent. The Anaheim Mighty Ducks and the Vancouver Canucks opened the season with two games in Tokyo. The Predators will open their 2000–2001 season in Japan with two games against the Pittsburgh Penguins.

Hockey attracts the most upscale audience of the sports leagues. According to a FOX Sports/TMG poll, nearly 53 percent of all hockey fans have a household income over $50,000. The sport's popularity is growing rapidly in every demographic, especially among women and the important youth segment.

Much of the explosion in hockey's popularity over the past decade can be attributed to one man: Wayne Gretzky. His impact on the sport where he has broken untold records has been at least as profound as, and perhaps even more than, Michael Jordan's impact on basketball. Hockey, however, had much farther to grow. As hockey veteran and Rangers forward John MacLean puts it, "When Gretzky was in LA and with the TV exposure there, whether you knew anything about hockey or not, you knew Wayne Gretzky played it. He had a major influence on expansion, especially on markets like Nashville, Florida, and Anaheim." Prior to Gretzky's stint in LA, it was just assumed that hockey and warm weather didn't mix.

Predators general manager David Poile also gives much credit to the Great One: "Without a doubt, it's because of Wayne Gretzky that hockey has grown so much and been able to succeed in so many places. It's one of the key reasons why we're in Nashville today."

THE FUTURE LOOKS EVEN BRIGHTER

Without the Great One, hockey will never be the same. And while all of the people involved in the game believe there will never be another Gretzky, they believe that he left hockey stronger than he found it, that he built a great base for future stars. Some of them are already on the ice, filling in where Wayne left off: Jagr. Bure. Selanne. Kariya. Forsberg. Sakic. Hull. Modano. Nieuwendyk. Shanahan. Robitaille. Hasek. Bourque. Leetch. LeClair. Lindros. Roenick. Pronger. Nolan. Sundin. Ronning. And someday soon, Legwand.

The future has never looked brighter for the NHL. And the future looks just as bright for Nashville and the Predators.

Cliff Ronning says he hopes to be around to watch David Legwand mature into one of the league's great players.

Jack Diller says he wants to be around to see the team grow traditions like those of the New York Rangers.

Tom Ward says he wants to be around to see the day that he has to run just one ad announcing when the few available season tickets go on sale, because like hockey tickets in Toronto and Montreal, they are passed from generation to generation.

David Poile, Barry Trotz, and Tom Fitzgerald say they want to be around to kiss the Cup.

And Craig Leipold says he wants to be around to see it all.

Breakaway

We've got a lot of new guys, and they always call me Mr. Leipold. Fitzy [Team Captain Tom Fitzgerald] and Cliff [Ronning] look at them and say, "No, no, no, it's Craig." I look at all of us as partners in this franchise.

It's been a dream year. Particularly the impact we, as a team, have had on the community.

I'm just having a ball. No one person should be having this much fun in life.

The honeymoon is over. The first year is always a honeymoon.

We knew that going in. There are expectations now. That is the challenge of year two.

I'm not going anywhere. I'm sticking around for the long term.

—CRAIG LEIPOLD

It's bitter cold in Moscow, and Alexei Dementiev wants nothing more than to stay in the warmth of his bed. It's Saturday morning, and Alexei hears his wife, Natasha, and his daughter, Vera, in the kitchen discussing their plans for the day. They'll go shopping and then to the ballet, but Alexei won't be joining them. He arrived home late the night before and needs to get up and get moving again. It was a short night. Alexei, European scout for the Nashville Predators, had been 150 miles outside Moscow the night before, scouting a player David Poile and the Predators coaching staff are interested in. It was a long drive home, and despite it being late spring, in Russia the weather is still unpredictable. Alexei drove most of the way home in snow.

But Alexei has little time today to worry about snow or the busy life of a scout. He has to catch an early flight to the Czech Republic to look at another player. It's still hockey season in Europe, and the only time to look at talent is when they're on the ice. Scouting is a demanding job, physically and mentally. And with David Poile as the ultimate recipient of his information, Alexei knows he must be thorough and accurate. He's proud of his work. He was one of the first in the Predators organization to watch and report on an emerging star for the Predators, Patric Kjellberg from Sweden.

This weekend he's particularly interested in two defensemen, a Russian and a Czech. He will send his individual player report to Stu Judge (scouting coordinator) in Nashville for entry into the sophisticated databases, and he is already making mental notes for his upcoming face-to-face meeting with Poile and several of the coaching staff. They'll be in Europe shortly after the season to watch some special hockey tournaments there. He finally stirs from his bed and heads for the shower.

An ocean away, Alexei's thoughts are being repeated many times over by his counterparts in the Predators scouting organization across North America. Paul Fenton, director of player personnel, heads the Predators' lifeline to the future. Paul has been a longtime hockey professional, and he was most recently with the Mighty Ducks. He was intimately involved with bringing Kariya and Selanne to Anaheim. Fenton and Chief Amateur Scout Craig Channell work closely together to develop draft pick recommendations for the Predators and their minor-league affiliate teams in Milwaukee and Hampton Roads (both known as the Admirals).

Channell, like Fenton, is a seasoned professional with a solid track record from his minor-league playing days, and has a practiced eye for young talent. Channell had the responsibility of guiding David Legwand's amateur development before Legwand joined the Predators.

The scouting staffers communicate daily—in person and/or through electronic means—about players and their future prospects for the Nashville Predators. Under Poile's direction, they've built a sophisticated computer system that would be the envy of many companies. Helping feed that system with detailed data about potential Predators are Fred Devereaux, who scouts the pros, and eight amateur scouts based in Europe, Canada, and the United States—Lucas Bergman, Luc Gauthier, Alan Hepple, Jim Johanson, Rick Knickle, Greg Royce, Darrell Young, and Glen Zacharias.

Over the course of the season they'll evaluate some 2,000 players, narrow the list to 200 prospects, and then pare it down to 100 for possible selection at the NHL Entry Draft (amateur) held each year in June. Of those, 50 will be invited to the Predators' preseason camp in September. In July, the Predators invite their young draft picks and some of the free agents to Nashville for orientation and conditioning.

In making their picks, the scouts are looking for size, strength, speed, hockey skills, character, and maturity. Most important, the Predators, a new team without significant bench strength developed over years, look for players who will give the team depth for a long time. For serious prospects, the scouts will visit the players' families, schools, friends, coaches, and just about anyone else who can help them evaluate the players' potential and desire.

A COMPLEX GLOBAL CHALLENGE

Hockey scouts face a challenge unlike that in any other sport. They largely evaluate and select youngsters who are in their late teens and are often as many as five or more years away from playing in the NHL. Few young prospects, like David Legwand, make the jump directly to the NHL. Other high-potential players, such as Karlis Skrastins and Rob Valicevic, will spend some time in the minor leagues to ensure plenty of ice time, readying themselves for the call to join the Predators. Unlike the players who feed the ranks of professional baseball, football, and basketball, most of these young hockey players won't have the luxury of a maturing process in college.

More and more of today's NHL players come from college, like the Predators' outstanding goalie, Mike Dunham (University of Maine), but most amateurs who hope to play professional hockey, like Sebastien Bordeleau and Scott Walker, choose the Canadian or European junior leagues. For young players it's a difficult decision. "It's tough when you're fifteen years old and you have to make a decision like that," says Bordeleau, who played in the Quebec Major Junior Hockey League. "It can be the biggest decision of your life. If I had gone into major junior and it didn't work, I'd have had to start college at twenty-one or twenty-two [he was being recruited by Clarkson University]. On the other hand, if I had gone to college and everything went well in school but I didn't get drafted, I'd be twenty-two with a degree, but my goal was to play hockey."

In the last few years players in the NHL have come from several continents, including two players from African nations. In the 1999–2000 NHL season there were players from seventeen countries, although the majority were still Canadian (56.3 percent) and American (16 percent).

The Predators scouting staff played a central role in selecting the twenty-six players at the NHL Expansion Draft that allowed Nashville to fill out a team roster. The scouting and hockey staff worked for more than a year to prepare for that draft. Every existing team in the NHL was allowed to protect eighteen skaters and two goalies on its current roster, and Nashville was permitted to select one player from the list of unprotected players on each team.

More than a year away from the draft, Poile, Trotz, Gardner, and the scouting staff started their work in preparation for the NHL Expansion and Entry Drafts that would provide them with the players for the Predators' roster. They scouted teams all year and evaluated individual player skills. One problem, according to Poile, was that they were never sure which players a team would protect. "Some general managers would help with information, particularly if they wanted to make some sort of a deal," says Poile, "while others wouldn't give us much information at all." In many ways it was like flying blind until the final lists were revealed.

However, with more than a year of intense preparation and analysis behind them, Poile and his team went into the draft as prepared as any group in history. In the weeks leading up to the draft, a general philosophy of favoring speed, skill, and youth was developed that guided their activity. Poile says, "We had developed a basic philosophy of how we would draft, and some key strategies that we would follow in the specific picks. Of course, some of this is guided by what the rules are, but we had some room to negotiate with individual teams as well. We were able to arrange some specific compensatory deals. For example, we wouldn't draft a certain player, and in return the other team would make some other players available to us."

A couple of days before the draft, Poile, Trotz, and the rest of the Predators team charged with drafting the roster assembled in Buffalo for their final, intense discussions. They established a "war room" and began plotting various player combinations on large flip-chart sheets tacked around the room. Poile keeps the charts to this day to remind him of that intense experience. "We went into the draft very well prepared and hopeful but realistic. We looked at various scenarios right up to the morning of the draft. You never get everything you want, but we did well. As we saw the list of available players and made our selection, that would often change our next pick. We were only allowed a certain number of defensemen, goalies, etcetera, so with each move we had to reevaluate our next pick," he says.

In many ways, an NHL Entry Draft is like a chess game, requiring the drafting organization to think many moves ahead, but being flexible enough with each move to reassess and change strategy depending on a "competitor's" reaction. The year of intense preparation and constant travel to scout all their potential draft picks paid off, however, as the lists of unprotected players became available. In the end, Nashville drafted twenty-six players, many of whom, such as Boughner, Bouchard, Cote, Dunham, Johnson, Vokoun, and Walker, became the nucleus of the Predators team. But each drafted player also became an opportunity for Poile to acquire other players in trade. With some last-minute trading and superb maneuvering, Poile and his staff were able to put together a team that not only survived the rigors of their first season, but also surprised the hockey world with their grit and determination.

David Poile is known for making deft trades, although he doesn't really like to make them. He remembers his first job as an assistant in Atlanta: "It seems like every day I'd be in to [Atlanta Flames GM] Cliff Fletcher's office, suggesting that we trade this or that player. After quite a few of my suggestions, he sat me down and talked to me about a GM's responsibilities in making trades, about all the ramifications for the players and the team. From the outside a trade may seem like an easy thing, but from the inside it's tough to gauge the impact on the individual players and the team's cohesion. Cliff taught me early on that you don't make a trade lightly."

Despite his reluctance to make trades, Poile is no stranger to them. In 1982, at thirty-two years old, just days after being appointed GM for the Washington Capitals, Poile made some of the NHL's blockbuster trades, getting Rod Langway, Brian Engblom, Craig Laughlin, and "iron man" Doug Jarvis from the Montreal Canadiens, a deal that paved the way for the Capitals' improvement.

In addition to their excellent selections in the draft, Poile and the hockey staff made several key trades to improve the team's current roster and to ensure its future. They signed several free agents, including NHL-proven Captain Tom Fitzgerald, as well as Rob Valicevic and Mark Mowers, both of whom had no NHL experience. After a career in the minors that almost didn't happen, Valicevic joined the Predators and immediately proved that Poile and the hockey staff were right. A low draft pick out of college, Rob had to be convinced by his brother to try out for the Louisiana Ice Gators of the East Coast Hockey League. There he became a star and then moved up to the Houston Aeros of the International Hockey League, where he starred again. When he joined the Predators in their first season, Valicevic quickly established his presence, scoring 4 winning or tying goals, and in his second season, he became the first Predator to score a hat trick. For that 3-goal effort, he went into the record books and received a cowboy hat from country music stars Brooks & Dunn in a ceremony at the arena.

And like the free agent signings, almost immediately the trades brought significant strength to the Predators' first-year lineup. Poile acquired defensive standout Drake Berehowsky from the Edmonton Oilers and the team's leading goal scorer, Cliff Ronning, from the Phoenix Coyotes. Drake brought the team's hardest shot to the Predators' power play and added mobility and finesse to the defense. Ronning, affectionately dubbed "Mighty Mite" by broadcaster Terry Crisp almost immediately on joining the team, has led the Predators in scoring, intensity, and unwavering focus. And when Coach Trotz assigned rookie David Legwand to the offensive line for the 1999–2000 season, he added on-ice mentoring to Ronning's responsibilities as offensive leader.

Ronning, who most thought was too small to play in the NHL, was given his initial chance with St. Louis, and he has never looked back. One of the league's most skilled stick handlers, he has also become one of its most respected playmakers. Having played for the Vancouver Canucks (near his hometown of Burnaby, British Columbia) as well as St. Louis, he thought he'd found a permanent home with the Coyotes. He hasn't had second thoughts about coming to Nashville, though, or about his new role with Legwand. He wants, he says, to be around to watch David Legwand grow into the great player he is destined to become.

THE OFF-SEASON: SCOUTING THE FUTURE

If the hockey season seems long for the hockey professionals, the summer is not much shorter. For some players, such as left wing Patrick Cote, the summer months are devoted to gaining strength and conditioning and practicing his off-ice pursuit (boxing); in 1999, he attended a skills camp in Europe. Others use the time to work for favorite charities or participate in youth hockey camps. Most players try to use the summer months to relax, play golf, or catch up on family or business matters neglected during the rigorous season. The hockey season has grown in recent years, and with conditioning and training camps and then play-offs, it can stretch into ten months.

For some, the summer off can be quite profitable. Assistant Coach Paul Gardner stays in Nashville for the summer to work on Predators activities and to participate in community events such as celebrity golf tournaments. In the 1999 Diamond Rio Celebrity Golf Classic (to support the American Lung Association of Tennessee), Gardner fired a hole in one in an early round. He won $10,000, but as it was widely reported in the media, he gave back much of it in the form of "entertainment" during the balance of the tournament.

For the scouting and coaching staff, along with the GMs, the summer is filled with an extensive debriefing of the season just past and a preview of the season ahead. It's the time for them to create the future. Poring over their huge statistical database, closely analyzing game videos, or comparing notes on players and strategies, they never seem to see the end of summer off-ice preparation. Contract negotiations and league business fill out the rest of the available time.

For David Poile and his staff in Nashville, hockey has become a seven-days-a-week, year-round job. A recent two-time selection as GM of Team USA for hockey's World Championships takes up what little time Poile has left, but he relishes the opportunity. "It gives me a unique opportunity to look closely at some of the world's best players," he says.

Many scouts for a professional hockey team, like those for the Predators, have other jobs—as coaches or staff with minor-league teams or even schoolteachers. Most, however, consider scouting to be their prime avocation, and they recognize that their judgments and decisions impact not only the future of a franchise, but also the lives of hundreds of young men. Most had productive professional or amateur careers on the ice, and they know what it takes to win. For the Predators scouting staff, winning is their prime goal. For the Predators management, winning is "job one."

The second year for an expansion franchise is often a letdown. The Predators hockey people were not overly worried about it, though. "The morning after our last game," says Assistant Coach Paul Gardner, "we met with David Poile on the subject of the second year 'jinx.' We talked several hours about it. We tried to analyze why it happened to others and how to prevent it from happening to us. We weren't going to get caught off guard because of not being well prepared. David has taught us that. He's the most prepared man I've ever met. Having some great talent among our younger players, such as Richard Lintner, Mark Mowers, Randy Robitaille, and Karlis Skrastins, doesn't hurt either."

"We've talked a lot about what it would take to win, on and

off the ice," says Craig. "Jack, David, and Tom Ward are very thorough. They don't leave anything to chance. Having been in business, I have a perspective on that side of the operation. But I'm a listener in the conversations about hockey. The team issues are absolutely David Poile's. It became evident early on, to both Jack and me, that David was a good strategic thinker. He isn't just a hockey general manager. He is a good businessman. David would be successful in the private sector, in any kind of business, because he is a stickler for details. He bases his judgments on facts. Lots of them.

"He built a scouting system that just absolutely blew me away. Everything is computerized. Whatever games our scouts see anywhere in the world, in Sweden, for example, by ten o'clock the next morning in Nashville we know everything that happened and how everybody we're interested in played. Everything is carefully laid out. With the players we are watching, the scouts note their strengths and weaknesses in virtually every game they play. Then someone else will check them out a couple of weeks later to verify the earlier observation."

Craig continues, "David and his hockey staff are just incredible. When we sat down on draft day, we were very well prepared. There is an old saying that really applies to David and the hockey people he's assembled. 'The harder you work, the luckier you get.' Combine all David's hard work and careful preparation with his ability to think strategically, several moves ahead, and you've got a surefire winner for the future."

A CUP IN THE FUTURE?

According to Craig, the Predators didn't set any goals for points or standings for the early years: "We didn't have any specific numerical goals for the first three years. Sure, we want to be competitive, but our major concern was establishing a strong base of youth for the future. We didn't want to push a young team too hard, to put too much early pressure on a young franchise. Also, we didn't want to set unrealistic expectations for our fans. We felt our fans would understand expansion and the concept of building a club for the long term. By the third year, though, our expectations are to be much more competitive, to be in the hunt for the play-offs. We set our minds on where we would like to see this franchise by that point.

"Jim Fitzgerald, who is the guy that I've talked most to about managing a pro sports team, coached me a lot about the strategy of a new expansion franchise. His approach was to take advantage of the building period in the first couple of years because it's healthy. Not so much healthy for you as an owner, but because the fans will be generally patient with you, and it doesn't put too much pressure on a young organization and young players.

"In the normal life cycle of a franchise you need to get better every year. But if you win 35 games the first year, that becomes your Year 4 in the normal cycle. So then, in Year 2, everybody expects you to win more than 35 games. Now, all of a sudden you have an arbitrary number that you've got to be at. It's just not realistic or sustainable in pro sports today," says Craig.

"Jim shared with me one of the problems he faced with the Milwaukee Bucks franchise [Fitzgerald was the first owner]. In their second year of existence they drafted Alcindor [the great Lew Alcindor, who later changed his name to Kareem Abdul-Jabbar], and they won it all. From then on, everybody expected that the Bucks always had to win. And in the following years, when the team had very good years, but didn't win it all, everyone thought there were problems.

"Unfortunately it changed the relationship between the franchise and the city. So they had difficulty developing a strong base of loyal fans who were there from the beginning because they loved the sport and the team. They had the types who would go out there because the team was winning. When they didn't continue to win it all, which is virtually impossible for any team in any sport, particularly an expansion club, their attendance dropped. I was an interested spectator at the time, but it wasn't fun to watch. Jim's message to me, one he'd learned from experience, was to take advantage of the early expansion period to really develop the club and your core fans. To grow them together. The best fans are the ones who will always be there. They're the ones who are proud to say, 'I was there when this team was in last place because I'm that kind of fan. I stuck with them from the beginning, so I can enjoy their success now.'"

Craig explains, "My philosophy, which is widely shared by the kind of people Jack, David, and I recruited to the Predators, is that we are here to win. And in hockey that means the Stanley Cup, period. We want to win it. But so do twenty-nine other franchises. And some, like Chicago, have been around since the beginning and haven't won one for a long time. In their case, since 1961. They have a great, proud, historic franchise, but in today's competitive professional sports business, winning doesn't happen easily or quickly.

"We want to be a contender, but don't feel the need to contend for the Stanley Cup in the first couple of years. We clearly overachieved where we thought we would get in the first year. That made it a little tougher in year two. We were obviously pretty pleased with the team's success, but it was within the range of where we wanted to be."

"In Florida, the Panthers went to the Stanley Cup Finals in their third year. It was very dramatic, but that's not what we are trying to do. Florida's doing well again now, but following that third year, they struggled. That's a good example of not using the growing period. They never took advantage of it. And after that great year, when reality began to set in, the fans were really restless. And in their sixth year, they struggled with attendance."

From a player's perspective, making a fast trip to the Stanley Cup can be a once-in-a-career opportunity. In today's competitive environment, some of the NHL's great players on long-established teams, such as Ray Bourque of the Colorado Avalanche, have never made the trip. On balance, though, players like the Predators' Tom Fitzgerald think the approach in Nashville is the right way to go.

Fitzgerald was a part of the third-year Panthers team that went to the 1995–96 Stanley Cup Final faster than any expansion team in modern history (other than the 1967–68 season that had all expansion teams in one division, thus guaranteeing one team a place in the finals).

"No question, we went for experience and a quick trip to the Cup," says Fitzgerald of his early days with the Panthers. "I'm not being critical. It's a matter of philosophy. With the Panthers, everything was geared to 'right now.' And it got us there. We did what we set out to do.

"But what did it cost us? We made some quick acquisitions like the Ray Sheppard deal. He was thirty-one, thirty-two years old at the time. You knew you could ride that guy's coattails to the Cup Finals. He was a real star, a winner. But how much longer was he going to play? And we didn't have a young goaltender in the minors like the Predators now have with Brian Finley.

"I personally benefited a great deal from the fact that the Panthers went to the Cup Finals so quickly," Fitzgerald says. "That was an experience that is hard to duplicate for a young player like myself. But I think the Predators' approach is much better for the team, the community, and in the end, the fans.

"Just look at our original draft and our second amateur draft. I think that Brian Finley was a superb draft pick. I think we've done a great job with building around youth, building for the future. Look at David Legwand. He's going to be around here for a long time. David is going to be one heck of a player when he's twenty-four years old. I hope I'm around to see it.

"To win over the long term, you need a goaltender as the backbone. You need a big-time goalie, and we've got two already in Mike [Dunham] and Tomas [Vokoun]. And we need a lot of young players in the system, ready to come up. The Panthers didn't have that.

"I think the Predators management, coaches, and scouts have done a terrific job that way. They want to build a lasting franchise with a winning tradition over the long term.

"I know that's all David Poile is thinking about," adds Fitzgerald. "He's thinking about constantly making us better. Building for the future. Sure, we are all concerned about getting off to a great start, maximizing what we have right now. We want to be competitive. Being competitive, working hard, and making the most of our talents are the essence of being a professional. But as captain, I'm really pleased that we are not giving up our young draft picks just so we can win right now.

"Actually we're winning a bit more now than maybe some would have predicted because the guys are learning together how to win as a team. We've quickly figured out what it takes to be a winner.

"At the time, Florida's management said they didn't draft to be a doormat in the league. They said they drafted to win right now. But in the end, that's not the right approach. Every team has to build. Florida's building now. But so are we. From the ground up. It's absolutely the right way to go."

Craig, Jack Diller, and David Poile are dedicated to the right way. They talk about it constantly and work at it endlessly.

"We've talked a lot about our style of play, and we set a series of goals for the first several years," says Jack Diller. "We really determined that the long-term health of what we were doing is best served by not trying to go for a 'quick fix' in the beginning, that we would build a team over time. At one point there was a rumor that we could acquire all the players from the Edmonton Oilers. But we decided that even if they were available, we wanted our own guys. Calls from our fans supported the decision. That was the game plan. We had a lot of talks about what realistic level we would be able to achieve. We talk all the time about where our team is and where it's going to be. Winning is a goal that Craig, David Poile, and I are constantly discussing."

"We looked at all the other new franchises too," says Craig. "The model that impressed us was the one Disney was using with the Mighty Ducks. They recognized that they were in the entertainment business, and so are we. They know how to build audiences that last over a long time. They've grown their team slowly but surely over the same period as Florida. They both came into the league at the same time, the 1993–94 season.

"The Ducks' philosophy seems to be to build around a couple of really good, premier players and surround them with a hard-working team. We've looked closely at them and paid attention to the philosophy that Disney is using. That same approach makes a lot of sense, particularly in this market. Our goal is to develop some of the same type of players as they have. They've got Paul Kariya and Teemu Selanne, two great players. They don't get any better than that. They are really fortunate to have players like that. It means good things for them over the long term.

"We looked at and had lengthy discussions about all the other models used in hockey. Of course, we looked particularly close at the other southern teams, how they operate their franchises, and how they built their teams, things like that.

"What we want to do, even before we start talking about the Stanley Cup, is to just be competitive. Fortunately we have a very young team. We've still got a lot of draft picks available. We've got a lot of great, young players who are either here or in the system in Milwaukee or Europe."

Craig continues, "Obviously we feel very good about our young players such as David Legwand, Randy Robitaille, and Karlis Skrastins. The hockey people already see things in David Legwand that they didn't expect they would see for some time. If we can get another one or two young players like that, who can contribute over a long period, we'll be fine. If we are lucky, we are going to be set for the next ten years in goaltenders.

"We think we are moving in the right direction. But we're not going to push it too hard, too fast. We've got to do it a step at a time. Our objective is to run the team like a business. If the franchise is going to survive and thrive in Nashville, we've got to make money, a decent return. We intend to survive, and we make no apologies for that. However, I have no intention or expectation that I'll get rich off this team. Frankly if I can just break even or make enough money to keep investing in the team, moving it forward, that is all that I want. In the first year, we were able to accomplish that. In the next couple of years we think we're going to be there as well," says Craig.

"*Forbes* magazine made some wild statement about how we did in our first year. They didn't get any information from us, so I'm not sure how they got their numbers. We did make a little money our first year, in fact, but on an $80 million investment, I'd have made more if I left it in a savings account. We did better in year two than our first year because we invested heavily in the start-up, and we had more revenue coming in. We had a full season of sponsorships. Some of the sponsors only joined us midway through the first year. Our TV contracts were better than year one because Pete and Terry did a great job for us. They proved we had a loyal TV audience.

"However, salaries were probably 25 to 30 percent more for the team than they were the first year. But that is to be expected.

"In hockey, you hope to break even or stay a little ahead year to year, and you look for capital appreciation, for the value of the league and the franchise to increase over time. It's the nugget at the end of the day. Frankly, though, I don't even think about it. Right now it's a long way off, and I have no interest in short-term rewards. I'm in this for the long haul. I'm committed to being in hockey, in Nashville, for a long time to come."

Craig emphasizes, "We've had a truly great start. This has been an experience beyond belief. When I say experience, I mean *total experience*. The hockey part has been great. Much better than I could have ever imagined. But I'm also talking about Nashville, the friends I've made here, the things I do here. I hadn't even dared to dream about the kinds of things that have happened to me. So I'm sticking around.

"From what I've come to learn, Nashville has changed dramatically over the last ten years or so. I like to think the Predators have been instrumental in some of those changes. The feeling of confidence around the city, of being in the big leagues, is tremendous. Of course, the Titans have been a big part of that too. They have a great franchise, and I think it is very complementary to us."

THE END OF A SEASON, THE BEGINNING OF A TRADITION

Many people in professional sports say they've never seen anything like the Predators' first season. "I had the feeling this special relationship was building throughout the process of applying for a franchise," Craig recalls. "I could literally feel it, and so could everybody else, when the NHL Governors were here for their visit. The unbelievable support we got from the business community and the fans during our season ticket campaign confirmed for me that the city wanted hockey, and in a big way. Then the fan response during the opening game just seemed to build and build. I couldn't get over it. It was a very special time."

Not everybody, however, had an opportunity to feel the growing sentiment that would ignite the team's first season. Like the rest of the Predators, Bob Boughner was much too busy in the early part of that first season getting ready for the Red Wings, Blackhawks, Blues, and the rest to notice the intensity building between the team and the city. At the end of that first game, however, he and the other players knew that they were part of something none had ever experienced before. "We lost that first game 1-0," he says. "I was astounded when the fans gave us a standing ovation! It's something I'd never seen or heard about before. It was an incredible moment."

But throughout the next nine months those incredible moments didn't seem to end. Everyone involved in the team and many in the city were at a loss to explain it.

Perhaps the "overnight sensation" of the Predators was the result of something from deep in the hearts of the Nashville fans that would embrace a group of twenty young men from nearly a half dozen countries and two continents. The players' original homes stretched from Vancouver and Burnaby, British Columbia, to Chelyabinsk, Russia; from LaSalle, Quebec, to Detroit; from Thunder Bay, Ontario, to Billerica, Massachusetts; from Windsor, Ontario, to Falun, Sweden; from Johnson City, New York, to Karlovy Vary, Czech Republic; and from Toronto to Vantaa and Kuopio, Finland.

Perhaps the fans knew that the magic of that first season was not some sleight of hand, but something that would endure. That David Poile and Barry Trotz and their hockey staff had plans for many more magical moments. That the long days of scouting and coaching and planning and nights short of sleep would pay off someday soon.

Perhaps they believed that this franchise, that grew out of a "hole in the rock," that chose as its symbol a fierce beast from the Ice Age, had come to stay.

Perhaps they realized that anything lasting, like the city itself, had to be built on a rock-solid foundation, but needed the vision of Mayor Phil Bredesen, along with Dick Evans and Terry London of Gaylord Entertainment, to give it meaning and direction.

Perhaps they sensed the dedication of Craig's early "get the franchise" team—Tom Sherrard, Sue Atkinson, Ed Lang, Russ Simons, Jenny Hannon, and Kevin Phillips.

And perhaps they understood better than anyone that nothing as entertaining as a night at a Predators game happens without the hard work and dedication of Jack Diller, Tom Ward, Gerry Helper, and the entire Predators staff.

Or perhaps, more correctly, it was the magical combination of all those things.

It ended, that first season, just about as it began. They skated into the record books with one of the league's highest "game days lost to injuries" seasons, but with the third best record ever (28 wins, 47 losses, 7 ties) for an expansion franchise. And despite their injuries, despite the fact that they were still less than a year old, the Predators stayed in contention for a play-off spot until the bitter end. And when they lost that last game, as they lost their first, the fans gave them a standing ovation. The *Tennessean* reported about the conclusion of that last game, "The fans stood and roared again as if the Predators had just captured the Stanley Cup. They remained as each player ceremoniously gave his jersey to a fan. During a highlight video scored to music with the lyric, 'I hope you had the time of your life,' they spontaneously began to chant, 'Let's go, Predators!'"

It is a chant that will be heard for many years to come.

We liked it. We loved it. We want some more of it.

And, yes, we did have the time of our lives.

About the Authors

CRAIG LEIPOLD is the chairman and majority owner of the Predators (Gaylord Entertainment holds a minority share). He is a governor of the National Hockey League and serves on the boards of directors of Gaylord Entertainment, Levy's Restaurants, and LaCrosse Footwear, among others.

Leipold is a graduate of Hendrix College in Conway, Arkansas. He began his business career with Kimberly-Clark and left to found Ameritel Corporation in 1984, a telemarketing firm that specialized in business-to-business sales contracts for major companies. He purchased Rainfair Corporation in 1987. He recently sold that company to focus on the sports market.

Leipold's philosophy of partnership with the Nashville community in operating the Predators was a major factor in the team's first-year success. He worked closely with corporate and civic leaders to gain the necessary support to convince the National Hockey League to award Nashville a franchise. To support ticket sales, he compiled a thirty-member task force aimed at corporate and suite sales. He teamed with Gaylord Entertainment in January 1997. He made a presentation to the NHL's Executive Committee and was awarded the franchise on June 25, 1997. The Predators began play in October 1998.

Leipold is active in a number of corporate and civic groups. He served as the chairman of the Wisconsin Sports Authority and was vice chairman of the Milwaukee Brewers Baseball Stadium Board. He is a past director of the Racine Area United Way, is past president of the Taylor Children's Home, and is currently a director of the Wustum Museum and the Midwest Athletes Against Childhood Cancer. He is a member of the Nashville Area Chamber of Commerce Board of Governors, the executive committee of the Middle Tennessee Council for the Boy Scouts of America, and the Board of the Marquette Sports Law Institute.

RICK OLIVER is a professor at the Owen Graduate School of Management, Vanderbilt University. He was previously vice president of marketing for Northern Telecom. He received his B.Sc. from Cornell University and his Ph.D. from the State University of New York (SUNY). He is chairman of the board of Symmetricom, Inc., and serves on the board of directors of five other public and private companies.

He is the author of *The Coming Biotech Age: The Business of Bio-Materials* (McGraw-Hill), *The Shape of Things to Come: 7 Imperatives for Winning in the New World of Business* (Business Week Books, McGraw-Hill), and the coauthor of *The Eagle and the Monk: 7 Principles of Successful Change*. He is a regular columnist with the *Journal of Business Strategy* and the American Management Association's monthly magazine, *Management Review*.

Dr. Oliver is a graduate of Leadership Nashville. He has been active in Nashville cultural and civic affairs, currently serving as a member of the board of trust of the Metropolitan Nashville Public Education Foundation, the Center for Non-Profit Management, and the 18th Avenue Family Enrichment Center.

He served previously as the chairman of the board of Harpeth Hall School, and as chairman of the board for the Nashville Institute for the Arts, the Nashville Opera, and the Davidson County Sheriff's Department Advisory Committee. For several years he served as chairman of the Athletic Advisory Committee at Cornell University and as vice chairman of the Cornell University Council.